The Loss of a Life Partner

The Loss of a Life Partner

NARRATIVES OF THE BEREAVED

Carolyn Ambler Walter

COLUMBIA UNIVERSITY PRESS
NEW YORK

Columbia University Press
Publishers Since 1893
New York   Chichester, West Sussex

© 2003 Columbia University Press

Library of Congress Cataloging-in-Publication Data
Walter, Carolyn Ambler.
    The loss of a life partner : narratives of the bereaved / Carolyn Ambler Walter.
        p.   cm.
    Includes bibliographical references and index.
    ISBN 0–231–11968–2 (alk. paper)—ISBN 0–231–11969–0 (pbk. : alk. paper)
    1. Bereavement—Psychological aspects.   2. Death—Psychological aspects.
    3. Loss (Psychology)   4. Grief.   I. Title.

BF575.G7 .W3435 2003
155.9'37—dc21

                                                                    2002031503

Columbia University Press books are printed on permanent
and durable acid-free paper.
Printed in the United States of America

c 10 9 8 7 6 5 4 3 2 1
p 10 9 8 7 6 5 4 3 2 1

This book is dedicated to my wonderful family—
Bruce, Kim, Brian, Steve, Matthew, David, Donna, Amy,
Eric, and my late husband, John Walter, who provided
the spirit for its inception and completion!

Contents

Acknowledgments

This book has been germinating for some time, and there are many whom I would like to thank for their contributions to its creation. First, this book would not have been written without the twenty-two partners who willingly shared their stories of the loss of a partner with me. Their stories and the creative ways in which they have constructed meaning from their experience of loss have helped to carry me forward in the completion of this work. I have tried to preserve the essence of what each partner shared with me, and I am grateful to all of them for their contributions to this book.

The idea for this book took root when I realized, during a workshop that I was giving on support groups for the loss of a young spouse, that there were no support groups for domestic partners. As I began to comb the literature, I realized that, other than Ken Doka's fine work on disenfranchised loss, this group had been neglected. Moved by my own experience of the loss of a spouse at a relatively young age, I sensed that my experiences in recovery did not match what I had learned about grief and loss in the earlier years of my education. I attended my first Association for Death Education and Counseling conference at the urging of one of my former students, Tony Griffith and, for the first time, heard the message that it is important to hold the memory of your partner in your thoughts and heart as you move forward in your new life. This is what the journey felt like to me, and I began to absorb the literature written by Klass, Silverman, and Nickman and by Robert Neimeyer for more ideas. I thank my colleague at the Center for Social Work Education, Dr. Alan Irving, for introducing me to John Michel, Executive Editor at Columbia University Press, who came to the Widener University campus for discussions with faculty who might want to write a book. John and I sat together and talked for two hours as we fleshed out the heart of the prospectus. John has been a support to me throughout the three years that I have worked on this book. I thank him for his help in keeping me going. Later, Enid Pearsons was invaluable as my copy editor.

I thank so many people, some of whose names I do not remember, for connecting me with bereaved partners who wanted to share their stories. The Samaritan Hospice in New Jersey—particularly Tony Griffith—was very helpful in my quest, as was the Association of Death Education and Counseling, which offered to place an ad in its national newsletter. Camp Rehoboth was another source of help in locating bereaved partners. Jeffrey Kauffman helped me to locate contacts for possible partners to interview and discussed the beginnings of the book with me.

Many thanks to Widener University for granting me two Faculty Development Options Awards so that I could complete the work on this book. Provost Buck, Dean Wilhite, and Associate Dean Paula Silver were all helpful in the pursuit of release time. I thank all of you.

I am also appreciative of all of the typists (too many to mention) who worked to transcribe the interviews of the partners from the audiotapes. The staff at my husband's office has helped with so many different parts of this process—I am most grateful to all of them! I would like to thank two graduate assistants, Diane Hall and Reinhild Boehme at the Center for Social Work Education at Widener University for helping me to comb the literature for material relating to the loss of a partner. Both of these graduate students went far beyond what I expected in helping me.

Finally, I am so appreciative of the wonderful support I have received from my family and friends (notably Janet Neer), but especially from my husband, Bruce, who married me while I was writing this book! My relationship with Bruce provides real proof that you can establish a wonderful, rich new relationship while transforming the relationship with your spouse who has died. Bruce has helped me with finding typists and with mailings of various parts of the manuscript, but most of all, by encouraging me to complete this work that has been so important to me.

Despite the growing number of books devoted to grief and loss, none integrate the literature about varying types of relationships and the bereavement experiences of partners in those relationships. This text juxtaposes the experiences of bereaved partners from marital relationships and those from domestic partnerships (same-sex and opposite-sex) in one work and examines the effects of both spousal loss and disenfranchised grief upon bereaved individuals.

The research on spousal loss is extensive and provides documentation showing that it can be the most stressful event in one's life (Holmes and Rahe 1967). What is far less extensive, however, is literature that examines the reactions of bereaved domestic partners. Here, we present and discuss excerpts of narratives of bereaved partners from widowed, same-sex, and opposite-sex relationships, based upon issues from the literature as well as from a postmodern perspective. This book provides the reader with a rare opportunity to explore the issues of partner loss in both traditional and non-traditional relationships. Socially sanctioned and disenfranchised grief are placed side by side, in an integrative manner, to validate the diverse types of grief that bereaved partners experience.

Because the number of adults choosing to live in nontraditional relationships is increasing, it is important to augment the literature that examines the issue of loss of a nonmarried partner. The most recent census report (Fields and Casper 2001) indicates that 7.6 million men and women responded to the census by indicating that they were living in a cohabiting relationship. This figure represents 3.8 million unmarried-partner households. According to the U.S. Census Bureau, "These numbers may underrepresent the true number of cohabitating couples because only householders and their partners are tabulated, and respondents may be reluctant to classify themselves as such in an interview situation and describe themselves as roommates, housemates or friends not related to each other" (Fields and Casper 2001:12). The increase in age at which both men and women are marrying has contributed to these statistics. For example, between 1970 and 2000, the number of women between twenty and twenty-four years of age who had not married doubled, and the proportion of women ages thirty to thirty-four years more than tripled. Similar dramatic shifts occurred for men.

Marriage rates in New York City are lower than at any time since the early 1970s (New Yorkers tying the knot, *New York Times* 2000). An increase in the social acceptance of couples who cohabit has helped to lower these rates. "These New York statistics mirror a national trend: the rate per thousand Americans who married in 1998 was 8.3, the lowest rate since 1958, when 8.4 people per thousand were married" (New Yorkers tying the knot, *New York Times* 2000:21).

Although there has been an increase in the amount of literature devoted to the loss of a gay male partner due to the AIDS epidemic, little, if any, literature exists on how lesbian women experience the loss of a partner. Chapters 5 and 6 present narratives of bereaved gay men and lesbian women. Although the bulk of the current literature addresses experiences of older widows, there is a small but growing literature on men's experience of grief, and some attention is given to the death of a young spouse. Narratives from men are included throughout the book. Chapter 2 gives a summary of the research on this topic. Chapter 8 discusses interventions with bereaved male partners. Chapters 3, 4, and 6 present literature about younger women and their experiences.

Although this book presents both classical and postmodern approaches to grief, the lens through which the themes of these narratives are seen is the postmodern paradigm. The narratives herein demonstrate how the bereaved have incorporated the death of a partner into their ongoing "life stories" to restore a sense of order and meaning to their lives. In addition, the book discusses how the narratives reveal ways in which various partners have used memories and continuing bonds with their deceased partners to help them cope with the grieving process and, in many cases, to help them establish new relationships.

INTERVIEWS

Twenty-two interviews of men and women who had lost their partners through death were conducted in the bereaved partner's home or, in a few cases, at national conferences. All but three of the interviews were face-to-face and took from one to two hours. Only bereaved spouses who had lost their partners at least one year prior to the interview were included. The number of years from the time of the partner's death ranged from one to sixteen. These bereaved partners come from nine different states in the United States. They were recruited from announcements in newsletters of organizations, such as the Association for Death Education and Counseling, and from hospice organizations throughout the nation. In addition, the "snowball technique" was used, in which bereaved partners were asked if they knew someone else who might be interested in participating in this project.

OVERVIEW

This text begins with a discussion of various theories of grief and how they inform our understanding of the loss of a partner. In particular, it describes and compares the classical (or traditional) and postmodern perspectives on grief. Traditional theories of grief discussed include those of Freud (1957), Worden (1991, 2002), and Bowlby (1977, 1980). Postmodern theories include those of Klass, Silverman, and Nickman (1996); Neimeyer (1998, 2001); and Rubin (1999).

Chapter 2 describes current issues surrounding the death of a partner, which are summarized from the literature on the death of a married partner, an opposite-sex partner, a gay partner, and a lesbian partner. These issues are later integrated into chapters throughout the book.

Chapter 3 presents excerpts from narratives of three widows and three widowers ranging in age from twenty-nine to eighty-nine. Kristen was only twenty-nine when her thirty-year-old spouse died in a tragic car accident that Kristen, a passenger, survived. This chapter discusses the available literature on young widows during an analysis of Kristen's experiences. John was thirty-seven when his wife died in a car accident, leaving him as the primary caregiver for three young children. Marion and Frank were each in midlife when their spouses died suddenly—Marion's husband of a heart attack while jogging and Frank's wife from a severe viral infection. Both Marion and Frank unexpectedly found themselves single parents to young children. Flora was eighty-nine when her spouse died at age eighty-seven. Flora and Jim had been married for almost sixty years. George was eighty-one when his spouse of fifty-two years died suddenly following an illness. This chapter integrates literature that specifically relates to bereavement for older spouses with George and Flora's stories during the analyses following their narratives.

In chapter 4, bereaved partners in opposite-sex relationships share their stories. This chapter begins with a discussion of the available literature on disenfranchised loss. Each analysis, following the narrative, explores how the narrative illustrates disenfranchised loss. The chapter presents seven narratives, from both men and women. Alisa was only twenty-three when her fiancé, Brian, died from heat exhaustion while jogging. Laura and Francine were in midlife when they lost their partners. Francine's partner was killed in a plane crash; Laura's partner died from cancer. Marie was forty-four and the main caregiver for Bert when he died from heart failure. Barry was a seventy-five-year-old widower whose partner, Julie, died of cancer at age fifty-seven. Peter, a retired schoolteacher, was fifty-nine when his partner, Marilyn, died of a severe viral infection. Ida was eighty-nine and had been widowed for seventeen years when her partner, Henry, died at age eighty-seven.

Before presenting the narratives, chapter 5 summarizes issues from the literature that face bereaved gay partners. Jim was forty-seven when his partner, Matt, died of AIDS at age thirty-eight. In addition, within a short time of that loss, Jim lost twelve of his best friends. Tom was forty-two when his partner died from an AIDS-related illness at age forty. David was forty-five when his partner, Brent, committed suicide. Don was fifty when his life partner of seventeen years, Eric, died of cancer. This chapter analyzes the narratives by examining how they reflect disenfranchised loss caused by reactions from community, family, and the medical profession. The analyses deal as well with other issues common to bereaved gay men.

In chapter 6, five bereaved lesbian partners share their narratives, following a brief summary of the limited amount of literature available regarding the issues faced by this population. The youngest bereaved partner, Pauline, was thirty-two when her young partner, aged twenty-six, was killed in a tragic auto accident. Gretchen, Denise, Lea, and Pat were all in midlife when their partners died. Gretchen and Carol had been living in a committed relationship for seven years when Carol committed suicide. Denise and Diane's twenty-year partnership came to an end when Diane died of ovarian cancer after a four-year struggle. Lea was a forty-six-year-old divorcée when her life partner, Corky, died of cancer at forty-seven. Each narrative is analyzed by examining how it reflects the issues of disenfranchised loss as well as issues from the scant literature on the death of a lesbian partner. The chapter also explores new ideas that emanate from the narratives.

Chapter 7 reveals themes that explore similar and diverse experiences among the various types of bereaved partners. These themes include (1) ambivalence regarding existing ties with the deceased partner, (2) discrimination experienced by surviving partners of nontraditional relationships, including discrimination from the medical profession, family, friends, and the community, (3) ways in which bereaved partners have used memories and continuing bonds with their lost partners to cope with grieving, (4) ways in which surviving partners have been able to develop new relationships while continuing bonds with the deceased partner, and (5) ways in which partners have been able to derive meaning from experiencing the death of their partners. Within each subheading, this chapter discusses the diverse ways in which various partners have faced these issues, using excerpts from a variety of narratives.

In chapters 3–6, each narrative is followed by an analysis that demonstrates how the case study elucidates the theory and issues arising from the loss of a partner. This analysis, by providing the reader with a perspective on how that particular partner's experiences deviate from or parallel discussions in the available literature, deepens the reader's understanding of the bereaved partner's experiences and struggles. In addition, the bereaved partner's experiences are observed through the lens of a postmodern approach to grief, which examines the ways in which bereaved partners have used their relationships with their deceased partners to enhance their ability to function in their current lives. Rather than presenting a phase/stage approach, the narratives illustrate how bereavement has affected the surviving partners and how they have chosen to derive meaning from traumatic loss. In addition, these chapters address new concerns or issues, not discussed in the literature, that emerge from the narratives. Each chapter terminates with a summary that synthesizes the experiences of the bereaved partners whose stories are included in that chapter.

Chapter 8 discusses interventions with all types of bereaved partners. It presents a summary of both the classical and postmodern approaches to interventions with bereaved adults, exploring the similarities and differences in these approaches. This chapter also gives a summary of the literature that describes both individual and group interventions with spouses. When possible, appropriate excerpts from the narratives are used to illustrate an intervention. These descriptions cover current literature regarding individual and group interventions with young bereaved spouses as well as with men. Traditionally, there has been little focus on these two groups of bereaved adults, but the literature on these groups is growing and needs to be addressed. Appropriate examples from the narratives illustrate some of the issues regarding intervention strategies with both of these groups.

Following these summaries, chapter 8 presents a very brief summary of the scarce literature on individual interventions with bereaved lesbian partners, with suggestions by the author for new directions that can be taken with this population. Since there is no literature on group interventions with bereaved lesbian partners, this chapter offers suggestions for creating such interventions, based on the narratives of the lesbian partners in this text and on what is known about bereaved widows. Next, this chapter summarizes the literature that addresses both individual and group interventions with bereaved gay partners. Excerpts from the narratives illustrate the issues. Finally, we provide a brief summary of the important factors to consider when working with gay and lesbian bereaved partners, including the importance of social support and community linkage.

The final chapter of this text discusses clinical implications for work with all types of bereaved partners. However, implications for bereaved partners from same-sex and opposite-sex partnerships are discussed in more depth, since these populations have received little attention in the literature. These implications are drawn from the previous discussions of both classical and postmodern grief theory, the experiences of the bereaved partners whose narratives are included in the book, and the existing literature about interventions with bereaved partners, including those who suffer disenfranchised grief.

These clinical implications can be extended to populations who have been separated from their loved ones for reasons other than death. Such losses can include partner or marital separation, divorce, and long-term separation as a result of war or other crises. A later section of chapter 9 includes a discussion of the clinical implications for those partners who have experienced death and long-term separation as a result of the tragic events of September 11, 2001. Although this text was conceived long before that date, any work on grief that is published following September 11 takes on new meaning for the reader who has been affected by these tragic events, which have so dramatically changed our worldview. Living with trauma and death, whether vicariously or directly, has become a way of life for most Americans. The events of September 11, their aftermath, and the narratives of the twenty-two bereaved partners who share their experiences in this text can provide all of us not only with an increased appreciation for the meaning of loss and grief, but with insights into how life-enhancing experiences can emanate from loss.

The loss of a partner is always highly traumatic. The beliefs, assumptions, and expectations regarding ourselves and the world around us are shattered. Bereaved partners are forced to make sense of experiences that seem senseless. This text provides a vehicle for a discussion of the unique ways in which bereaved partners can move forward in their lives while reexamining their relationships with their deceased partners. The diverse narratives presented in this text help the reader to understand that although each person's loss and bereavement is uniquely experienced, certain aspects of these experiences are shared by others.

Because the narratives provide riveting examples of the loss of a partner, this book can offer valuable insights to both a professional and lay audience. A serious loss of any type, but particularly loss of a partner, undergirds many of the issues faced by clients served by helping professionals. Not only social workers but psychologists, counselors, hospice workers, psychiatric nurses, and psychiatrists can benefit from these narratives. Understanding loss and grief is a focus of concern for practitioners who work with all types of client problems. In addition, as a supplemental text, the book has value for instructors and students who are participating in any program that offers a course on grief and loss. Finally, other bereaved partners, their families, and their friends will gain much from reading the poignant narratives of bereaved partners of all ages and all lifestyles. *The Loss of a Life Partner* provides a vehicle that can enable people to connect with the lives of those who shared their stories in this book.

The Loss of a Life Partner

Chapter One

Theories of Grief: How They Inform Our Understanding of the Loss of a Partner

Grief is the expression of a profound conflict between contradictory impulses—to consolidate all that is still valuable and important in the past, and preserve it from loss; and at the same time, to reestablish a meaningful pattern of relationships, in which the loss is accepted. Each impulse checks the other, reasserting itself by painful stabs of actuality or remorse, and recalling the bereaved to face the conflict itself.

MARRIS (1986:31, 32)

CLASSICAL PARADIGM OF GRIEF

During the twentieth century, the model of grief that dominated the literature and the layperson's understanding of the loss of a partner was drawn primarily from the psychoanalytic theories of Freud (1957), Bowlby (1980), and Kubler-Ross (1969). In Freud's view, the bereaved partner must sever bonds with the dead person to have the energy to reinvest in life and in new relationships. This model presupposes a limited amount of energy present for the work of grief. Simos, in her description of grief work with adults, states, "Living demands that they (the bereaved) detach their emotional investment from that which no longer exists so that they will have energy for living in the present" (1979:35). For successful mourning to occur, the bereaved partner must "disengage from the deceased and let go of the past" (Klass, Silverman, and Nickman 1996:4). "Grief, as Freud saw it, frees the ego from the attachment to the deceased" (Klass et al. 1996:5). In the classical paradigm for understanding the grieving process, the emphasis is upon cutting the "bond with the deceased so that new attachments can be formed" (Klass et al. 1996:7).

In the classic texts "there is a major theme emphasizing detachment achieved through the working through of feelings, and a minor theme emphasizing the continued presence of the dead and a continuous conversation with and about them" (Walter 1996:8). I believe that the classical modernist authors have typically underplayed or ignored this minor theme because the secular and twentieth-century culture was likely to discount the possibility of a meaningful relationship between the living and the dead.

As Klass, Silverman, and Nickman (1996) have suggested, psychoanalytic theory does not explain the nature and extent of the changes that occur in the relationship between the surviving partner and the deceased loved one. Psychoanalytic theory uses the concept of internalization to describe the transformation of the bond with the dead. Following a loss, people attempt to continue receiving gratification from the lost loved one by internalizing the person's image and relating to this now "internal object" as if it were the actual person (Freud 1957). However, psychoanalytic theory developed the idea that internalizing the lost partner is only a preliminary stage to letting go of that partner (Klass et al. 1996). Fenichel (1945) used the concept of *introjection* to describe a process in which the lost partner was held more closely during the early phases of grief so that he or she could be given up at the end of the grieving process.

This model is rooted deeply in the logical positivism of our modern culture, which emphasizes reason and observation as well as "a faith in continuous process" (Gergen 1991). This approach to life places heavy emphasis upon goal-directedness, efficiency, and rationality. In applying this model to grief, Klass et al. (1996) suggest that this view urges people to recover from their state of intense emotion and return to normal functioning as quickly as possible. In this view, grieving is seen as an interference with daily routines so that it must be worked through.

Many theorists (Kubler-Ross 1969; Worden 1991, 2002; Bowlby 1980; Simos 1979) describe a number of tasks that need to be confronted by the bereaved partner in order to return to a normal life. For example, Kubler-Ross (1969) discusses five stages of anticipatory grief in the dying person. These stages are (1) shock and denial, (2) anger and irritability, (3) bargaining, (4) depression and beginning acceptance, and (5) true acceptance.

Worden

In both editions of his classic work, Worden (1991, 2002), a well-known specialist in grief work, claims that it is essential for the bereaved partner to accomplish four tasks "before mourning can be completed" (1991:1, 2002:27).

These tasks include (1) accepting the reality of the loss, (2) working through to the pain of grief, (3) adjusting to an environment in which the deceased is missing, and (4) emotionally relocating the deceased to move on with life (Worden 1991:10–18; Worden 2002:26–37). Although Worden believes that there is no ready answer for when mourning is finished, in his view, "mourning is finished when the tasks of mourning are accomplished" (Worden 1991:18, 2002:45).

Worden (1991, 2002) describes the normal grief reactions of "uncomplicated mourning." Sadness is the most common feeling found in the bereaved partner, whereas anger, though frequently experienced, can be one of the most confusing feelings and may be the root of many problems in the grieving process. Worden believes that anger may come from a sense of frustration and/or helplessness, because nothing could have been done to prevent the death, as well as from a primitive response that human beings have developed to cope with the loss of someone close. Bowlby has described this behavior as part of our genetic heritage and claims it symbolizes the message, "Don't leave me again!" (Worden 2002:13). Guilt, self-reproach, and anxiety are other common reactions to the loss of a partner. Two major sources of anxiety stem from the belief of the bereaved partner that she will not be able to take care of herself on her own and from her heightened awareness of her own mortality.

Worden (1991, 2002) further discusses the sense of loneliness and helplessness that is pervasive in grieving partners. Yearning for the lost partner is what Parkes (1972) calls "pining" and is a common experience of survivors, exemplified by the widows who were interviewed. Worden (1991, 2002) also refers to those bereaved individuals who experience positive feelings of emancipation and/or relief because the person who died had been difficult to live with or burdensome to care for.

The cognitive patterns that mark the early stages of grief but sometimes persist for many months include disbelief ("I can't believe it happened"), confusion, preoccupation with thoughts of the deceased, a sense of the presence of the lost loved one, and hallucinations, both visual and auditory (Worden 1991, 2002).

Physical behaviors frequently associated with normal grief reactions include disturbances of sleep and appetite, absent-minded behavior, social withdrawal, dreams of the deceased, and avoidance of reminders of the deceased. The bereaved person may also search and call out, become restless and overactive, cry, visit places or carry objects that remind him or her of the deceased, and treasure objects that belonged to the deceased (Worden 1991, 2002).

Bowlby

One cannot approach the study of bereavement without attention to the work of John Bowlby (1977, 1980) and his theory of attachment. Bowlby's attachment theory provides an understanding of how human beings forge strong affectionate bonds with others. He provides a way to comprehend the intense emotional reaction that develops when these bonds are threatened or severed. Bowlby proposes that the importance of attachment, together with the security it provides, undergirds the extreme distress ever present when that bond is broken.

Bowlby (1977, 1980) includes data from neuropsychology, ethology, developmental biology, and cognitive psychology to develop his thesis that important attachments come from a need for security and safety. These attachments develop early in life, are usually directed toward a few specific individuals, and tend to endure throughout much of the life cycle. Bowlby (1977, 1980) argues that forming attachments to significant others is part of normal behavior because attachment behavior has survival value. Since the goal of attachment behavior is to maintain an affectional bond, situations that threaten this bond encourage specific reactions. "The greater the potential for loss, the more intense these reactions and the more varied" (Worden 1991:8). In these circumstances, such behavior as clinging, crying, and angry coercion is used to try to restore the attachment bond (Bowlby 1977). If the danger is not removed, the individual experiences withdrawal, apathy, and despair.

In Bowlby's work on loss of a spouse he discusses the following four phases of mourning: (1) numbing, which can be interrupted by intense distress and anger; (2) yearning and searching for the lost spouse; (3) disorganization and despair; and (4) some degree of reorganization (1980:85). A central task of the third and fourth phases is for the bereaved spouse to find a way to reconcile two incompatible urges—the urge to cling to the deceased spouse and the urge to separate (1980).

Although Bowlby (1977, 1980) takes a more classical approach to understanding grief and loss with his stage approach, he provides some early thinking about the persistence of the relationship to the deceased spouse and the importance of normalizing the widow's tendency to see and "speak" with her deceased partner long after the actual death. Bowlby (1977, 1980) clearly believes that the loss of a loved one is one of the most painful experiences any human being can suffer. "To the bereaved nothing but the return of the lost person can bring true comfort" (Bowlby 1980:8). However, for Bowlby (1980), talking to the deceased is important, because this experience helps the bereaved partner to eventually let go of the deceased partner.

Bowlby believes that a bias affects much of the older literature on how human beings respond to loss, in that "there is a tendency to underestimate how intensely distressing and disabling loss usually is and for how long the distress . . . commonly lasts. . . . There is also a tendency to believe that a normal, healthy person can and should get over a bereavement, not only rapidly but also completely" (1980:8).

Bowlby suggests that healthy grieving has a number of characteristics that were once thought to be pathological. Grief involves suffering and an impairment of the capacity to function. "The processes of mourning can be likened to the processes of healing that follow a severe wound or burn" (1980:43). Just as in the healing of a wound, the processes of mourning may, in time, lead to the capacity to make and maintain love relationships or may impair this ability.

All the theories discussed earlier emphasize the importance of separating from the lost partner as representing the heaviest workload of the bereaved partner. The following section presents a new paradigm of loss and bereavement that questions this emphasis.

POSTMODERN PARADIGM OF GRIEF

Klass, Silverman, and Nickman (1996); Neimeyer (1998); Walter (1996); and Rubin (1999) give voice to an emerging consensus among bereavement scholars that our comprehension of the grief process needs to be expanded beyond the dominant model, which holds that the function of grief and mourning is to sever bonds with the deceased, thereby freeing the survivor to reinvest in new relationships in the present. Instead, they view these bonds as a resource for enriched functioning in the present.

Within this new paradigm, the understanding between the self and its relationship to others has been challenged. This perspective also recognizes the possibility of "multiplicity in perspective" (Gergen 1991). The modernist, or "old," paradigm espoused a model of grief based on a view of the world that stressed how separate people are from one another. Klass, Silverman, and Nickman (1996) claim that "A central feature in the modern Western world view is the value placed on autonomy and individuation" (1996:14). Traditionally, human development theory (Erikson 1963) has focused upon autonomy as the stated goal of human development. Relationships with others within this traditional perspective are perceived instrumentally, so that a person establishes a relationship to have security, intimacy, or other needs met. When an important relationship no longer fills such needs (because of divorce or death, for example), the relationship should be severed. Within this model there is little room for the importance of interdependence or the idea of living in a "web of relationships" (Klass et al. 1996:15). Within the "modernist" or classical paradigm, individuals are understood to have a limited amount of energy for any one type of relationship, so that in order to have a new relationship one has to "give up the old one" (Klass et al. 1996:15). By contrast, the postmodern paradigm of grief allows for beginning a new life while continuing a relationship with the deceased. In fact, the "continuing bonds" with the deceased can enrich the new life of the bereaved partner.

A postmodern, or narrative, approach to understanding the process of loss and grief is presented in the works of Klass et al. (1996), Neimeyer (1998, 2001), and Attig (1991). This paradigm questions the universal stage theories of adaptation to loss, as well as the description of the universal symptoms of grief, because they miss the particulars of an individual's struggle that is uniquely his or her own. Neimeyer suggests that although there is some support for a stage theory of mourning derived from comparative developmental research on loss, the "most recent research on grieving has failed to find evidence for the validity and reliability of such a model" (1998:4).

From an examination of the works of Kubler-Ross (1969), Wortman and Silver (1989), and Corr (1993), Neimeyer (1998) suggests that research has provided little empirical support for the existence of distinct psychological stages, or for a "determined sequence of psychological states" (1998, 2001:84). Instead, he finds that the emotional reactions to loss seem to vary greatly between individuals. Neimeyer's 1998 study of empirical evidence, as well as his clinical observations and personal experience with loss, lead him to reject some of the assumptions of traditional grief theories and to move away from some of the clinical practices derived from those assumptions.

Neimeyer

Neimeyer believes that the "attempt to reconstruct a world of meaning is the central process in the experience of grieving" (1998:83). He outlines criteria that he believes to be useful in understanding the process of grief from this alternative perspective, proposing that people seek to construct meaning systems that are internally consistent and socially supported, and that offer a degree of security in helping them anticipate and participate in the important experiences that comprise the narratives of their lives (1998:87).

This proposition undergirds the criteria that he sets forth in his work. The following passages represent Neimeyer's thinking:

1. Death as an experience can "validate" or "invalidate" the belief systems that we have created over time. Death may also represent a novel experience for which we have made no mental constructions. What is important is the extent to which a particular form of death resonates with our current mode of integrating experience, rather than the observable characteristics of the death itself. For example, it is misleading to describe certain types of death (e.g., violent or sudden) as inherently traumatic for the bereaved, except insofar as they are very much at odds with the belief systems of that individual or family. The important emphasis needs to rest upon considering the extent to which certain ways of interpreting loss can lessen or "exacerbate its impact" (Neimeyer 1998:88).

2. Grief is a very personal process and can be fully understood only in the context of our ongoing process of "constructing and maintaining our most basic sense of self." When events disrupt our sense of self and world, we tend to respond by attempting to interpret them in ways that are consistent with our basic worldview and sense of identity. When these attempts prove unsuccessful and our basic sense of self is threatened, we are forced to reestablish another. This proposition provides caregivers with a deepened appreciation for the "unique significance of a bereavement experience for each client" (1998:90), urging the caregiver to move beyond what a particular loss "feels like" to any given bereaved person. Neimeyer further contends that we need to appreciate more deeply the extent to which losses of those we love can create profound shifts in our sense of who we are. Through the process of loss of a loved one, whole facets of our past that were shared with the deceased are "gone forever," if only because "no one else will ever occupy the unique position in relation to us necessary to call them forth" (1998:90). The grieving process involves not only relearning a world disrupted by loss, "but relearning the self as well." This is a view similar to that proposed by Lopata (1996) and Silverman (1986) in their studies of widows.

3. Grieving is an active process that needs to be viewed as a period of "accelerated decision making" rather than a passive process of "waiting

out" a series of predictable emotional transitions. This view is important to embrace, despite the fact that bereavement is a "choiceless event"—one that few would choose to experience. Neimeyer finds fundamental to the grief process "the vacillation between engaging versus avoiding grief work" (1998:91) proposed by Stroebe and Stroebe (1987), Marris (1986), and Simos (1979).

4. Grieving requires the bereaved to reconstruct a personal world that again "makes sense" and restores a sense of meaning and direction to a life that is forever transformed. The griever seeks opportunities to tell and retell the stories of his or her loss and in so doing "recruit social validation for the changed story lines" of their lives (Neimeyer 1998:94).

5. "Affective grief responses are traditionally treated as merely symptomatic, as problems to be overcome with the passage of time or the administration of treatment" (1998:94, 95). Neimeyer adopts the view that feelings have a function and need to be understood "as signals of the state of our meaning making efforts" (1998:94) following challenges to the way in which the griever has created his or her worldview prior to the loss experience. This understanding of emotions can be contrasted with the discussion of feelings "characteristic" of the loss experience discussed by Worden (1991, 2002) earlier in this chapter.

6. Adjustment to loss can only be understood in a broader social context in which the bereaved constructs and reconstructs his or her identity, as a "survivor of loss in negotiation with others" (Neimeyer 1998:96). The reconstruction of a personal meaning of the world following a loss must take into account "ongoing relationships with real and symbolic others, as well as the resources of the bereaved themselves" (1998:98). The bereaved are faced with the task of transforming their identities in order to redefine their "symbolic connection to the deceased, while maintaining" their relationship with the living (Neimeyer 1998:98). Attempts to reconstruct their identities may be similar or dissimilar to the perceptions of immediate family or more distant social relationships.

Klass, Silverman, and Nickman

Klass, Silverman, and Nickman (1996) emphasize the importance of "adaptation and change" in the bereaved partner's relationship with the deceased, following death (1996:18). These researchers question the concept of closure in the grief process and do not view it as "a psychological state that ends nor from which one recovers" (1996:18). Although Klass et al. recognize that the intensity of feelings may lessen while the bereaved becomes more future- than past-oriented, they propose a model in which "the emphasis should be on negotiating and renegotiating the meaning of the loss over time" (1996:19). The bereaved partner is changed forever by the experience of the loss of his or her partner, and part of the change is a "transformed but continuing relationship with the deceased" (1996:19).

It is impossible to understand the process of loss without recognizing what is lost. When a partner dies, not only the person but the social role is lost. In addition, the "self in that role and the role itself are lost as well" (Klass et al. 1996:18). Although the bereaved partner's construction of an inner representation of the deceased is in part a continuation of the old relationship, to a greater degree it must be a different relationship. Thus, to the researchers who have studied grief from a postmodern or social constructionist viewpoint, the Freudian and post-Freudian concepts of identification and introjection seem insufficient to describe what these researchers are observing in bereaved partners. Klass, Silverman, and Nickman (1996) identify ways in which the bereaved partner can maintain a connection to the deceased, and they have challenged the "modernist" practice of encouraging the survivor to disengage from the deceased partner. Their focus is upon how to change connections—how to hold the relationship in a new perspective, both cognitively and emotionally. This model also emphasizes how the bereaved partner constructs meaning from the experience of loss. When this approach is applied to clinical work with the bereaved partner, new kinds of intervention emerge, which will be discussed in the final chapter of this book.

Some studies have documented the number of ways in which a relationship to the deceased spouse is cherished and possibly nurtured. Schuchter and Zisook concluded that ties are strongly held rather than broken. These researchers found in their study of 350 widows and widowers that

> The empirical reality is that people do not relinquish their ties to the deceased, withdraw their cathexis, or "let them go." What occurs for survivors is a transformation from what had been a relationship operating on several levels of actual, symbolic, internalized and imagined relatedness to one in which the actual ("living and breathing") relationship has been lost, but other forms remain or may even develop in more elaborate forms.
>
> (SCHUCHTER AND ZISOOK 1993:34)

This process of sustaining and transforming bonds to their relationship with the deceased, while forming a new identity and a new life, provides the lens through which the case studies presented in this book will be viewed.

INTEGRATING THE PARADIGMS

Rubin

S. Rubin, in his seminal work on "The Two-Track Model of Bereavement," has presented an approach to an understanding of grief and loss that combines the merit and value of both the classical (or modernist) approach and the postmodern approach. Rubin believes that the bereavement process involves a "disruption and achievement of new levels in homoeostatic functioning" (1999:684). He suggests that a similar disruption also occurs in the bereaved partner's relationship to the deceased, which "also requires reorganization" (1999:684). According to Rubin, "the response to loss must be understood as it relates to both the bereaved's functioning and the quality and nature of the continuing attachment to the deceased" (1999:684). In Rubin's presentation, the first axis reflects how people function naturally and how this functioning might be affected by the upsetting life experience that loss may entail. This axis concerns itself with anxiety, depressive affect, somatic concerns, familial relationships, self-esteem, work, investment in life tasks, and meaning structure.

The second axis focuses upon the ways in which the bereaved are involved in "maintaining and changing their relationships with the deceased" (Rubin 1999:685). Although the bereaved may not always be aware of the nature of this relationship and may not appreciate its extent and their investment in it, Rubin sees this component as critical for what happens with the bereavement response across the life cycle.

This second axis is concerned with (1) the extent of the imagery and memories that the bereaved person experiences, as well as his or her emotional distance from them, (2) the positive and negative affects associated with the memories of the deceased, (3) the extent of the preoccupation with the loss, (4) the indications of idealization of and conflict with the deceased, and (5) how all of these indicators provide a view of the nature of the bereaved's "cognitive and emotional view of the deceased" (Rubin 1999:686). Rubin is also interested in how the bereaved partner memorializes the deceased and how he or she transforms the relationship into something more than the mourning process (1999:687). The bereaved partner can accomplish this transformation of the relationship through "informal or formal memorials" or through identification with the deceased. This transformation process enables the bereaved partner to place the memory of the deceased "into the fabric of the bereaved's life" (1999:687). This second axis speaks to the issue of the postmodern construction of grief as conceptualized by Neimeyer (1998), Walter (1997), Attig (1991), and Klass et al. (1996).

The narratives of partner loss included in this book focus upon the bereaved partner's changing relationship with the deceased. Although this book on partner loss is not particularly concerned with the degree of resolution of grief achieved by the bereaved partner, Rubin believes that when the bereaved can establish a more comfortable and open connection with the memory of the deceased, there is a greater likelihood of moving toward a resolution. Furthermore, the experience of the deceased and the relationship to him or her should not "remain fixed in time," but instead must shift for the bereaved to have sufficient energy to invest in his or her current functioning (Rubin 1999). The involvement with the deceased should not provide a replacement for relationships in the present, but serve only as a complement to them (Rubin 1999).

Rubin believes that as time passes there is a "reduction in the intensity of the focus on the reworked attachment to the deceased" (1999:698). As the bereaved achieves a new organization in his or her life, a balance is attained with regard to the bereaved partner's continuing relationship with the deceased. The extent, intensity, and frequency with which the deceased is now remembered, and the feelings that are highlighted by thinking of the loss, become "relatively fixed markers of the nature of the ongoing relationship with and attachment to the deceased" (1999:699). When the memories and thoughts are available in a balanced way and provide a measure of strength, warmth, and solidity to the experience of the bereaved, Rubin believes that it is possible to consider that some resolution of the loss has occurred.

Although the classical approach to grief emphasizes the need for the bereaved person to disengage from the person who has died, most of the theorists who represent this more traditional paradigm recognize that the bereaved person goes back and forth between two ways of functioning with regard to his or her relationship with the deceased person. This "holding on" and "letting go" process is described by many theorists (Marris 1986; Bowlby 1980; Simos 1979; Stroebe and Stroebe 1987).

Research by Stroebe, Schut, and Stroebe (1998) finds mourning to be based on a "dual-process" model, in which the bereaved accommodates to the loss by an ongoing shift back and forth between two contrasting modes of functioning. At times, the bereaved engages in exploring, experiencing, and expressing the full range of feelings associated with the loss in an attempt to grasp its meaning for her life. At other times, the bereaved "tunes out" the waves of acute grief that may return in order to focus upon the many external adjustments required by the loss.

Although Simos uses a phasic approach to understanding grief, she also believes that the bereaved do not readily abandon someone in whom they have invested so much energy. Instead, she suggests that the bereaved are thrown into a state of confusion—that they are "torn in two directions and keep going back and forth in their minds between the past and the present" (Simos 1979:35). Even in Freud's analysis of loss there is reference to internalizing lost "objects," relating to them as if they were the actual person, and making the lost image a part of themselves (Hamilton 1989).

Similarly, Bowlby (1980) speaks of "two incompatible urges"—one of yearning and searching for the lost person and one of ridding oneself of the painful memories of the lost person. Bowlby describes a widow who "tried sleeping in the back bedroom to get away from her memories and how she missed her husband so much that she had returned to the main bedroom in order to be near him" (1980:92). However, Bowlby believes that a major task of the mourning process is to find a way to reconcile these two "incompatible urges."

Bowlby's theory (1977, 1980) suggests a resolution or reconciliation phase of the mourning process, which is one of the concepts with which the theorists representing the new paradigm take issue. The postmodern perspective does not envision "a period of letting go," because the relationship with the deceased is transformed and carried with the bereaved for an indeterminate amount of time. In fact, it is this very transformed relationship that aids the deceased in moving forward and forming new relationships and/or in making meaning from their experience with loss.

The premise adopted in this book emphasizes elements common to the postmodern paradigm—that is, attempts to understand how the relationship with the deceased is transformed and how this contributes to new "meaning making"—without negating the possibility that phases and stages may occur.

The interviews of bereaved partners from traditional and nontraditional lifestyles reported in chapters 3–6 of this book demonstrate how bereaved partners incorporate the deaths of their partners into their ongoing life stories to restore a sense of order and meaning to their lives. These interviews also demonstrate how grief is an expression of conflicting impulses in which the bereaved partner preserves the past while concurrently reestablishing "a meaningful pattern of relationships in which the loss is accepted" (Marris 1986).

Chapter Two

Loss of a Partner: Current Issues

REVIEW OF LITERATURE ON LOSS OF A SPOUSE

Loss of a spouse has been dubbed by Holmes and Rahe (1967) as the most stressful of all losses. The literature and research on this issue underscore the emotional, mental, and physical pain experienced by widows and widowers in our society. Schuchter emphasizes the acute reactions of numbness, followed quickly by intense heartache, and points out that, as the reality of the loss sinks in, "the survivor experiences an increasing sense of loss" (1986:2). This sense of loss is intensified because the grief is not only for the person who has died but for the connection to the spouse, as well as for the bereaved person's plans, hopes, and dreams for a future with the spouse.

The adaptation to the loss of a spouse greatly depends on the survivor's ability to find some means of integrating the "real loss" and the continuing form of the relationship. A myth seems to prevail in our society that new relationships cannot be developed until bonds with the lost spouse have been severed. As Schuchter explains, "a survivor's readiness to enter new relationships depends not on 'giving up' the dead spouse but on finding a suitable place for the spouse in the psychological life of the bereaved—a place that is important but that leaves room for others" (1986:116).

However, the bereaved partner may be intensely ambivalent about these continuing ties. A bereaved spouse, confronted by the reality that the dead partner is gone forever, will do whatever it takes to sustain the relationship. Conversely, evidence of the partner's prior existence can easily trigger very painful feelings. The bereaved spouse faces a continuing dilemma—whether to be comforted by reminders of the deceased partner or to avoid them. Continuing ties to the dead spouse can be maintained by celebrating anniversaries and rituals, by developing living legacies, by communicating with the deceased, by holding on to the deceased's possessions, by keeping symbols of the relationship (wedding rings, marital bed, married name), and by spending time with relatives (siblings, parents, children). For Rubin, continuing ties with the deceased are reflected in memories that the bereaved experiences, in positive and negative effects of memories of the deceased, and in ways in which the relationship with the deceased is transformed into something more, through the use of identification and informal and formal memorials (1999).

According to Walter (1997), common themes with which both widows and widowers struggle include loneliness and isolation, an identity shift from we to I, changing relationships, handling rituals and marker events, handling anger, and taking responsibility for oneself. Often the bereaved spouse is unprepared for the degree of isolation following the death of a spouse (Kinderknecht and Hodges 1990; Lopata 1996). The literature reports that there are two types of loneliness common to bereaved spouses. One results from the "loss of daily intimacies of shared routines and private moments," as well as the loss of family holidays and sexual intimacy (Yalom and Vinogradov 1988:435). The other arises from "no longer being the single most important person in someone's life, nor of having a significant other with whom to share important experiences" (Yalom and Vinogradov 1988:436).

Following the loss of a spouse, a significant change occurs in relationships—with friends, immediate and extended family, in-laws, and social networks. "For bereaved spouses, particularly in the younger age group (under 55), dating is a very important, difficult, and conflicted issue, made more difficult by all of the changes in social norms and mores within the last twenty to thirty years since these adults last dated" (Walter 1997:77). Loyalty to one's dead spouse contributes to one's struggle with dating. The idea of loving someone new can evoke a wide range of feelings, ranging from a perception that this is a signal of healing and a readiness to move forward to a perception that this is a betrayal of the marriage, almost as if loving someone new might invalidate the love for the departed spouse (Walter 1997).

Another difficult task when forming a new life is handling such important marker events as anniversaries, birthdays, holidays, weddings, and graduations, which were once shared experiences. Bereaved spouses have to cope with their reactions to these events and then try to carve out a variation of the old experience in their new world as a single adult.

Handling anger and other negative feelings is an important but difficult part of the grieving process. Bereaved spouses often struggle to hold on to the positive aspects of a relationship that they desperately miss. It is difficult for them to confront the fact that they are angry at their spouses for leaving them or that there were negative aspects of the marital relationship that they must let go of, not just positive aspects (Walter 1997). This difficulty is magnified by society's tendency to sanctify persons who have died, putting them on a pedestal (Lopata 1979). Yalom and Vinogradov (1988) found that bereaved spouses were more able to direct anger toward physicians who had missed a diagnosis or had been insensitive to the needs of the patient and/or family. Expressing anger toward the deceased spouse for abandoning the partner, or for persistent denial while ill, was much more difficult.

Finally, the death of a spouse confronts the remaining partner with his or her own mortality. While there are usually increased fears about being alone and concerns about physical safety and health, many bereaved spouses use increased awareness of death in a positive way. "The death of their spouses served . . . to teach them existential responsibility—that they, and only they, have ultimate responsibility for their life and happiness" (Yalom and Vinogradov 1988:143). This is particularly salient for bereaved spouses who married at a young age and may have viewed their marriage as the key to lifelong happiness. It is not easy to move from feeling abandoned by one's spouse to taking responsibility for one's life (Walter 1997).

Loss of a Husband

Lopata speaks of the importance of understanding that what happens to a wife when her husband dies "depends on the degree of her dependence on being married and being married to that particular husband, the degree of disorganization in her various roles and support systems, and her status as a widow" (1996:15).

Lopata also challenges the conflicting myths that sudden death is more difficult than prolonged dying and that the reverse is true. Lopata argues that

the difficulties and experiences are so different that they cannot be compared. With sudden death, as in the case of a young husband who dies from
a heart attack, the spouse is left with varying degrees of "unfinished business." The suddenness of the death also forces the trauma into a shorter period of time than most people can absorb; too many things happen too
quickly, leaving a feeling of helplessness. On the other hand, although a
prolonged serious illness provides the caregiving spouse with a forewarning
of possible death, some researchers (Roach and Kitson 1989) have concluded that there is no significant impact from forewarning, or length of husband's illness, on psychological distress. These researchers explained their
finding in terms of the hope that the spouse holds on to until the moment
of death, so that the reality of the impending death is not grasped from the
seriousness of the illness. In addition, while caring for an ill spouse, a
woman often experiences great stress and anxiety, which can contribute to
difficulties in adjustment after her husband dies.

Roach and Kitson (1989) also report that losing a husband at a young age
is more distressing than death in later years. This finding is supported by
Neugarten and Hagestad (1976), who found that the older the woman at the
time of her husband's death, the more likely she was to have "rehearsed"
widowhood. On the other hand, "older wives may be more dependent on
the husband than are younger ones, so age by itself appears not to be the de-
termining factor as to the strength of the grief reaction" (Lopata 1996:76).

Lopata (1996) cautions against trying to find generalizable patterns of normal grief, because there are such great variations in how individuals respond
to bereavement. However, she does discuss five dimensions of the response
to bereavement, which she has distilled from her own research as well as
from other studies of widows and widowers (Schuchter 1986; Shuchter and
Zisook 1993). The first dimension involves the intense emotional and mental reactions to the loss of a spouse. They include shock, pain, anger at the
dead spouse (and everyone or anything connected with the death), and
guilt. These emotions do not necessarily occur at the same time and can be
accompanied by positive feelings, even at the most difficult times. "In the
right circumstances, the bereaved can feel joy, peace, or happiness as oases
amidst the sorrows" (Shuchter and Zisook 1999:30).

The second dimension entails coping with the emotional pain and the
strong emotional reactions (both avoidance and exposure) to stimuli that
trigger grief, as well as coping with activity and involvement with others.
This dimension is similar to that reported by Bowlby (1980), included in
chapter 1 of this text.

The third dimension focuses on the "continuing relationship with the dead spouse" which can include memories, dreams, rituals, continuing contact through conversation, and other ways of preserving the relationship with the deceased in the survivor's life.

The fourth dimension involves "changes in functioning, such as withdrawal from social settings and loss of work motivation and interest" (Lopata 1996:102). This can lead to a deterioration in health. The fifth dimension is concerned with changes in relationships with family and friends, who are either brought closer or distanced, and with romantic relationships.

Lopata questions Lindemann's (1944) assumption that one of the main tasks of grief work is to cut ties with the deceased. She points out that this is difficult to do "because the present time for human beings rests on memories of the past, and the widowed woman's past contains the dead husband" (1996:116). Lopata asks, "How can the widow cut ties with the deceased and yet preserve his memory?" (1996:116). This question is similar to that raised by the postmodern theorists, Klass et al. (1996), Neimeyer (1998), and Rubin (1999), who believe that there is never really a period of letting go, because the relationship with the deceased is transformed and carried with the bereaved for an unknown amount of time.

The Chicago area widows interviewed by Lopata provided her with an answer in the form of "reconstructed memory" (Lopata 1996:116). She found a tendency among Americans to reconstruct the deceased in "one-sided ways" and discovered that many women had developed "an extremely idealized image of their husbands and their lives with them" (1996:117). In addition to being culturally approved, this idealization, or sanctification, of the deceased husband performs important functions for the widow. First, it helps her to believe that she was a worthwhile person if such a man married her. This is important because one questions one's self-esteem during grief. In addition, this process converts her husband into a person who is not critical or jealous and who remains in the memory as a "positive critic" of how she manages money or copes with her children. Lopata (1996) points out that among the disadvantages to this process of sanctification are that it discourages friends and potential mates, who may remember the husband as a normal person with irritating habits, and who may become impatient with this new idealized image. Finally, it is difficult for another man to compete with this ideal construction. It is this author's belief that sanctification, although it has its benefits, prevents the widow from moving forward and integrating the positive and negative aspects of her relationship with her late husband.

Lopata (1996) and Silverman (1986) speak about the identity loss and the issue of re-forming a new sense of self while continuing a bond with the deceased partner. Lopata found that the major element of change following widowhood usually occurs in the woman herself. She refers to the importance of "reconstructing the self-concept," which she found to be one of the most important tasks of the mourning process. Lopata claims that since marriage brings forth a "reconstruction of reality, including the reality of the self and of the spouse" (1996:120), the death of the spouse, particularly for the woman, creates a great disruption in the widow's social relationships that formed her "social anchorage." Lopata believes that the widow needs to create an identity composed of emotions from the past as well as developing new attachments and feelings. This is an extremely difficult task, which takes a great deal of time, because "it means learning to live without the deceased and the future they had constructed for themselves as a couple and that the woman had constructed for herself individually" (Lopata 1996:124). In addition, social relationships and other complex social roles need to be modified in varying degrees, depending upon the widow's degree of involvement in them and the changes in her life circumstances and social identity.

The widows who were interviewed by Lopata (1996) early in their bereavement responded with negative self-perceptions when asked how they had changed since the deaths of their husbands. They felt incompetent to face situations and problems that were previously handled by their husbands. On the other hand, women who were interviewed later in their widowhood were much more likely to report positive changes to the self. Lopata (1996) reports that a quality of resilience is one of the major findings of most studies of widowed women (Lieberman 1994; Matthews 1979). Although widows are devastated at first, most of them are able to "work through memories of the past and tie in the present to a reconstructed future" (Lopata 1996:125).

Schuchter believes that the "most profound changes that occur in the bereaved are those that reflect their personal identity" (1986:263). Because every aspect of one's capacity to cope is tested, Schuchter claims that the "bereaved often find themselves thinking, feeling, and behaving in ways that may previously have been foreign to them" (1986:263). It is these new experiences as well as the changes that occur in the survivor's social identity that can lead to a permanent alteration of his or her self-concept.

Schuchter (1986) and Kauffman (1994) discuss the significance of the loss of the "mirror" aspect of the relationship with the spouse, in which one spouse can reinforce the positive self-image of the other partner. With the death of the spouse comes the loss of this mirror, and often with it, the loss of the sense of being important, special, beautiful, loved, or even lovable. In Walter's work on the loss of a spouse, one widow (aged forty-seven at the death of her spouse) lamented, when invited by the group leader to share what had been most difficult for her, "I no longer feel special to anyone" (1997:74).

One of the most difficult shifts in identity is from being part of a couple that has been "reality for long enough that it is usually a stable part of one's self concept" to being single (Schuchter 1986:266). The idea of being single requires a change that most spouses would not choose and is not easily accepted. Schuchter (1986) reports that, while the bereaved spouse is adopting the self-image of a single person, he or she is also changing from thinking and acting as a couple to operating as an individual. Many couples have adopted lifestyles that are often other-oriented in their motivations and it is difficult for some to tolerate a more self-oriented position.

However, Lopata (1996) found that widows in her study reported dramatic changes in life style, self-concept, emotions, and relationships with everyone from the past. The widows who were most likely to express satisfaction after the period of mourning had been able to create and define new needs and to modify self-defined old needs. Lopata believes that the capacity to diminish ties with the deceased spouse and yet still preserve his memory is accomplished in the form of "reconstructed memory" (1996:116). This process seems similar to the one advocated by researchers working within the new paradigm of bereavement, which emphasizes the importance of continuing bonds with the deceased, referenced in chapter 1.

Lopata (1996) reported that by the end of two years of bereavement, most widows and widowers were able to perceive their loss as promoting growth and experienced a positive change in their self-esteem. Widowed spouses seem to gain strength—not only from coping with the pain of loss but also from acquiring independence and autonomy. Walter reports that members who participated in groups for widows and widowers believed that one of the most helpful experiences within the support group was that they "learned to be good to themselves and to take care of themselves" (1997:80).

Loss of a Wife

Although the research mentioned earlier concerned widows, men must also work on identity issues following the loss of their wives. There are fewer documented studies of men's grief, but researchers who have examined gender differences have generally found more similarities than differences (Brabant, Forsyth, and Melancon 1992). Brabant et al. (1992) found that men, like women, experienced a severe loss of their sense of identity. This research questions the societal notion that the wife is less central to the husband's life than the husband is to the wife's. Walter (1997) affirms this, observing that in one support group for bereaved spouses, all five men in the group reported a loss in their sense of self. "The men in this group experienced their wives as central to their lives and perceived that their identity as a spouse had been critical to their sense of themselves. One forty-five-year-old widower poignantly said, 'I feel like half of me is gone now that my wife is gone—we made all our life decisions together' " (Walter 1997:76).

In one of the few qualitative studies done to date of how men experience the loss of a spouse, Carverhill found one core aspect, related to the redefinition of self-identity, that was revealed across all the participants in the study.

> At some point in the loss story of each widower, he stops and asks himself: Who am I? Or Who am I not? . . . The widower's process of relearning or redefining his self-identity is, I propose, a core meaning of the lived experience of male spousal bereavement. The event of losing his spouse forces the widower into an unfamiliar journey of introspection, where he discovers that he is changed. . . . Whatever they had previously defined themselves as in terms of the relationship to their spouse is now in serious question.
>
> (CARVERHILL 1997:14)

The men in Carverhill's study believed that they had not only lost a partner but the "mirror image of the many roles that their spouse played: companion, lover, friend, traveling partner, co-parent" (1997:14). These widowers found that their jobs were not in fact who they were, although they had previously believed that much of their identity was related to their occupational roles. In some cases the widower found that it took the death of his spouse for him to realize how much of himself was actually defined through his relationship with her. These men were forced to examine and change their own values and priorities and spoke of how work had lost its "inherent meaning because there seemed to be no purpose towards which to work" (1997:14). This research seems to refute any idea that the wife is less important to the husband's life than the husband is to the wife's.

Campbell and Silverman found that many men, following the death of their spouse, talked about "feeling that you're not, in fact, separate, that somehow two have merged into one, that you have become one organism, two halves of one whole." They suggest that, to the extent that a widower experienced this sense of oneness with his wife, he may well feel that in some way her death was his death. One widower spoke of a sense of "personal annihilation that came on occasionally," while another spoke about it in terms of "feeling he'd met his own death" (Campbell and Silverman 1996:230).

Much of the research on loss of a spouse has been concerned with the consequence of the loss on the physical and mental health of the bereaved. In a review of research findings on the differences in consequences between widows and widowers, Stroebe and Stroebe (1983) found that spousal loss tends to be associated with higher mental illness rates, higher rates of serious illness, and more physical disabilities for widowers than for widows. Widowers are also identified as having higher death rates and a higher likelihood of committing suicide in the first months after the deaths of their wives (Campbell and Silverman 1996). Widowers who care for dependent children had higher rates of clinical depression than did widows in similar situations. Following the death of a wife, fathers have to learn to deal with household chores as well as developing new parenting skills (Worden and Silverman 1993).

Studies of widowers indicate that they remarry at higher rates than women and that they often marry earlier than widows do (Lister 1991; Campbell and Siverman 1996). Campbell and Silverman found that the widowers they interviewed did not always seem to have sufficient experience, skill, or understanding of their needs to find help. Given their socialization, which predisposes them to think of themselves as self-sufficient, men may not be aware of the full meaning of their loss and cannot acknowledge their feelings or needs. Carverhill also points out that the image of a widower is very much "incongruent with socialized male role expectations" (1997:15). Admitting a need for some kind of assistance or expressing fear, as by crying, seems opposed to the societal view of masculinity, which is represented by the need for control and independence. However, Carverhill's 1997 study provides evidence that, contrary to the widely held notion that men do not want to discuss their loss experience, these widowers expressed the need and desire to tell and retell the story of their loss.

GENDER AND GRIEF

In contrast to younger and midlife partners, it has been found that there are no gender differences in older widowed people on measures of emotional well-being (Feinson, 1986). Lund, Caserta, and Dimond (1993) found that competencies, tasks of daily living, and adjustments to spousal bereavement in later life were similar for both widows and widowers. The differences between men and women may not be so much in the way they experience grief as in how they respond to it (Campbell and Silverman 1996). Some authors (Balswick and Peek 1971) have found that men have feelings but cannot express them. They also discovered a group of men who did not admit to experiencing feelings at all. It has been documented that men generally disclose far less than do women about their relationships with others (Campbell and Silverman 1996). However, rather than putting men at a greater disadvantage when coping with grief, perhaps this means that there are other ways to respond to grief. Martin and Doka (2000) challenge the popular gender stereotypes. These researchers examine the following two specific patterns of grieving: (1) an intuitive pattern, in which individuals experience and express grief in an affective way, stereotyped as female, and (2) an instrumental pattern, where grief is expressed physically or cognitively, stereotyped as male. These researchers also introduce a third pattern that represents a blending of the two. According to these authors, these patterns are related to, but not determined by, gender.

Brabant, Forsyth, and Melancon (1992), in their study of bereaved male spouses, found that after the deaths of their wives most men described themselves as feeling sad and numb. They were depressed and hurt by the loss and tried to handle their pain alone by keeping busy and by using prayer. These men thought a lot about their wives but did not share these thoughts with others. These authors believed that although men may have very strong feelings of attachment, they may not articulate their needs as women do.

Campbell and Silverman (1996) suggest that we need to legitimize different ways of expressing grief and that some of this work can be done effectively without the involvement of others in a traditional sharing relationship. These authors found that men respond to the death of their wives in many ways. Professional helpers must realize that bereaved men (and women) do not all need the same kind of help. In his new text, Doka (2002b) suggests that the "counseling community tends to disenfranchise instrumental grievers as a result of their lack of strong affective response" (2002b:14). Golden and Miller (1998) believe that talking about the loss, crying, and sharing one's emotions with another are not the only ways to heal.

Men grieve in a multiplicity of ways. Some men are able to use the more feminine mode of talking about pain with family and friends. This mode is one in which the bereaved might emphasize "interaction with intimate others" and express his emotions verbally, by talking about the past and sharing emotions (Golden and Miller 1998:5). Other men do not find that talking about their grief is necessarily a safe thing to do. These men tend to prefer to express their grief through action rather than interaction. They prefer to heal by changing the future rather than by talking about the past. Because this style uses fewer words, it is often less easy to perceive, but it is no less powerful.

In short, some men who are genuinely grieving may not express their emotions. "Men sense the public display of their emotions can cause concern or discomfort for those who aren't used to seeing them act this way" (Golden and Miller 1998:14). Many men feel shame for shedding tears or otherwise showing emotional distress when others are around. This reaction is justifiable when we see how society has treated political candidates who have shed tears. Doka argues that the "larger community disenfranchises" grievers who do not meet the expectations or rules for grieving that society has created for the bereaved (2002b:14).

Other men respond more cognitively to their loss. They're trying to figure things out—to discover an explanation or come up with a plan that will help them to deal with what has happened. "A larger percentage of men than women are likely to choose this rational approach" (Golden and Miller 1998:18). Men often take a problem-solving approach to their experience of loss. They identify the trouble, analyze it, and develop a strategy to handle it. Finally, they're ready to take concrete steps to solve the problem. A man might read all he can regarding what he's facing , including research on the Internet.

Some men are drawn toward the future as a way of dealing with their loss. A common way to do this is to respond actively, tangibly, and physically. This needs to be respected as a genuine grief response. What a man does with his grief can be a form of talking without the words and even a form of "crying without the tears" (Golden and Miller 1998:21). Men are often active, for example, in setting up foundations or memorials for their deceased spouses.

Social support has frequently been documented as mitigating the negative affects of the stress of bereavement (Stylianos and Vachon 1999; Faberow,

Gallagher-Thompson, Gilewski, and Thompson 1992). Campbell and Silverman report that "when their participation in the available social network was working, men and women adapted equally well to their spouse's death" (1996:8). The problem seems to be that most men lack extensive contacts within the community. Men are less likely to admit a need for companionship, and many have never had a male friend. For many men, the "only confidants many of them ever had were their wives" (Campbell and Silverman 1996). When men do have friends, they are allies rather than confidants. Thus, when their wives die they are lost. "In addition to everything else, they have lost public access to friendship networks which might have sustained them" (1996:8). However, although Campbell and Silverman (1996) found that men have difficulty in accepting help, all of the men in their study found what they needed—in friends, in family, and in themselves.

Campbell and Silverman found that when men go in search of help they are often referred to professionals. Although this type of assistance is important, it is usually not sufficient. However, there is some research indicating that men are finding it easier to join mutual help organizations. Organizations such as the Widowed Person's Service report that it is often difficult to involve men, but once they participate, some of them become very committed (Campbell and Silverman 1996).

REVIEW OF LITERATURE ON OPPOSITE-SEX PARTNER LOSS

Other than Doka's work on disenfranchised grief (1989, 2002) there is no literature on this growing population of opposite-sex cohabiting partners. This material on disenfranchised grief will be presented in more detail in chapter 4, integrated with the stories of bereaved cohabiting opposite-sex partners.

Doka suggests that disenfranchised grief occurs when partners experience a loss that cannot be "openly acknowledged, publicly mourned, or socially supported" (1989:4). Societies have norms about grieving that specify when, who, where, how long, and for whom people should grieve. Doka (1989, 2002b) notes that our society places more attention upon kin-based relationships and roles. The closeness of nonkin relationships is neither understood nor appreciated. Partners who cohabit do not share with married partners the societal sanctions that allow them to receive support for their grief. In addition, the emotions of a bereaved partner (such as anger, guilt, sadness, and loneliness) are often intensified in a nontraditional relationship. The lack of social sanctioning and social support may well cause the bereaved who have been partnered in nontraditional relationships to become alienated from their community.

It is important to examine the meaning that the relationship had for the bereaved partner as well as the degree to which the relationship is accepted or rejected by others. When the relationship is accepted, there is greater possibility for social support from family and friends, and this facilitates the resolution of grief (Doka 1989, 2002b). Doka (1989) suggests that in modern American society, many cohabiting heterosexual relationships may be open and accepted and may involve heavy degrees of commitment and affect. To this degree, the grief experienced by bereaved partners may be similar to that experienced by many bereaved spouses. However, in many cases, sources of traditional support may not be available.

REVIEW OF LITERATURE ON SAME-SEX PARTNER LOSS

Gay and lesbian partner loss can be related to the literature on disenfranchised loss. As Doka (1989) has pointed out, disenfranchised grief occurs when (1) the relationship is not recognized or sanctioned by society, (2) the loss is not recognized, and (3) the griever is not recognized. In his new text, Doka includes two additional categories "concerning the circumstances of the death and the way individuals grieve" (2002b:14).

Gay Partners

Most research on bereaved spouses has focused on heterosexuals, especially elderly widows and widowers. In the late 1970s, research describing the intimate relationships of gay men began to emerge with attention to AIDS and the special problems of homosexual partners of persons with AIDS (Shernoff 1998). Prior to the advent of AIDS, there were only two professional articles that addressed bereavement issues of gay individuals, one by Shernoff and the other by Schwartzberg (Siegal and Hoefer 1981). According to Shernoff (1998) "when a gay man's partner dies, his trauma is often exacerbated by the lack of mainstream culture's recognition of his relationship, his loss, and his being a widower" (1998:27). Because there is little validation by our society for same-sex relationships, gay widowers may be more apt to "encounter scorn, ostracism, fear, or blame" (Schwartzberg, 1996). However, Shernoff (1998) makes it clear that not all bereaved gay partners experience disenfranchised grief. When a gay partner has not hidden his sexual orientation, he is more likely to have a network of supportive friends who will help him during the mourning process. The gay partner who claims that his live-in lover was "just a roommate" is much more susceptible to experiencing disenfranchised grief than a partner who has support from the gay community (Shernoff 1998).

For some gay men, shame about being gay emerges as an issue when the trauma of losing a partner "reawakens previously internalized homophobic feelings" (Shernoff 1998:30). If the gay widower devalues or minimizes the relationship, that is one indication that disenfranchised grief has merged with internalized homophobia. Shernoff believes that if these reactions are not challenged by the psychotherapist, the bereaved partner is "at risk of regressing to a less developed stage of gay identity formation" (1998:30).

Guilt is an important aspect of most adverse grief responses because the survivor's belief that the death was somehow his or her fault can be a way of coping with grief. Guilt can also emanate from conscious or unconscious feelings of hostility towards the deceased. "Guilt seems to play a large part in most losses. It may be a small nagging remembrance of something that should have been done or a full-blown, persevering guilt stemming from ambivalence associated with a lifetime of rejection or other hurts" (Sanders 1989:64).

The guilt feelings experienced by gay men who have lost a partner take a different turn. Boykin examined the guilt feelings of gay male AIDS survivors. Some men felt guilty about infecting their partner with the AIDS virus, even though the act was totally unintentional. The survivor may also feel guilty about not having taken his partner to the hospital soon enough. Conversely, "there can be guilt around having encouraged the deceased to undergo painful and prolonged medical procedures which were neither helpful nor necessary" (Boykin 1991:251). Like heterosexual partners and spouses who have survived the death of a partner, the gay widower often feels guilt about being disloyal when he begins to feel attracted to others after the death (Boykin 1991; Murphy and Perry 1988). Murphy and Perry found that gay men who had lost a partner often verbalized feelings of guilt, particularly when they had not been present at the time of the partner's death. Most of these men had spent every available minute caring for their partners and found it extremely painful when their partners died away from them. The survivor might express this by saying, "If only I stayed instead of going home," "I promised I'd be with him," or "I never said the final 'I love you' " (Murphy and Perry 1988:458).

Several researchers (Boykin 1991; Sanders 1989; Murphy and Perry 1988) have identified general survivor guilt as an important issue for gay men who have lost partners. The conception of "Why him?" and "Why not me?" was present in all of these studies. According to Boykin (1991), there was a trend toward a higher degree of survivor guilt scores in the HIV+ and/or AIDS subgroups. This is consistent with traditional grief theory (Bowlby 1980; Lindemann 1944), which claims that survivors try to blame themselves for the death of their loved ones and feel guilt about still being alive. Because the gay widower is often quite young, given the AIDS crisis, these men are often experiencing a major loss for the first time and finding it nearly impossible to comprehend that grief is a time-consuming process. Perhaps survivor guilt is one of the coping mechanisms for denial of the intense pain within this group of young men.

Ferrell's 1992 study found that managing the care of the partner with AIDS greatly impacts bereavement outcomes. Those who participated in the study were consciously aware that the "managing care process" had affected their progression toward bereavement resolution. "All participants acknowledge a positive psychosocial growth as a result of the managing care experience" (Ferrell 1992:88, 89). One participant commented, "I'm at peace with myself, and I think that caring for him (the partner) has made me a better human being and has given me a better perspective on life and death" (1992:89)

Some studies (Dean, Hall, and Martin 1988) suggest that the stress of helping a loved one through the course of illness and death may be a cause of emotional and physical distress that then negatively impacts one's bereavement process. However, Ferrell found that most participants felt that managing the care of their partner was a more positive experience. One participant said, "Because I did it (provided care) to the best of my ability, not perfectly, and I did everything humanly possible that I could to help him, it made the grieving easier. It was not a totally horrible experience" (Ferrell 1992:89).

Two critical factors in making this care more positive were the caregiving partner's ability to take care of himself and his ability to share care of the partner with family and friends. Taking care of oneself is described as "evaluating the ability to cope with the demands of caregiving" (Ferrell 1992:70). Most of the participants had decided to pursue personal plans, such as career or school, while providing care for their ill partners. In addition, they used such coping mechanisms as occasionally removing themselves from the situation by "submerging themselves in their jobs, actively involving themselves in religious groups or self-healing groups, drinking alcohol and taking other drugs, becoming involved in athletics or various forms of community activities" (1992:70, 71). Finally, the caregivers were able to adopt a positive view, which enabled them to maintain some control over a situation in which the fear of loss is overwhelming. As has been reported in other studies (Oktay and Walter 1991), some participants reported that the strategy of caring for oneself was a growth process, which fostered a more productive lifestyle.

A real problem for gay widowers is that, because they are subject to homophobia, society offers them less opportunity to grieve. As Shernoff indicates, although sexual orientation has nothing to do with the dynamics of grief, the "ramifications of homophobia can greatly complicate the grieving process of a gay man" (Shernoff 1998:29). Shernoff describes a thirty-nine-year-old man who was unwelcome at his partner's funeral and had to move out of the apartment they had shared because there was no will bequeathing it to him. Murphy and Perry point out that many family members deny how important the deceased was to the bereaved lover" (1988:456). Furthermore, gay widowers have little or inadequate support from their family and friends and their work environment. People don't fully acknowledge gay relationships and often react out of fear of AIDS. Given that many friends of gay men are young people who have had little or no experience with losing a loved one, friends of the gay widower frequently have no idea how to behave with him (Murphy and Perry 1988).

Dworkin and Kaufer review theory and research about multiple losses due to HIV infection. These researchers are critical of traditional theories about the grief process, which tend to focus on an individual's response to a single episode of loss and "fail to capture the experience of multiple loss by an entire community" (Dworkin and Kaufer 1995:42). A chronic state of mourning describes the bereavement process of gays and lesbians who experience losses due to HIV/AIDS. When the onset of mourning for one loss overlaps with the end stage of mourning for another loss, the implications for complicated reactions are clear. "Not only are gay men losing those with whom they have shared strong emotional ties, but they are also losing acquaintances, role models, and coworkers at a very fast rate" (Dean, Hall, and Martin 1988). Neugebauer et al. (1992) studied bereavement reactions among two hundred and seven gay men between the ages of eighteen and sixty who had experienced multiple loss. They found that the men who had experienced the greatest number of losses reported more experiences of searching for the deceased partner and preoccupation with his memory than those who had experienced fewer losses.

All bereaved partners, whether heterosexual or homosexual, need to make sense of the loss and fit it into their assumptive world. Because AIDS most often strikes individuals at the prime of life, emotions related to the meaning of life, sickness, and suffering are particularly difficult to accept. These issues are confronted more gradually as people age. Without adequate life experience to cope with their losses, those partners who are infected with HIV/AIDS must confront and integrate these issues rapidly. "One's value system must be reworked to incorporate the meaning of multiple losses and suffering" (Dworkin and Kaufer 1995:47).

Grief suffered by a gay partner reactivates emotions that were involved in establishing one's gay identity. "In experiencing such loss, one's identity, self-esteem, and body image are challenged" (Dworkin and Kaufer 1995:47). Gay men mourn not only the death of their partners but the possible loss of their own health.

Lesbian Partners

Although there is ample research on widows and a growing literature on both heterosexual and homosexual widowers, there is a severe lack of research on lesbian women who have lost their partners through death. Lesbian women who have lost a partner are truly "silent grievers."

Lesbian Relationships

Jones cautions readers not to oversimplify the complexities of women's experiences. "There is no such thing as the typical lesbian couple" (1985:97). Most empirical research has concentrated on younger, educated, middle-class white women. Very little is known about lesbians from other backgrounds. According to Jones, a great majority of lesbian women are involved in a relatively stable relationship at any given time. Peplau and Amaro (1982), following an analysis of seven studies, concluded that about 75 percent of lesbian women are in relationships at any given time, with from 42 to 63 percent of all lesbians surveyed living with their partners. "Most authors seem to agree that lesbians tend to establish relatively long-term relationships" (Jones 1985:97). A nationwide study done by Mendola (1980) established trends toward long-term relationships in which "95 percent of the respondents expressed the belief and hope that they would grow old with their current partners" (Jones 1985:98). Several studies indicate that lesbian women look primarily for companionship and affection from their relationships. Jones reports that research has suggested that there is an ease of intimacy and mutual interdependence within lesbian relationships. The closeness and sharing of activities may account for how satisfied lesbian respondents are with their partners (Jones 1985).

The existence of lesbian communities within a sometimes hidden culture has been well documented. "Homophobic or heterosexist values are common within the majority heterosexual culture who are uninformed about or openly hostile toward lesbian individuals and institutions" (Deevey 1997:13). Lesbian women lead "double lives" as they work among the heterosexual majority, but develop hidden networks of support, activity, and resources within lesbian communities (Deevey 1997). Lesbian women and gay men create families from the networks they develop. Although they often substitute for "blood family," the kinship networks in lesbian communities differ from traditional heterosexual nuclear families (1997). The review of literature on lesbian kinship suggests that we can not assume heterosexual models of family relationships to be universal.

Factors identified as complicating bereavement in the heterosexual population include issues related to the death, the relationship, and the social/cultural context. A death that is in some way unjustified (because of youth, human cause, or suddenness) is known to be more difficult to accept. If the relationship was in some way ambivalent, because of unresolved anger or miscommunication, grieving may be prolonged. The sociocultural context provides permission and rituals for mourning. "If the relationship is hidden, or socially condemned, the rituals of mourning may be unavailable to help in the healing process" (Deevey 1997:21). For many lesbians, the normal emotions of anger, sadness, denial, and fear may be prolonged or intensified.

In Deevey's (1997) qualitative study of lesbian women who lost a partner, she found that the theme of "disenfranchised grief" identified by Doka (1987) emerged from some of the narratives. During Deevey's interviews, 83 percent of the lesbian survivors presented with intense grief, or intense negative affect. Some of the most painful narratives concerned lack of social support, which accounted for 83 percent of the survivors. In Deevey's study, "one woman returned alone to her hometown for the funeral of her first lover; she did not know the current partner and faced the ongoing hostility of her mother and sister who had always mocked the relationship" (1997:86). Jones (1985) also found that support and recognition during lesbian bereavement was more mixed than expected. Interactions with the women's families, with their partner's families, and with such professionals as doctors, nurses, funeral directors, and clergy were varied (Jones 1985). Deevey concludes that although it is encouraging that lesbian women in both studies had "positive as well as negative experiences during bereavement, the unpredictability of caregiver and family responses remains a source of stress and fear in the daily lives of many lesbian women" (1997:88).

Jones (1985) corroborates Deevey's (1997) concerns by reporting that a lesbian woman who has experienced the death of a long-time lover is likely to receive a much wider variety of responses from the community. "Lesbian women who have lived well-closeted lives may find, upon the death of their lovers, that the majority of members of their larger social network are not even aware of their bereaved status" (Jones 1985:8). Family and friends who are not aware of the nature of the relationship between the grieving spouse and her partner will not necessarily be supportive or approving of expressions of grief from a lesbian woman. Lesbian women who are grieving the loss of a long-term partner are most likely to be perceived as belonging to the category of "friend" of the deceased (Jones 1984). In a novel about a lesbian couple who had lived closeted lives, the bereaved partner, Harriet, was surrounded by a community that failed to support her grief because they did not recognize the life partnership that she and Vicky had shared (Sarton 1993). Harriet remarks at the beginning of her story: "When Vicky died our friends took it for granted that I would simply go on living, gardening, and reading for pleasure in our house; that I would go on unchanged by her death, as though I were not recovering from an earthquake" (Sarton 1993:9).

Other issues that emerged as representative of disenfranchised grief included being excluded from attending the funeral (in most cases separate ceremonies were held by the lesbian survivors) and practical and legal difficulties. One lesbian survivor reported that she removed all evidence of the couple's lesbian lifestyle before the brother arrived. "One surviving partner had arranged power of attorney, but due to changes in the law, the paperwork was not valid, so she could not be part of a legal suit against the driver whose negligence caused her partner's death" (Deevey 1997:86).

In one of Deevey's case studies, Amanda, a retired schoolteacher, was interviewed eight years after Kate's death of a brain tumor at age forty-nine. The couple had lived together for twenty-four years and had raised three children together. Amanda said, "Initially it was like I had lost half of myself," and added that she felt "very alone." Amanda, wanting to isolate herself after the death of her partner, chose not to attend group meetings at the hospice because she didn't want to "air" their relationship.

Jones refers to grief as a part of the development of a lesbian identity or the "coming out" process. She indicates that as a "stigmatized and often invisible minority, lesbian women must give up many of the privileges of heterosexuality which they had assumed since childhood to be theirs" (1985:93). Such privileges include the freedom to speak openly of one's partner without censure, the wedding ritual in which family and friends celebrate the union, and the opportunity to bear children in an atmosphere of support. Bowlby (1980) and Rando (1993) report that unresolved grief can create problems in the way a person functions, making future losses more difficult. Jones (1985) raises the question of whether lesbian women who have not resolved the earlier grief associated with the loss of "heterosexual privilege" will have a more difficult time with the loss of a lesbian partner.

Integration of the Bereavement Experience in Lesbian Relationships

Jones's study (1985) examined how lesbian partners understood their experience of bereavement at the time of the interview. Jones found that although the time that had elapsed since the death of their partner varied from one to fifteen years, there were common themes in the responses. "The most frequent theme was of having incorporated some of the dead partners' positive qualities within themselves" (Jones 1985:193). Several women in Jones's 1985 study described a "conscious sense of having 'taken in' valued parts of their partners' personalities. One woman reported, "I've also found that in losing her, I've also taken her in. I mean, truly, now she is a part of me, part of my personality." It's almost like a physiological process. I don't know how it happens, but I'm like her now. At least half of me is" (193).

Another aspect of "taking in" was having a comforting sense of the dead partner's presence. One participant observed, "Sometimes, in times of stress, I will not only think about the way she would handle things, but think about her as a comfort to myself. . . . There's something very affirming to me, in the fact that she was in my life" (1985:193). Bowlby (1980) reports that this kind of admiring identification is compatible with healthy mourning.

Another major theme reported by Jones is that several women spoke of gaining an "awareness of mortality" and its meaning to them. This realization made them more willing to take risks. For example, one woman said, "I don't have very much fear, . . . which means that I can take risks with equanimity. . . . I'm not afraid of being humiliated, I'm not afraid of looking like an idiot, I'm not afraid of dying. So, that leaves me a lot of room to take risks" (1985:194).

In *The Education of Harriet Hatfield* (Sarton 1993), Harriet, a sixty-year-old lesbian woman who had lost her partner, took many risks following the loss of a woman who had been dominant in her life. Harriet opened a community bookshop in a low-income neighborhood and risked her life to keep the bookstore open when members of the community threatened her security.

A third major theme, found among the responses in the 1997 study by Deevey, was an awareness of one's strengths, a feeling of confidence that the surviving partner could "weather major life difficulties." One woman in Deevey's study remarked, "It brought me the awareness of who I was as a person. Because it really put me right there at rock bottom of who I was and whether or not I was strong. Because I never knew whether or not I was a strong person . . . and I realized that I really could deal with things" (1997:195).

Harriet Hatfield frequently speaks of how much she has changed since the death of Vicky, who had "always been a power . . . and I was simply an adjunct to that power, doing volunteer work to keep busy, and managing the household for her" (Sarton 1993:9). Near the end of the novel, Harriet speaks to her brother of the changes that have occurred within her since Vicky's death, saying, "I am more myself, I am more of a whole person now than when I was a kind of appendage to Vicky. She dominated our life and I willingly went along with it. . . . We were also shut off from a lot of things. So it is not so much mourning and missing her now as building and moving forward into what feels like my real life" (Sarton 1993:295).

Adoption of Partner's Roles

Jones also found that none of the women in her study perceived their relationships as stereotypically "butch-femme" (1985:254). Although more than one half of the women interviewed claimed that there had been some degree of task-splitting within the relationship, "none of the women experienced the difficulty in adopting the partner's roles which widows characteristically endure" (1985:254). The lesbian women who did have to learn new tasks expressed the same sense of pride and mastery that heterosexual widows have mentioned as one of the long-term satisfactions of coping with the problems of bereavement (Lopata 1979).

Support Systems

Almost all the lesbian women in Deevey's study found friends to be extremely helpful. The size of the friendship network varied from two to twenty and served a function similar to that of a family. Approximately half the lesbian women found their families helpful, while the remainder found them to be neutral or unhelpful (Deevey 1997). Most of the women whose families were unhelpful or hurtful had either concealed their sexual orientation from them or were aware that the families disapproved of their lifestyle. In contrast, the two women who found their families most helpful had never formally told their parents they were lesbians but assumed their parents knew.

SIMILARITIES AND DIFFERENCES AMONG TYPES OF PARTNER LOSS

Widows and Lesbian Partners

Jones found that the experience of bereavement for lesbian women paralleled the experiences of heterosexual widows in many ways. "The process and length of grief of the women in the study confirm the findings of previous research." However, the major differences were found in social networks and in the "amount of psychic energy needed to adjust to a new social identity and adopt roles previously accomplished by the partner" (1985:250). In contrast to heterosexual widows, who found family members to be more helpful than friends during their bereavement (Glick, Weiss, and Parkes 1974), lesbian women found friends to be the most helpful group. Just as Oktay and Walter (1991) found in their study of breast cancer patients, lesbian women referred to their friends as family. Diane, a forty-six-year-old lesbian woman diagnosed with breast cancer, derived support throughout her cancer experience "from her close network of women friends who became like family to her." Diane said, "I have a lot of friends. . . . Every weekend and on all the holidays someone would come to visit. . . . So at some incredibly deep level I realized that I had family" (Oktay and Walter 1991:137).

Although friendship groups of the lesbian partners were composed primarily of other lesbian women, they also included gay men and heterosexual men and women. The friendship network served a function similar to that served by the family for heterosexual widows. Friends provided practical and emotional support during the final illness and the first few weeks of bereavement (Jones 1985). However, as seen in similar findings about heterosexual widows, almost all of the lesbian women found that the amount of support they received dropped away shortly after the first month (Jones 1985).

Lesbian women seemed to need much less psychic energy than heterosexual widows to adjust to a new social identity and take on roles formerly
assumed by their partners (Jones 1985). Because there is no word for a lesbian woman to parallel *wife* or *widow*, "the amount of self invested in this
kind of conception of self is smaller . . . and needs to change less dramatically" (Jones 1985:250). In addition, because lesbian partners shared more
equally in role assignments, the bereaved lesbian partner appeared to be less
disrupted in her daily functioning by the loss of a partner than were widows, whose husbands were often totally responsible for home repairs and a
major portion of the family finances.

Deevey concludes that until more is known about the experiences of lesbian survivors, "we should not be too quick to compare lesbian bereavement experiences to the experiences of heterosexual widows" (1997:110).
Risk factors for complicated grieving, such as ambivalent relationships or
sudden death, may or may not be similar. Deevey is adamant that counselors
who are working with a lesbian partner must be aware of individual and
cultural differences, even within lesbian communities.

Widows and Gay Men Whose Partners Died from AIDS

In his work with gay men who lost partners, Ferrell (1992) found that
they experience the common grief reactions identified earlier in studies by
Lindemann (1944), Bowlby (1977), Freud (1957), and Parkes (1972).
"However, the problems of loss and grief that are present in the general
population are often compounded for survivors of AIDS-related deaths"
(Ferrell 1992:25). In AIDS-related deaths, identification with the deceased
is more intense and long lasting because of the survivor's fear of developing
the disease from exposure to the partner. "The fear or unfounded belief that
one has the disease easily complicates the grief work, in that before the initial loss is resolved, anticipatory grieving for the survivor begins" (Ferrell
1992:26).

In addition, stress may be compounded for survivors of AIDS-related
deaths. Added to the common issues of grief that every survivor experiences, gay survivors face problems of stigma and homophobia. Their grief
is also compounded by their youth. Surviving partners of gay men with
AIDS not only grieve for an untimely death but also deal with their own
mortality. This task is not age-appropriate for adults between the ages of
twenty and thirty-five. Their lack of exposure to major life events makes
them more vulnerable to the consequences of stress.

CHAPTER SUMMARY

This chapter provided an overview of the current literature about various types of partner loss—loss of a spouse, loss of a same-sex partner, and loss of an opposite-sex partner. The chapter concluded with a brief summary of the literature, examining issues that are similar for widows, gay men, and lesbian women as well as issues that are different.

Chapter Three

Loss of a Spouse

YOUNG WIDOWS AND WIDOWERS

According to the National Center for Health Statistics (Rosenberg 1991), more than 73,000 women between the ages of thirty-five and fifty-four became widowed in 1991. If younger women were included, this figure would escalate. Data from the new census will push these figures even higher. Although sufficient literature exists that speaks to the issues and challenges for middle-aged or older widows, little is available regarding the issues that face younger widows and widowers.

Walter (1997) discusses some of these issues as well as interventions for widows and widowers under age fifty. The most salient issues include shifting one's identity from couple to single person; adjusting to changing relationships with in-laws, friends, and social networks; dating (which raises the issue of loyalty to the deceased spouse); and confronting one's own mortality. Levinson reports that "for young widows, the death of a spouse places them in a category out of synch with their developmental life stage," which can increase the sense of aloneness they already experience because they feel different from their peers (Levinson 1997:278). Shaffer (1993) and DiGiullio (1992), in their studies of young widows, concur with Levinson that the loss of a spouse at a young age is clearly an example of a nonnormative event.

Shaffer (1993) points to the impact of the secondary stress inherent in the "off timeness" of the event, exemplified by the lack of comfort from others of a similar age who have been through a similar experience, the lack of role models to demonstrate how to cope, and the lack of previous experience with the loss of loved ones. All of these factors lead to a heightened sense of isolation and lack of support. DiGiullio adds that the woman who is widowed in her thirties or forties "has not been socialized to anticipate what being a widow will be like, and she has few role models for young widowhood" (1992:99).

The primary finding of Shaffer's 1993 study of twenty young widows was that the grief and phases of bereavement reported by these young widows follow the general pattern of mourning and recovery described by Bowlby (1980), Kubler-Ross (1989), and others. Her study not only confirms the sequence of phases described by Bowlby but validates earlier findings that "while recognizable stages may be common to most people, the length and duration of each stage varies among individuals" (127). She adds that grief is also characterized by positive opportunities for self-expression and growth that are not always associated with mourning in general. For the widows in this study, grief was characterized more by "positive shifts in life perspective and by a theme of metamorphosis and rebirth" (1993:128). Such transformations may be related to the youth of the women experiencing such deep suffering and loss. Loss at an earlier time may allow them to remake their lives and "start over" in a way that might seem unrealistic to an older widow, who has lost a spouse later in life.

The following story of a young widow illustrates some of the issues just presented as well as the theory on grief presented in chapter 1.

Kristen

Kristen was twenty-nine years old when her husband, Carl, died at age thirty. They had been married for two and one-half years. The young couple was returning home from a vacation in Florida because Kristen had been notified that her grandmother had died. "We were coming home a day early from our vacation for Carl to sing at my grandmother's funeral. We left about 6:15 on Sunday morning, and we were in my brand new Ford Explorer. Carl was driving and I had leaned my seat back—not all the way, but just enough so that I could lean against the back of the seat. He had been acting like he was a little bit tired, but we had only been on the road for about 40 minutes at the most. I kept asking, 'Do you need me to drive?' He said, 'No, I'm OK.' I said, 'Are you sure?' He said, 'I'm fine. We'll stop up here at the next gas station, get some coffee, and get gas.' So I sat back and closed my eyes. I was not asleep. I was just simply enjoying the ride when I heard the sound of gravel under the tires. I thought that he was pulling off, like he had said, or pulling over. I thought he had decided he was too tired and was just pulling over on the emergency lane to let me drive. I heard that sound and sat up and by the time I sat up we were already flipping. My only thought was, 'I'm just gonna die, I'm just gonna die.' We flipped two times, nose over end, and then five times over side. We came to rest driver's side down, in the grass on the other side of the highway. We had gone off in the median and then five times across the road into the other side of the road.

"Carl never made a sound. I have *no* idea what happened. I didn't see anything. There were no other cars. Nobody saw it. Nothing. . . . When I realized that we were done flipping, I looked down at him, because I was up—suspended over him. I looked down at him and he was bleeding a little bit. I let myself out and I climbed out the back window. I remember sitting and trying to dial 911. I was shaking really bad, and this is all from a view above me." (Kristen believes that she had a dissociative experience at this point.) "I don't remember doing this myself, but remember seeing myself do it. In fact, I remember hearing somebody scream and then realized that it was me. I remember trying to dial 911 three or four times and I kept dialing the wrong number and I was getting frustrated. Then I put the phone down, to just catch my breath, and I started smelling smoke. I got scared and I moved further away from the car. I knew that he couldn't get out. He was trapped, and so I knew that there was nothing I could do. I guess I was cognitive enough at that point to know that I needed to get away from the car, and then, when I looked up, there was somebody standing there. He was in jeans and a navy blue shirt with a little emblem on it, like a police officer. I thought, 'I don't think I ever called 911. How did this guy get here already?' I came to find out an off-duty firefighter had come over the hill just as the car had come to rest. He never saw it. He just saw the tires were still rolling and spinning. He instantly cut across the median and came over. He actually checked Carl before I even got out of the car. I was still in the car when he got there and I don't remember any of that. When I climbed out of the car, he said he was standing there, and I had no memory of it. He said that when he got there, Carl was dead. So, him being a fireman paramedic, I feel completely confident that Carl never suffered.

"I didn't know what to do. I'm twenty-nine years old. . . . Thirty-five minutes earlier my husband and I were eating breakfast together." Kristen suffered both a head and nose injury. "They were working on me and I was getting very, very angry, 'cause nobody was helping him, because I know he needed help and I was OK. I mean, I was bleeding, but I was gonna be OK . . . just a few minutes earlier he had been alive, and now they are telling me he is not coming to the hospital. So they took me to the hospital. I have no memory of anything after they told me Carl was dead. I really didn't remember much of anything for about two weeks." Although Kristen suffered a concussion, she was never admitted to the hospital. She was taken to the hospital and put in a room where they treated her nose injury, and then Kristen sat in the hospital chapel for nine hours while she awaited the arrival of her parents, whom she had contacted. During these long nine hours, Kristen never received any support from hospital staff regarding her emotional needs and now knows how terribly she was treated.

Kristen was able to reach some of their friends who lived in Florida, and they stayed with her until her parents arrived. Carl's parents were also contacted, but when they called Kristen at the hospital, they were upset that there would be an autopsy, which is required by state law. When Carl's parents contacted Kristen at the hospital en route from their home, they said to her, "What are you doing? Where is our son? Where is our son? Where did they take him? You should have stayed with him."

Although Kristen appreciates the support she receives from Carl's parents (whom she has known all her life), "a lot of times I wish that we weren't so close. So I could just move on. But other times, I'm so grateful, because they love me, and I have total support when I can't find support from anybody else. Because nobody has gone through this, I have no peer support system. I have a big support system, but no one that I can just sit down and just talk to about being a widow at thirty."

As part of her own mourning process, Kristen needs to talk about Carl with her in-laws. And yet, she feels torn. She can't move on because of their presence in her life. "After Carl died, they joined my church. We are all very active in our church. I just started dating again three months ago, and this is where I have met this guy. It makes me a little bit frustrated, because I can't just be with this new person without being concerned that I am hurting them. But at the same time, I am kind of happy that they are there because they are seeing our relationship develop."

Kristen and her boyfriend, Brian, have discussed the difficult situation, and Kristen has decided that she would rather have her in-laws see her dating than not know. "It wouldn't be fair if we suddenly say, 'Oh, by the way, we are getting married.' It's gonna hurt them. No matter what. I explained to Brian that it's not about him. It's about Carl. It's really not about me, it's about Carl. . . . I'm thinking how it's hurting them (the in-laws), because for me to see their pain, . . . and you know, it's just, it's real difficult for me. . . . I've always been overly sensitive about other people's feelings. I kind of have this radar, emotional radar, around people. . . . I can sense feelings and stuff. I don't want to hurt them, and I think a lot of it is because I have been hurt so bad. I feel very guilty that I survived and their son didn't . . . not that they don't love me, but they can't help but wonder, 'Why did she walk away and he died?' I know that it's never been said, but that's just human nature. So I feel there's a real tight bond and a lot of times there's just a lot of angst and maybe a little bit of anger."

Kristen has had to rework her relationships with her own parents since Carl's death. Since returning to graduate school she has been living with her parents to save some money. "My mom and dad had a really hard time because my mom wanted to be my primary support system. And she would say, 'I understand, I understand.' I would say, 'Do not tell me you understand if you have not been through it. Do not tell me.' What I've had to do is to draw some boundaries. I realized through some of my psychology classes that my mom and I were enmeshed with each other and we needed not to be. So I've had to make some real conscious decisions about not letting her in any more than she should be. I do need to be able to hear and let her talk, because she's grieving, too. I have to realize that. This man was a part of her life for his whole life, too. He was my husband and he was her son-in-law. So I've had to let her grieve in her way. I had to realize I am not sixteen any more. I am a thirty-one-year-old woman. You can't really tell me what to do and not to do. She could share her opinion with me, but I had to realize that's my mom's opinion. That's about my mom. I met widows younger than my mom. I formed this really tight bond with them and I tried with my mother, I really did. But we could not relate. . . . We really struggle. But my mom and dad absolutely love me. And I really couldn't have done this without them. . . . So, I realize that my support system, even my in-laws, has just been invaluable to me."

Kristen can openly discuss her anger at Carl about being left to deal with all the details, her anger at "losing her sense of innocence and about a lot of stuff that isn't really Carl's fault." Kristen copes with her anger by jogging.

But she also deals with it by talking to Carl. "I just unleash it on him. It helps me a lot. It helps me to just talk to him. You know, just tell him, 'I'm pissed off.' I'm the one that is left here to suffer. He never had to suffer. . . . Now my mom, my dad, my brothers, niece and nephew—we all have to look at this every day." Kristen does believe that she suffers from survivor's guilt. Her work with animals helps her to cope with this reaction. "I am actually a certified veterinarian technician. And so pets are a huge source of . . . unconditional love for me.

"I am pretty open with my parents about how I feel about some of the things that happened. And my mom and dad are real good letting me vent some of that. But they are very angry, too. A couple of times my mom has overstepped. I don't know what it is, but when she starts getting too personal, I say, 'You can't say that about him. I can say that about him.'" Kristen has had to endure her in-laws' anger. "I said one night, I think it was the night of the funeral . . . and I got up and I said something weird Carl said to me. His Dad said, 'Tell me, what do you think happened?' And I said, 'Really, Carl fell asleep.' And his mom reacted by saying to me, 'Don't you ever say that my son made a mistake that cost him his life.' I said, 'OK.' So now I don't go there. I mean she laid down that boundary."

Like many young widows, Kristen's identity was deeply affected by the loss of her husband. Their relationship had been long-term and intimate. She and Carl "grew up together. . . . Really and truly, the hardest thing about losing Carl was that I lost my friend. We met when we were in first-grade Sunday school . . . five years old. We grew up together. We didn't start dating till I was twenty and he was twenty-one. We dated all through his business school. We were only married for two years and eight months when he died, and I still miss my friend a lot. I really don't have any memory of my entire life without Carl. Not necessarily as my boyfriend or as my husband, but when I think of things . . . we grew up in church together and we are a very tight church. We went to camp every summer and he was always there. So it's really difficult. It's more to me like losing a brother, because we really did grow up together. I mean, we graduated from high school together. We were just really good friends. So I realized after he died that it wasn't just my entire life up to twenty; I also spent a decade with this man in some form as a boyfriend. And I didn't have any kind of skills on how to date, you know. I realized I missed that whole twenties thing when you do all that stuff.

"What happened to me is that at twenty-nine, there was not a single place where I could go to get help. The AARP had a center, but I wasn't

. . . sitting around with a bunch of 'old' people. That's how I felt. You know, they've been married for fifty years. I didn't want to hear. 'Oh, honey you were only married two years, so you can't hurt as bad as I must be hurting.' I wasn't about to go there. So I packed my stuff and I told my mom and dad; I said, 'I am leaving and I don't know if I am coming back. If you can find me a place that I can go talk to people, you call me. But until then I need to get away.' You know, I've had to sell our house. There's a whole lot of stuff that I had done that I needed to get away from. So I went to the Bahamas. While I was away, my mom and dad found a Methodist hospice. They contacted a social worker, and she agreed to let me come in on some of the grief-support groups, even though I wasn't involved with hospice." Kristen believes that they allowed her to attend hospice because of the "urgency of it." She now realizes how many risk factors she had for complicated mourning—her young age, the sudden onset and extreme trauma she experienced with the loss of her husband, and facing her own near-death experience.

Kristen joined a local grief support group sponsored by a hospice. "The closest woman in age to me was fifty. Which, the first time I went, I was very angry about that, but I had to really do some soul searching and say, 'All right, Kristen, you are only twenty-nine. How many of you do you really think there are?' So I made myself go. I went for the twelve weeks. I don't know what I would have done without that group. It was just the universality. It is just being able to sit in a room with three other women— there were just four of us—and just talk about what we are going through. Nobody understood. I just needed to talk about the practical stuff. People did not want to hear that I was mad at Carl. . . . This kind of mysticism of what a widow was about was all of a sudden placed on me and I didn't really know what it was. It really helped me to be with what I considered young women that were going through the same thing. I began to just completely looked forward to the groups. I thought, 'I can't wait to go. I need to talk to Pam about so and so.' We just formed a really tight bond. The therapist was fabulous. But she really was just there to facilitate stuff. We were the ones that were doing the work. And just hearing their stories . . . I can't even describe how meaningful that was."

Kristen joined the group about four months after Carl died and described how it helped her get through that difficult first year. "It got me through the first set of holidays . . . my wedding anniversary was during that time. It was just orchestrated really well for me. I had my anniversary, then I had Thanksgiving, then I had Christmas, then I had New Years, then I had his birthday. So there were just these sequential things I had to deal with first. The women were there to support me. And even though my mom and dad really tried, they couldn't help me. All of a sudden I wasn't included in the group of my married friends any more. I felt that the young women were very threatened by me. . . . All of a sudden, when their husbands wanted to help me (they would come over and help me cut the grass), I just got this instant feeling of 'you're crossing a line, girlfriend.' These are people that Carl and I have been friends with for years. They have been in our home. All of a sudden I wasn't included in any of the functions anymore. I just got completely cut off. I was supposed to be friends with all these single people, but I didn't feel single. And really I was thrown into this void, and these women (in the support group) were really the only women that I could connect with to help me."

The death of her husband has deepened Kristen's desire for personal and professional growth. She has left her job doing research on endangered species and has decided to pursue a master's degree in counseling psychology. "It was during these counseling sessions that I realized that our city needed something. I also realized that because those women could share their stories with me, I could share my story with other people. I never read the obituaries before. I read the obituaries every day now. And I see these people—thirty, thirty-two, twenty-five—and I see they were married. There is somebody out there now that's going exactly through what I am going through, and they are not going to find anybody, just like I didn't find anybody. So I really started feeling this need or drive to help people." Kristen is now in her second semester of graduate work and will soon begin her internship with a hospice. "I am going to be working with the chaplain." Kristen has vivid memories of her own ER experience immediately following Carl's death. "I just think of another me sitting in the room all by herself. Maybe . . . a need to talk. But just having somebody acknowledge. Nobody ever even acknowledged what had happened. I just needed somebody to sit with me or to just come in and say, 'Here's my card.'" Kristen also plans to cofacilitate grief support groups for adults and children. "My real interest—I mean, if I had to say this is the one thing I want to do—I really would like to open a grief center. There is not a place that comes to mind in this city that when someone dies and someone is left behind they can go and get support. Who do you call? I would like there to be a place like that. So this experience has completely changed my life."

Kristen is now forming a new sense of identity, which she has forged from her experiences with death as well as from her old identity and her work with animals. Her "dream grief center" includes providing animal therapy because she knows that her own animals provided her with much comfort following the loss of her husband. The hospice center is willing to support her with research to examine how animals can be beneficial to people while they are grieving.

Kristen spoke of how she has integrated her memories of Carl into her new life. At about twenty months following Carl's death, Kristen started to feel better. "When I think of Carl now, I can think of happy memories. I am not really angry any more. Kristen also believes that seeing Carl's parents about twice a week helps to keep Carl's memory alive. "And I've been real open with talking about Carl. I don't want people not to talk about Carl. So people talk about him in front of me. And it makes me feel really good. And I really and truly . . . I know Carl is gone forever, but it's almost just like he's just on vacation. I mean I still feel close to him. . . . There's some days now I realize I go to bed and I am like, 'Wow, I didn't even relate something to Carl today.' My parents believed that after Carl died, a filter got put on my thought process that was just Carl. Everything I did, everything I said, everything I experienced had to go through that Carl filter. And it's not there anymore. Maybe it's still there, but some stuff goes around it."

Kristen speaks about relocating Carl's memory in a place where it is accessible to her. "I think he'd be OK. I think he would have said a long time ago, 'Come on now, get on with it,' but I really wasn't ready. I felt like people were encroaching on him. I needed to put him in a place where I could have someone come in and not get involved in him. I feel like I finally emotionally relocated Carl, which has been a difficult, time-consuming task. A lot of it is psychological—I've just learned how I can have a memory of Carl and I can have a life without him."

Kristen also spoke of how she is integrating her memory of Carl with her new relationship with Brian. She now realizes what another woman in her support group was saying about forming a new relationship. "And it's not that you've forgotten him. It's not that you've moved on without him, because you can't. It's just that you are in a place where you can have somebody else and you can have him too, and they're not all mixed up. I think that's important for the other person, because Brian is very sensitive about my in-laws. He does not want me comparing. He says,

'I'm not going to be a replacement.' I said, 'I don't want you to be a replacement. You can't replace Carl, period.' But it dawned on me when I
was talking to him about it one night and I said, 'Comparing you and Carl
is like comparing apples and oranges. And it's not because you're apples
and he's oranges. It's because *I'm* different and I am so grateful that that's
happened.' Every once in a while, he'll open the door for me, and Carl
always opened the door. I wonder, 'Does he love me as much as Carl did?
Is he going to do this for me? Is he going to be able to do this for me?'
But I'm very scared about doing it again. Very scared. Because loving
somebody means that I am taking a risk again of losing that person. I
know how it feels. I told Brian, 'You just don't know the risk that we are
taking. You don't know.' He said, 'Well, if you don't take risks you might
be missing out on something really great.' And I said, 'I know that. I am
completely aware of that, but because I walked down this road it really
scares me.' I could see myself very easily just walling up—getting involved
with school, my job and profession, and just doing my thing and never
letting anybody in. But I don't want to do that. Because Carl and I did
have such a close relationship, I know how rewarding it can be. I want to
be able to have that."

Kristen's personal growth has also been amazing to her. "I am a much
healthier person now. I have much more insight into who I am. This relationship that I have gotten involved in—everything is just out on the table.
I live with a sense of urgency, now, every day. . . . I don't want you to ever
question that I didn't care about you. . . . No more games, no more 'What
about tomorrow? We won't be able to do this tonight; we'll do it next
week.' That's crap now to me. I am going to live right now, this moment,
here, now, today. And I feel very free. When I lay my head down on my
pillow every night I feel like, if I don't wake up in the morning, that I dealt
with things.

"The other thing that has happened, though, is that I don't have as many
close friendships as I did. It's because I don't have a lot of superficial relationships any more. It's not that I don't care about a lot of people, but I
have a couple of just real close people in my life. For the most part, I am
happy for the things that have happened in my life since Carl died. I am
not happy that Carl died. But if Carl were to come back, Carl and I would-
n't be married, because I have changed so much. I mean I would still love
him, but we wouldn't be able to relate on the same level, because we
danced that . . . dance. I am just not that kind of person anymore. We'd
just have to be open and honest and say, 'Let's deal with this stuff.' I just

don't think he could deal with it, and that's OK with me. That's the part about it that's so weird—that it's OK with me. I don't have this pining and, 'Oh, Carl, just come back,' because I realize that if Carl came back, we wouldn't be together. I am just a different person, and I am grateful for that. I read books about this stage and I thought I would never be able to say that I am happy for what happened, but that's exactly what I am saying now. I am happy for me."

Kristen believes that some of her professional growth has emerged from her new status as a single woman. "Carl made me feel—not that he purposely made me feel inferior—but because of his position I felt like I was just a wife. I mean I was pretty significant in my own right. But I just really never had to exercise my strength. I am attracting people to me that are also strong. Brian said, 'One of the things that attracted me to you is that, if you can handle this, you can handle anything.' But he's right. I found that that's attractive, but on the other hand I also attract some pretty yucky people, too, that just want for me to take care of them. I know enough about myself now to be able to call people on stuff like that. I know the right questions to ask . . . you just get to a point where you know the questions and you have this list of things that are important. . . . If they are not going to fit into my new life, then I'm not interested. I also want somebody to love me for me. Because that's one significant thing that Carl and I had— we were really good friends.

"I feel grateful for who I am, and I think that Carl would be happy for who I've become. I've been able to use him not being here to turn into a better person. I believe I am a better person now, with more goals, a lot more insight, and a purpose to my life. I'm not just living. 'All right, what am I going to do today?' Because I might not be here tomorrow. I know I freak people out about that. I've literally been given a second chance at life. I should not have walked away from that car. I looked my own death in the face as well as my husband's demise right in front of me. There's this song out by Steven Curtis Chapman about the next five minutes, and it's 'I'm going to live the next five minutes like it's my last five minutes because the next five minutes may be the only five minutes I have.' I feel that way. If you think about it too much it can be stressful, but for me it's very liberating. I've never lived in the here and now—realizing how great that can be."

During a follow-up conversation with Kristen, about one year after my initial interview with her, Kristen announced that she had remarried. "I got married, and Carl's father walked me down the aisle with my own father on the other side. Carl's father died eight weeks after my wedding and told me

that the happiest memory he had of his last months of his life was 'your getting married and seeing you happy again.' "

Analysis

Kristen's case provides an excellent example of how her relationship
with her deceased husband, Carl, shifted over time. Kristen spoke of "relocating Carl's memory in a place which is accessible to her now." Prior to that
time Kristen's whole life was "filtered through Carl." As Rubin points out,
for Kristen, the memories of Carl have become "relatively fixed markers of
the nature of the ongoing relationship with and attachment to the deceased"
(1999:699). When memories are available in a balanced way, they provide a
"measure of strength" and allow the bereaved to move forward in their lives
(Rubin 1999). Kristen has certainly demonstrated this process in her ability
to invest in a new career and dedicate her life to helping others with their
traumatic experiences. Furthermore, Kristen's remarriage and the involvement of her late husband's father in the wedding ceremony provide evidence
that Kristen is using her continuing bonds with her deceased husband to help
her forge a new life. Klass et al. (1996), Neimeyer (1998), and Rubin (1999)
discuss how continuing bonds with the deceased are used as a resource for
enriching the functioning of bereaved partners in their present lives.

Kristen's story points to the discomfort level experienced by the young
widow when she "becomes aware of increasingly divergent interests between herself and her coupled friends from the marriage. Friends and family may have expectations of the young widow that may be at odds with her
own wishes" (Levinson 1997:281–282). Levinson also reports that the
young widow may find an increasing gap between herself and her coupled
friends for two reasons. First, young married women are often afraid that
their husbands will make advances toward their widowed friends. Second,
they fear that the young widows will make advances toward their husbands.
Kristen clearly recognized this reaction when she got an instant feeling from
her friends of "you're crossing a line, girlfriend," and got completely cut off
from old friends. She reported that the issues of her coupled friends and
even her mother seemed frivolous compared to the challenges she faced.
According to Levinson (1997), this pushes the young widow into a search
for new ways to meet her yearning for unfulfilled internal needs and to initiate interpersonal change. Kristen began to become friends with the
women in her support group and then began to date. This pattern is corroborated by Levinson, who points out that, while the young widow is in-

volved in her new relationship, she continues the mourning process, "reframing her mental image of her deceased spouse in the context of this relationship" (1997:283). Kristen clearly spoke of "moving on with Carl's image." Kristen says, "It's just that you are in a place where you can have somebody else and you can have him (Carl) too, and they're not all mixed up." Kristen says, "I've emotionally relocated Carl."

Kristen also spoke of her difficult relationship with her mother, who "wanted to be her primary support system." Young widows and women facing life-threatening illnesses find it difficult to cope with their own drive for independence and their parents' (often their mothers') wish to protect them. Oktay and Walter (1991) found this to be true for women in their twenties who were diagnosed with breast cancer.

Levinson (1997), DiGiullio (1992), and Shaffer (1993) all speak of the young widows' attempts to re-create new lives. Interview data from Shaffer's study indicates a remarkable change in personal identity and self-definition. "The data provide strong evidence that while the loss experience represented a time of intense struggle and instability, it also initiated a transition in self-concept"(Shaffer 1993:113). The loss experience also contributed to increased self-awareness, self-definition, and the establishing of a new identity. Specifically, the widows' self-perceptions changed significantly, becoming more specific and well defined. The widows attributed this change to "challenging circumstances that had required them to stand alone and rely on themselves throughout the grief experience" (1993:114). Kristen clearly speaks of the personal and professional growth that has emerged from the loss of her husband at age twenty-nine. She has changed her career plans from animal research to grief counseling. More important, her own personal growth has "been amazing" to her. "I am a much healthier person and have much more insight into who I am." DiGiullio states that "early widowhood challenges one's internal assumptive world, a system of beliefs one has about life" (1992:99). Just as Kristen changed her professional and personal world, "the young widow must give up her view of the world and develop another in a short period of time" (99). Kristen speaks of being happy about who she has become "because I'm a better person now, with more goals and deeper insight into the purpose of my life."

In Shaffer's 1993 study, the widows reported that the bereavement experience required them to identify and clarify important new values as well as to alter their commitments to previously established long-term goals. There was universal agreement that the grief experience impacted their view of themselves, their relationships with others, and their relationship to life in general. Just as Kristen did, they most valued their new definitions of self and their commitment to new ways of being. Prior to the deaths of their husbands, widows in Shaffer's 1993 study believed their values to be largely influenced by their spouses' interests, as well as compromises resulting from a "marriage identity." Kristen speaks clearly of never having to exercise her strength as a "person in her own right" because "I felt like I was just a wife." Now, following Carl's death, Kristen embraces goals and values important to her—ones with which Carl may not have agreed. Just as Kristen described in her story, "personal values were less focused on exterior accomplishments than before the loss" (Shaffer 1993:122). Less importance is placed on maintaining the approval of friends and family.

For young widows, "Personal autonomy, an enlarged capacity for caring, a keen appreciation of human relationships and a strong sense of the preciousness of life" (Shaffer 1993:122) were the most highly valued aspects of postloss value systems. Kristen certainly spoke to her newfound appreciation of savoring every moment of her life. This is corroborated by Kessler's 1984 study, which generated the following categories of change and personal growth following bereavement: (1) an increased capacity for empathy and caring; (2) a heightened appreciation of human kindness and loving contact with people; (3) a strong sense of the preciousness of life, with an increased willingness to take responsibility and take risks; (4) perceived increases in inner strength and independence; (5) the capacity to relate to people with intimacy and honesty; (6) a keener desire to live fully in the moment, with a renewed affirmation of life; and (7) a willingness to confront the reality of a loved one's death and one's personal mortality. Shaffer (1993) concludes that the young women in her study demonstrate the possibility of going beyond survival of a spouse to engaging in a life that is more full and complete than might previously have been possible. Kristen actually states this in her story of the loss of her young husband, when she talks about how she has grown in her personal and professional self in ways she could never have imagined.

Finally, Shaffer points out that her current study confirms Weenolsen's 1988 findings that, although spousal loss significantly disturbs aspects of a person's life, the crisis may lead to a significant "re-creation of the self" and the building of a new life with increased capacity for growth and change. Furthermore, insofar as the loss of a spouse at a young age is viewed as a traumatic experience and a significant stressor, it appears to initiate a significant transition that impacts a young woman's life in far-reaching ways (Shaffer 1993:132). Weenolsen (1988) noted that the impact of a loss of identity significantly affects the way women re-create meaning in their lives.

This research also confirms Lopata's 1986 findings that some widows see themselves as more autonomous, competent, and self-reliant as a result of grieving over the loss of their husbands.

Although little literature is available on the experiences of young widowers, the following case illustrates some of the issues of the male experience with grief.

John

John was thirty-seven when his wife, also thirty-seven, was killed in a car accident. They had three children—a son aged nine and two daughters, eleven and thirteen. John and his wife, Bobbie, met at a college orientation dance "before college even started," dated for four years, and then married right after graduation. John and Bobbie were married for fifteen years before Bobbie's sudden death. John is a psychologist, and Bobbie was a "stay-at-home mom" who was involved in many community activities, both at home and at school. In fact, the day she died, she was driving to the childrens' school to help with a gathering for the teachers.

"She was driving there and stopped to make a left turn and some eighteen-year-old kid behind her came up, probably going too fast, and hit the rear right corner of her car. It pushed her across the street and a car coming the other way hit her head-on. It was right in town; the speed limits weren't real fast. This brings me to the mystery—this was 1979, when seat belts were in the cars but nobody cared very much whether you wore them or not. She always wore them, but she was not wearing her seat belt that day, which was surprising to me. I don't understand that. As a result, she got thrown across the front of the car and hit her head on the door handle on the other side. Basically, there were no injuries. She wasn't cut, bruised, or bleeding, but because she hit her head on the door, there was a brain-stem compression and her brain died. It was a freak thing. If she had been wearing her seat belt, she probably would have walked away fine. I was working at the time and got a call that my wife was in the hospital. I drove to the hospital, and she was there in the hall on a gurney, waiting for X rays. She was talking, and I told her I was glad that she was OK and that I loved her. She just sort of coughed and passed out. They ran her into a crash room, and they said she had a hematoma and her brain was swelling. They did brain surgery right away and drained it to relieve the pressure. She stayed in that coma for ten days, and then she died and never came out of it." John believes that the ten-day coma was a good thing for him because it wasn't a sudden death. "There was a long period of mourning and a period of kind of getting used to the fact."

Following his wife's death. the most difficult thing for John was dealing with the children. During the interview, John cried and said, "I had to do all that I could to assure them that their life would not change or be disrupted as a result of this. That was very important to me. I didn't want them to have to give anything up or suffer any more than they had to give up their mother." John also had great difficulty sleeping and often cried himself to sleep at night wondering what to do. He did not take medication or go to a therapist. "It wasn't intolerable, and it was something I had to endure. I didn't want to numb myself and dull myself. I cried my way through it—my family rallied and helped me. My mom came and lived with me for about a month to help with the children and everything else. My job was real tolerant of time off, so I was able to stay home and get things done."

In describing his coping mechanisms, John said that as a psychologist looking at himself, "This was a learning experience. Part of it was my training, my personality style, and my family. . . . There were people there to help, and it was important to know that there were resources available if I needed them, and that helped me cope. But more important, for myself, I needed to be there for the kids. When you have someone to take care of, you don't have time to worry about yourself." John's young son was very close to his mother, but he didn't understand much of what had happened. John's oldest daughter cried a lot, but his youngest daughter didn't cry at all. "It took her a month or longer before she was actually hit with the impact of it all."

John began socializing about three months after Bobbie died. "On the one-month anniversary of Bobbie's death, I said to myself, 'We're not married anymore, and there's no reason to wear a wedding ring. It took about thirty days, and then I just took it off, and that was a struggle. For a while, I wore it around my neck on a chain. I didn't really want to break that tie. Eventually I realized . . . it was a symbol, and I didn't need a symbol. I stopped wearing that. But that was an interesting struggle—around the ending of the marriage—the symbolic ending of the unique relationship. Physically, it was over. I knew that. . . . I had to recognize in my mind to put that relationship away. . . . She wasn't there to be a companion anymore." When John received a call from a friend who invited him to a party, he decided to attend. "I wanted to meet some people. I realized I was single, and as a single person, I ought to be going to parties, meeting people, and dating. I didn't feel like that was a bad thing to do, although I hear other people say, 'I'll never date again; this hurts the memory of my spouse.' If I died I would want her to go out on a date. That would be silly, to expect her to sit home and wear black the rest of her life."

John's friends and family were very encouraging about his decision to date. Even his thirteen-year-old daughter said, "You can if I can. Dating is something that people do. . . . I want to do it, you go ahead and do it." John tried to protect his children from "latching on" to anyone he dated only briefly. "I had to keep a distance between them and whoever I dated, and I also wanted to model good behavior. . . . I didn't want to give them the idea that just because you are dating someone you're committed to them." Until the children moved out on their own, John never allowed any women he was dating to sleep in his house. However, John did spend overnights with some women he dated and had babysitters stay with his children. He would always be home by 5:00 A.M. to help the children get ready for school, and they never knew he was gone. "It was a long time in our house before they were ever aware that I was in a relationship and spending nights with people. There was certainly no evidence of that. It was important that they understood that that was an important value for them to hold." John doesn't recall that the memory of his wife interfered with his new relationships. "I never felt like I was cheating. I never felt like I was doing something wrong or that my behaviors were inappropriate or that I was dishonoring my wife's memory. That didn't mean she left my mind. Even now, there's still a picture of her in my bedroom. I have a girlfriend of several years, now. Her picture is right up there with it. It took a long time for it to get there. . . . I don't feel like I'm dishonoring either woman. I don't think that was ever a problem." John's struggle was always making sure that the women he dated were appropriate for his children. "Their mother is very special and cared about them a lot and the kids always came first. Anybody I dated had to understand that."

John seems to have adjusted to rearing his three children, and when people tell him, "Boy, you did a great job," John's response is, "I didn't do anything. I just did what I had to do. What were the options? There wasn't a choice of having to do a good job or a bad job, you just did what you had to do. I was lucky that the children turned out as well as they did." John does remember some difficult times, "because one parent couldn't do what two parents could do. I had to work, I had to make other arrangements for them to go to soccer and softball. Somebody had to drive, and I would have to come home and pick them up. I had to do my share, whatever that was." John is very proud of his three grown children, who are all married, with college degrees, and have children of their own. "They're all independent and, to my knowledge, reasonably successful. . . . I'm pleased with the way they all turned out, considering what might have happened."

John stays connected with his memories of Bobbie by staying in touch with her parents, aunt, and cousins through phone calls and Christmas cards. He also honors the memory of his wife on the anniversary of her death by lighting a candle in the Jewish tradition. John has also carried his relationship with Bobbie into his work with the Girl Scouts. "My wife was very active in the Girl Scouts. She was a leader . . . a member of the board of directors. . . . After her death we started a memorial fund in her name. About a year later they asked me to be on the board of directors of the local council. I took that job, and I'm now a life member of the Girl Scouts. . . . It's really in her memory that I got involved in that. I wouldn't have done it on my own." John also believes that he has incorporated some of his wife's values and "put them into practice because she wasn't there to do it." John believes that his wife's death has changed him, because prior to Bobbie's death "I wasn't much of a dad because I didn't have to be, because she was so much of a mother. She did so much for them and with them. I thought it was important, but I didn't have to do it. . . . I learned from her that it was important to show certain attention to the children . . . getting my daughter to music lessons became a reason for being at that point."

John has used his personal experience with the death of his wife to expand and enrich his professional practice as a psychologist. Before the loss of his wife, John did not do much work with bereaved partners. Now he has developed a specialty in this area and has served as a consultant to a widow and widower's counseling center. This center is reaching many young bereaved spouses "where the death came as a shock. . . . It was interesting, when they came in and said they didn't know where to begin, and I gave them a list of things they might be feeling, they said, 'Wow, how did you know that?' I shared some of my life with them, and that was useful. . . . Treatment moved a lot more rapidly." John loves his work with bereaved spouses and believes that he has "credibility." Although his professional training has been helpful to him he believes that "To know something and to feel something is very different. The pain, the emotional upset, the thoughts that go through your head—I couldn't get from a book."

Although John's mother says she thinks about Bobbie every day, he now goes "for long periods without feeling connected . . . then sometimes, even now, I would be driving in a car and I could puddle up a little bit, with no reason, rhyme, or connection, but something struck something somewhere. . . . As time progresses, things get better, but they never get totally better." John is involved in a serious relationship with a woman he has known for several years and is planning to build a home with her in the very near future. At this point, John is uncertain about marriage. Because John married at such a young age and never lived on his own prior to his marriage to Bobbie, he says, "I never really had a life that was my life to do with as I pleased." John believes his relationship with Ellen is "a mature friendship. We have a good time, we talk, we don't argue. We don't have to struggle about having enough money to send the kids to camp, and we don't have to worry about who does the shopping. We can be friends."

Analysis

John's story illustrates Carverhill's 1997 findings that widowers are often forced to examine and change their own values and priorities and to reevaluate the meaning of work in their lives. John speaks of incorporating some of his wife's values and "putting them into practice because she wasn't there to do it." Before his wife's death, John was not that involved in parenting because his wife did so much for and with the children. Following her death, John believes that he changed his priorities because he recognized how important it was to be with his children. Instead of work as his reason for being, "getting my daughter to music lessons became a reason for being at that point." John also reorganized his work schedule as well as his personal life so that he could attend to the needs of his three young children.

John's story also illustrates Worden and Silverman's 1993 findings that following the deaths of their wives, fathers have to learn to deal with household chores as much as developing new parenting skills. John spoke of how difficult it was for him to deal with the children after Bobbie's death and how he cried himself to sleep at night "wondering what to do." Perhaps John was suffering from a depressive reaction, which is more common for widowers than for widows who care for dependent children (Worden and Silverman 1993). In John's case, he had been less involved as a parent prior to becoming a single father and felt overwhelmed by the tasks at hand.

In some ways, John's story also illustrates some of the findings about men and grief, as he developed an "I can do it myself" approach, refusing medication or therapy for his depressive feelings and his difficulty with sleep. Golden (1996) found that men tend to grieve in a private, quiet manner, don't want to be a burden to others, and want to maintain their independence. However, John does not fit this pattern regarding maintaining independence because he graciously accepted the very supportive help of his mother, who came to stay for one month following the loss of his wife.

John also stated that "when you have someone to take care of, you don't have time to care for yourself." This expression is illustrative of the research on male grieving patterns, which indicates that since men are often placed in the roles of protector and provider, it places them in a double bind with regard to using an "open mourning" approach to their grief. Although John often cried himself to sleep at night during the first few months following Bobbie's death, he never cried in public or in front of his children. "The roles of protector and provider don't mix well with the expression of tears" (Golden 1996:62). Men have been conditioned to be strong and to take on the role of "making it safe" for the members of their family (Golden 1996). John clearly speaks of his efforts to keep his children from experiencing a change or a disruption in their lives following the loss of his wife. Although John did not say this, it seems obvious that he made sacrifices for his children in his work and personal life.

Golden has noted that many men use action as a way to activate "the grieving process and move toward healing" (1996:83). John was certainly active in his professional, personal, and family life following the loss of his wife. One of the forms of action often used by men is the creation of a memorial for the deceased loved one (Golden 1996). Soon after Bobbie's death, John started a memorial fund for the Girl Scouts in his wife's name and still contributes to the fund. He also became very active in the Girl Scouts and says that "it's in her memory that I got involved as a board member."

John's narrative demonstrates the dynamic nature of the grieving process in which he can go for "long periods without feeling connected to Bobbie" and yet can be driving a car and "puddle up" with tears with little or no reason. John says, "Things get better, but they never totally get better." This is the voice of a man who has been widowed for almost sixteen years; yet we hear the same dynamic as in Kristen's story and the stories of other widows and widowers presented in this chapter.

Although John has been widowed for sixteen years, he has used his work with the scouts as a way of continuing his relationship with Bobbie, his deceased wife. He also continues to have a relationship with Bobbie's family and is quite involved with his three adult children and his six grandchildren. Bobbie's emphasis on the importance of family life has been incorporated into John's life. John's decision to remain single following sixteen years of widowhood is rare, according to the literature, which states that men remarry earlier and at higher rates than widows (Lister 1991). This decision may be related to John's desire to experience the independence he did not have during his early adulthood, since he married early, and to the loss of his wife in his thirties.

John has derived meaning from his early experience with the death of his wife by using his own grief experiences to enrich his professional practice as a psychologist. John now specializes in and serves as a consultant to widows and widowers. According to Rubin, John's new specialization may reflect the ways in which "the loss of a person has been transformed into something beyond grief and mourning" (1999:687). This integration of personal loss with one's professional life is similar to Kristen's change in careers, from working in animal research to counseling bereaved and traumatized adults and children. It seems significant that, in both cases, these bereaved spouses were in early adulthood when the death occurred, and for both individuals, it was a traumatic, sudden death.

From the literature cited in chapter 2 on the loss of a spouse, the following case study demonstrates how a widow copes with the loss of her own identity, which was intertwined with that of her husband. Marion's story illustrates how intense the loss of a spouse can be, in that it involves not only grief for the person who has died, but also for the part of the bereaved that was connected to the spouse (Schuchter 1986). This case study also speaks to how memories and the continuing bond with the deceased can help in coping with the grieving process.

Marion

Marion is a forty-six-year-old widow who lost her husband, Sam, three weeks before he was to turn forty-five. Marion and Sam were married for fourteen years but had lived together for almost nine years before they got married. Marion is Caucasian and Sam was African-American. Marion, a part-time teacher in a private school, likes her current job because of the hours and the people with whom she works. She has two children, ages ten and thirteen. Her youngest child has a serious disability and attends a special school. With her new job, Marion feels that she can be more available to her children because she is more of a support person, without as much responsibility. Marion used to work at a city welfare department, where Sam worked too, but they had met through friends before he started working there. Marion's husband died very suddenly, at age fifty-seven, from a heart attack while he was running. He was healthy at the time of his death, but ten years previously he had had a heart attack and bypass surgery.

"Sam was a marathon runner. It was the first day of spring break, and we went bike riding with my daughter in the morning and came back and we had lunch. Then my daughter and I went shopping, and he went out for a run, and he never came back. I was worried around dinnertime when he didn't come back, but kept thinking that he was going to call with a flat tire or . . . something happened, and then I was really panicking and there was nothing I could do. I was just waiting here, and I never heard anything. I called my parents and my father, and I drove around looking for the car. We were looking for a needle in a haystack, you know. It was ridiculous. Then I called the police, and they said they couldn't do anything because the man doesn't have to come home and check in with his wife. They did suggest calling hospitals and the medical examiner's office. I started calling around, and I called the medical examiner's office. . . . They asked me for a description, and I described him, and they said, 'He's here.' My father and I went down there—it was about 3:00 a.m.—and it was him. He was there. He didn't have any identifying information on him because he was running—he was just wearing his running clothes and he had his keys." Marion later contacted a friend who was a doctor and was told that Sam had died instantly from a heart attack while he was running and never knew what had had happened to him.

Having married at a young age, "I spent my entire adult life with him, so it was a real shock to my identity—it was very confusing. I had been 'Marion and Sam' my entire adult life and now, I'm suddenly, I'm Marion. I was so closely identified with him, and we spent all our time together. Other people told me we were unusual that way, that we didn't have separate things that we did. We did everything together, and when we had the two kids, it was the four of us. We just talked about everything all the time, especially because of some of the difficulties of an interracial relationship. We had all of that to deal with as well as my son, who was born with a serious disability. Then Sam had a heart attack when my kids were almost four and eighteen months old. We just had lots and lots of stuff to deal with through our entire relationship."

When Sam died, Marion went into shock. "I felt like I was dead. I just gradually had to regain who I was." What helped Marion to cope with Sam's death was being able to think about who Sam had been to her and to rely on memories of Sam to comfort her. "A lot of who he was helped me because we had talked through so many things. His death was another thing that I had to go through without him, but I could almost hear what he would be telling me to get through it. . . . Like at night, when I felt like I was going crazy, and I would remember something that he said when he was talking to a patient who had serious emotional problems. He said, 'You think you're crazy. I'm crazy too. I just have it under control.' And I just kept thinking, 'It's okay to be crazy, I just need to keep it under control. I can let myself be crazy, just within certain limits.' That kind of helped me through all the feeling crazy that I felt."

For the first year following his death, Marion found herself talking with Sam all the time. Even two years later, Marion talks to Sam "when I'm trying to figure something out, I ask Sam, 'What should I do? Just help me with this.' Sometimes when I pray, I'm praying sort of to him. It's easier for me to pray to him than it is to pray to God, because God doesn't have a face, but he (Sam) does. . . . I pray to him to watch us and take care of us and help us." Marion also reported that what also helped her cope with her grief was "the kind of person he was and the fact that I knew he didn't want me to be grieving. He was a positive, upbeat person, and I knew he would not want me to sit around being depressed."

Marion also reported that her spirituality and taking care of her children helped her to cope with her grief. "I had to put myself into taking care of them and their being a priority. Even if I wasn't going to do things for myself, I was going to do things for them. With regard to her spirituality, Marion reported, "I've never been a person of blind faith. I've always been real questioning, and after his first heart attack . . . we became more spiritually aware, praying more. Sam grew up in a very spiritual family, and he was always kind of in prayer himself . . . walking a walk that had to do with the Lord. That's how we made all of our decisions—in terms of what was the right thing to do and not necessarily what would make the most money. We started praying a lot after he had the first heart attack . . . but I was always skeptical. I wanted to believe, but I was always skeptical. But after he died, I had an experience the morning of the funeral where I actually felt him come back. I felt him tell me that everything is going to be okay, and then he left. And in just that moment, I believed. Now, I believe that there's life after this life . . . actually that is probably the real life, and I believe that we're going to be together again. I believe all those things and that really helps me a lot. The purpose of this [his death] is because he was finished with what he had to do here, but I'm not finished with what I have to do, and I have to do it by myself, in a sense, in order to be ready for the next side."

Marion believes Sam's death has changed her. She reported that she is no longer afraid of dying. Following her husband's death, Marion wanted to die. "I wanted to jump in the ground. I wanted to go through the looking glass, like Alice in Wonderland, and get to the other side. I still feel that way, but it's on a back burner. The one thing that gets me through is I know I will die some day. I'm not afraid of it like I used to be. . . . I don't want to suffer a lot—no one does—but I'm not afraid to go because I know for sure now. I believe that there is the other side, where I'll be going." Sam's death has also made Marion "realize that I can do things without him. Not that I want to, but I can. I can make decisions without him, so it makes me feel like I'm stronger than I thought I was."

Marion is also expanding her social network. "I'm reaching out to other people more, rather than just our unit here. We're kind of an isolated unity. And I need people now. I have ten people that are each doing one small part of what Sam did for me." Marion talks with her brother, who lives in the Midwest, every day, whereas before Sam's death, she spoke to him once a month. Her family's strengths are more apparent to her now. "My father is a mechanical genius. If something breaks, he's excited about fixing it. The kids stay with my mother, sometimes, and both of my parents like that. We never left them with anyone before. We never had babysitters, so occasionally they'll stay with my parents. I went away for the weekend five months after Sam died. I did it for me, and I left the kids with my parents for the weekend. They had never been away from me that long. So, it's making me branch out and appreciate the fact that people can't be everything to me the way I felt Sam was to me, but everyone can do something, and maybe that's okay—for me to be with other people." Marion has also become closer to some of her neighbors—particularly those who are widowed. She has reached out to others that she might not have known or spoken to before Sam's death.

There has been a major shift in the relationship between Marion and her parents. "I didn't speak to my parents for ten years because they objected to my being involved with a black man. I gradually started opening up and connecting with them after the kids were born, to the point that they were really upset when Sam died. They were with me through the whole ordeal. They drove me everywhere and paid for the whole funeral. My parents opened up their whole house and took in Sam's family, who came in from all over the country. It was unbelievable—in some ways it felt like my wedding. That's because the two families had never come together, and it just boggled my mind to hear what his brother and sister and my brothers and my family talked about. . . . My parents were unbelievable, and just the contrast of not speaking for all that time—to just opening up and being gracious—it was incredible."

Marion has had fears of forgetting Sam, which she worried about immediately after he died. She said, "I don't want to forget what he looks like; I don't want to forget how important he was to me. That's why I didn't throw away his stuff. His shirt and hat he had hung in the kitchen, he just put it over the kitchen chair before he went out to run—I left it there for a year. I didn't move it, and I finally moved it, and I still have it hanging on a hanger upstairs. It took me a year to throw out his toothbrush. I went through and threw out all the stuff I knew he didn't like, but stuff I knew he liked, I still have, and . . . I guess eventually, little by little . . . some of his clothes I wore and still wear. I wear his T-shirts, and now my son can wear some of his clothes." Marion feels that Sam is more "with her" when she wears his clothes. "I feel like I'm like him. As a matter of fact, my daughter made up a name for me after he died. She said to me, 'Now you're both (of) my parents.' Whenever I say or do something that's sort of like he would have done, she'll call me that name." Marion and her family keep continuing bonds with Sam through talking about him and by wearing his clothes. Although Marion had a big fear that he was "just going to disappear," she's gradually finding that he's not disappearing. "When we talk about him, it's more, 'Oh, he would have liked this,' or 'We went there with him,' or 'We passed by where we lived when we first met.' . . . He comes up all the time." Marion is comforted by her discovery that although "some minor things [about Sam] do get lost, major things don't—they seem to be permanently here—they're just not going anywhere. So, that's kind of a relief."

As a way to preserve bonds with Sam, Marion has asked her brother to type some stories that Sam wrote about his growing up in the South, "which will be mostly for the kids—I mean, it's not something to be published or anything like that, but it will be for them to know something about how he grew up and how he sees things. That kind of life no longer exists, which is why he wanted to write it. That kind of community they had in connection to the environment—they were basically self-supporting."

Analysis

Marion's identity was intensely intertwined with that of her husband, and his death dealt a severe blow to her sense of self. However, although Marion felt that she had "lost herself" after Sam died, she has been able to reconstruct a new identity as a single woman by incorporating some of the strengths of her relationship with Sam, as well as by keeping her connection with him alive, yet transformed. As Schuchter describes, Marion's "readiness to enter new social relationships depends not on giving up the dead spouse but on finding a suitable place for the spouse" in her own psychological life (Schuchter 1986:116). Marion's grief work also corroborates Lopata's (1996) and Silverman's (1986) findings that reconstructing the self-concept is one of the most important tasks of the grieving process, which involves continuing a bond with the deceased partner during the reconstruction phase.

Marion's story demonstrates the importance of understanding "the quality and nature of the continuing attachment to the deceased" discussed by authors (Klass et al. 1996; Rubin 1999) in the postmodern tradition. Rubin states that "an approach that emphasizes the continuing relationship to the deceased, while remaining attentive to the indicators of functioning that are disrupted, has particular value" (1999:684). Marion reports that she and her family have maintained and changed their relationships to Sam by talking with him and changing their lives in order to incorporate some of Sam's beliefs. Marion has integrated some of Sam's strengths, especially his faith, which has helped her to cope with her grief and her need to move forward. Marion has found a way of keeping Sam's "story" alive by asking her brother to record stories Sam had written about his early family life. Memories and thoughts of Sam seem to provide a measure of strength and warmth for Marion and her children, which, according to Rubin, is a significant sign that the memories have found an "appropriate resting point in the life of the bereaved" (1999:697). Marion's memories and thoughts of Sam are available in a way that provides her with a sense of comfort and strength.

Richards's 1999 study of gay men who have lost a partner reviews the following themes that were apparent in interviews in which the relationship with the deceased partner was maintained: (1) stating that the deceased is in some way a part of the self, (2) maintaining an active relationship through memory, (3) feeling guided by the deceased partner, and (4) experiencing the presence of the deceased partner. All of these themes were present in Marion's interview about the loss of her spouse.

The following story illustrates how a widowed father in his forties copes with his own grief while he cares for his young daughter. Like Marion, Frank clearly expresses his grief—for the loss of his wife as well as for that part of him that was connected to her. Frank's story also reveals how a bereaved partner will do whatever it takes to sustain the relationship with the deceased spouse. Yet evidence of the partner's prior existence can easily trigger very painful feelings. Thus, as Schuchter (1986) explains, the continuing dilemma of the bereaved spouse is whether to be comforted by these reminders or to avoid them.

Frank

Frank was forty-nine years old when his wife, Sarah, died suddenly at forty-nine from a rare form of pneumonia. Frank now cares for the couple's daughter, Cara, who was four and a half when her mother died. Frank says that both he and his daughter still think of Sarah as being " forty-something." Frank and Sarah were married for twelve years. Both had been married before but did not have children from their previous marriages. At forty-five, they adopted Cara, who was two days old. Sarah retired from teaching to be a "stay-at-home mommy."

Frank told the following story about Sarah's illness and death. "I think from the moment she got sick, I didn't realize what it really was. There was something that clicked inside of me that I had a little girl and that mommy was in the hospital, but I was just going to keep things rolling and I think that is the general mentality I had. . . . It became obvious that we were in deep trouble with this pneumonia. It was flu season in the middle of winter. I tell the story like this: Cara came down with the flu. My daughter, our daughter, Cara, came down with the flu. It was one of those times where if you went to her preschool class, out of the seventeen kids that were there, there were only two kids that week because the whole class had the flu. Cara was sick for a whole week. On Friday, Cara was okay. On Saturday night, we had a babysitter because we were going to go out. About the middle of the day, around 1:00 on Saturday afternoon, Sarah said to me, 'You know what? I think I have what Cara had. I think I have the flu. I don't feel well.' So I said, 'All right' and we didn't go out. Monday I went to work. I guess Cara went to preschool. Monday, Sarah took herself to the doctor because she felt so bad and she wanted to find out what was going on. I talked to the doctor, who said that Sarah had what everyone else had he saw that day. She had flu symptoms. He took a culture and did everything he was supposed to do, but he didn't prescribe antibiotics. You know, there's a controversy today about the use of antibiotics. . . . There's proantibiotic doctors and antiantibiotic doctors. He was of the mind, you know, 'Don't overuse it.' That was on Monday.

"On Wednesday, Sarah said she felt terrible; she never felt this bad before. And I said, 'Well, you know, it's the flu . . . I don't know.' Thursday morning she gets up with me at 5:30 in the morning. She says, 'You can't go to work today. You have to get me back to the doctor. I feel terrible.' I said, 'Sarah, I'll go to work, I'll put stuff away, tell my boss that I'm taking half a sick day, and get back as soon as I can.' So I actually went to work that Thursday, put my stuff away, came back, was back by 10:00. But Cara wasn't feeling well that day. As a matter of fact, Cara was home. Cara and I helped mommy into the car. She couldn't breathe. She said she couldn't breathe. She was so weak. We went back to the doctor's, and this time it's a medical center—there's five doctors. This time, a female doctor . . . the woman doctor, took one look at her and she said, 'Turn around and take her down to the emergency room down at City Hospital.' I said, 'All right.' So I take her down there. It takes hours to admit her. . . . Sarah seemed to be okay, more or less. She was being admitted and all that stuff people do in the emergency room. Cara was restless—this, that, and the other—so you know what? I said, 'Cara, this is going to take hours. It's going to take hours.'

"Cara and I went down to my school. For some reason, I knew something about pneumonia. People get pneumonia and they get better. If it's really bad, they go to the hospital. . . . I mean, I wasn't that concerned. . . . You know what I mean. We get back to the emergency room about 5:00 and she's just about admitted, and we see mommy on her bed, and I guess she had a plastic oxygen mask on, an IV. They had changed her clothes. She didn't look that bad. Um, it was chaotic in that room. Sarah's sitting there with an oxygen mask on, and then some of the doctors started surrounding me . . . started telling me about some kind of pneumonia.

"Meanwhile, Cara is pulling at me. I do remember them saying that it is really serious and that there were high mortality rates to it. Then again, I'm surprised at my own story, in that I'm saying one thing—that they were telling me that it was serious—but yet, I wasn't considering it serious. Like I said, I had to get Cara out of there. It was becoming an inappropriate place for Cara to be. 'I got it, we're going.' We said goodbye to Mommy, and I think, by taking Cara to the hospital and seeing Mommy in the hospital— Mommy looked okay— that served us well in the next three weeks, because Sarah never regained consciousness. That Thursday, when we said goodbye to Mommy in the emergency room and people running around . . . I remember Cara hugging at my pants. Then by the second week, we knew we were in deep trouble, and I stopped going to work. But I kept Cara going to school. I wanted to keep things going—that I was just going to keep on going. We were going to recover from this, so we were going to go on.

"By the end of the second week, the doctors called me in and said that we had reached the point where eight out of ten people don't make it, and the doctor asked me if he could have my permission to try extraordinary measures, and I said, 'Well, go ahead.' By Monday, we pretty well knew what was going to happen. By the end of the second week, we knew what was going to happen. I was called for a conference again, I was given two choices. We can either pull the plug right now or we can go the other extreme. The other extreme was even more experimental—all the different ways and continue what we're doing, and of course the middle way, the moderate way is probably the best way for me anyway. So I said, 'Just let it run its course,' and she died three Thursdays later." Frank began crying at this point in the interview and then said, "Uh, it's funny, I haven't been so emotional in so long."

One of the hardest things for Frank, aside from losing his wife, was having to tell his young daughter what was happening. "How do you tell a kid that this is going to happen?" Frank sought help from a friend, a social worker, who suggested using parts of a book written to help children understand death. "Mary [Frank's friend] helped me put together four brief statements to tell . . . I had to prepare . . . I couldn't up to this point . . . but I had to tell Cara what might happen so that when it did happen, it wasn't just like that . . . snap. . . . Mary helped me get together a few lines to tell Cara. We still use it today. Cara and I say, 'I love you . . . I love you, I will take care of you, and I will make you feel safe.' I wrote them out in big letters, because I didn't know whether I would stammer and I didn't want to. I didn't want to lose the importance and the power of the words. I took a legal tablet and wrote the four sentences out in big letters, and I put them on the floor. . . . 'Cara come on,' and sat her down on the sofa and just as natural as I could, read the four lines. 'The medicines are not working,' you know, that sort of thing. 'The doctors have tried this, that, and the other, but she might die.' Cara wailed. Cara actually wound up like a little baby . . . you take them out of the crib and you walk back and forth at two in the morning and then they fall asleep. That's what I did with Cara, because she started to wail so much, I would walk and she actually fell asleep in my arms that night."

Frank sought the help of a therapist "when I knew I was in deep trouble, here, with how was I going to tell a little girl, I called a therapist that I had seen. . . . I still go. I still go because there's still lots of issues in my life." Frank used to speak of his wife in therapy more than he does now, three years later. For Frank, the issue around his daughter's loss of two "mommies" has been of greater concern. "There's always been this double issue, the loss of first mommy, the loss of adopted mommy. . . . I'm okay with laughing . . . this is a story that happened a few weeks ago. We walk out of Pathmark and there are women and daughters selling Girl Scout cookies. I walk out, and a woman comes up to me and she says, 'I know you. I recognize your daughter from a picture you showed me. I took care of your wife.' And she says to Cara, 'I took care of your mommy.' She was one of the nurses in the ICU. This was almost three years ago. She recognized us. And Cara says, 'Well, what was that about?' I said, 'That was the nurse that took care of mommy in the hospital.' My daughter went, 'My first mom?' I said, 'Sarah, mommy, my wife.' She got her mommy mixed up. So later, we had another brief talk about who is what. I set it straight and she was fine. A couple days later, Cara said something about mommy to me and I actually got mixed up. I got my own terms mixed up. I think that's so funny. But the issues I deal with in therapy now are more about Cara. Just two nights ago, Cara said, 'I don't have to listen to you, you're not my real biological father.' You know these are more practical issues that I've begun to deal with."

To cope with his grief, Frank has also used a support group for younger spouses who have lost their partners. Frank has processed some of his work on the memories of Sarah in the group. The following passage demonstrates some of his ambivalence regarding those memories. "I said in the group, 'It's an interesting phenomenon . . . what do you remember, what do you hold on to, and what do you let go?' It's a tough question sometimes—it's an interesting question sometimes. It doesn't have to be tough all the time. You know, with me, now, it's like in a way, sometimes I don't want to remember because it makes me so sad. So who wants to be back there? . . . I'm a veteran in the group, in that most of them are in their first or second year, and I'm coming into my third. I told them, 'It's a conflict I'm interested in. I don't want to avoid the conflict. By going to the group, it puts me in touch with feelings I had a while ago, and they're not active feelings now. In a way, I'm glad for that. Who wants to be down like that? But there's that remembrance that you do want to hold on to. There's that person that you want to know, you want to remember [at this point Frank was crying], and like I said, I really do. With me, anyway, it really is always a little conflict. Oh, God, now I'm really sad.' I don't want to be sad and open up everything." Frank talked about how the support group has helped him to move forward by being "there" with him. "These six other people, they know that darkness that I'm talking about, and it's good to be in a group of people that know that darkness. And they are not immobilized by it—that's good to see." Frank describes the darkness as "unspeakable" and says, "There's this unspeakable sadness associated with it." Frank struggles with how to "not forget her, but not be sad with her memory. Without it debilitating me, without it sitting me down and saying, 'Oh, gosh, I can't do anything today.'" Frank does have "some nice memories of her" and says, "Maybe I should think of them a little bit more than the other things. It's trying not to have that darkness, to have the memory without the darkness, without the blackness."

The support group has also helped Frank with decisions about how to move on with his life. In particular, he was discussing what to do with Sarah's clothes and said to the group members, "My God, I can't stand it anymore, I'm just doing it. I'm getting rid of it because I need some stuff in back of it, and I've just got to get rid of it, and it's time for it to go. I haven't looked at it, and I went to it, I opened the door, and I put everything back . . . closed the door, and it's still there. You feel the need to do it, and you then do something better that day. I think the group helps me not be immobilized by it (the darkness—the grief)."

Frank believes that some details of the last few weeks of Sarah's life are fading. Just after Sarah's death, Frank said, "How could I ever forget that? You know, you honor that person. But then there's a part that says, 'Well, let go. Let it go a bit.'" Frank admits, "I don't think I've quite found it yet—the balance between holding on to the memories, remembering the good times, but without going back to, for me, what is a very dark place that immobilizes me. I'm fifty-two years old. I have a little daughter. I want to do the best by her. I want to do the best by me. Being immobilized doesn't do any of us any good."

Frank openly discussed his ambivalence about dating other women, which seems to be related to his memories of Sarah. At present, he believes that he's "a little bit too involved with one person right now, and somehow I let that happen. I'm not totally involved. I still have a relationship with Sarah." Yet, Frank is aware that dating is different for him than it was the first year after Sarah's death. "In the first year I was emotionally involved with Sarah. That's exactly what I would say when people ask me about dating, and if I went out with someone and what happened. Nothing happened the first year because I was still emotionally involved with Sarah, in either remembering or fantasizing. I remember all these wonderful romantic things we did together. Sometimes I would shake my head and say, 'If Sarah were alive, I wouldn't be remembering this right now.' I'm not sure it's all that accurate, but it's this halo effect.

"It's amazing, but your memory becomes selective. 'Gee, I'm not as emotionally involved with Sarah as before. In fact, only half of what I was before.'" Frank clearly remembers how, in the early days, "there was no room for anybody else. There was no room, I mean, Sarah's in there." However, Frank needed adult company, and that was the only purpose for dating in the early days. Now Frank says, "I think there's room for somebody else, but I can't imagine having the same feeling. You know, I can't quite imagine being in love. That's exactly what I mean, in that all-encompassing way. I think I would need a little bit more time for that. Not that Sarah's in there like she was before, but she's still a little bit in there and there's still the memories."

Frank sees significant changes in his personality since Sarah's death. "Once in a while, . . . you know, what I'll say at a red light: 'You used to do a lot of crying in the car.' It's a very private place. . . . I would cry, and I'd look at people watching me, and I would cry. . . . I would shake my head, and I'd say, 'Thank you Sarah. Thank you for making me grow up.' And I do mean that in some ways. I think at times I would let Sarah deal with the hard stuff, and now I have to do it. There's nobody around but me. It's me. I think I'm maturing. . . . I do think it's affected my personality. I don't think I'm quite as goofy as I was before. I'm not as lighthearted as I was before. I'm more vocal. There's a weightiness that I feel. And I don't appreciate it." Yet Frank believes that the maturing process has been good for him. He is currently on sabbatical from his teaching position and believes that taking the sabbatical was a direct result of Sarah's death. "There's a little bit about my mentality and my thinking that says, 'Do it now because you don't know . . . wait till you retire—well, there's no guarantee you're going to be there.' I think that affects me. I think it's matured me. It's provided me with an opportunity to find my own adultness. On the positive side, I'm the captain of my own ship. There's something about that that I do enjoy. I think it keeps me in the here and now. I think it sharpens your wits. I think I do try to be true to myself more than I did before. I think I don't care as much about what other people think of me as much as I did before. I think I put my own and my daughter's best interests really foremost right now, with a degree of focus and concentration that I didn't have before." Although Frank has stated that he regrets the decrease in lightheartedness since the death of his wife, he says "it's just an excellent way for making me grow up. I have to deal with tough stuff, sometimes, and unpleasant stuff, and that's what the real world is about. Maybe I wouldn't be doing that if Sarah were around. I had a little buffer there."

Frank's plans include marrying again if he finds the right woman. "People asked me two years ago if I'd get married again, and I said, 'Heck, what are you talking about?' Now it's something a little bit more concrete that I can consider and I actually do lean that way. I didn't plan to have this kid on my own. I don't envision me to be single the rest of my life. I'm not sure I would like that, but there's a degree of freedom that I feel I need to find my own way. That's what's developed, and I might as well play it out."

Analysis

Frank's experiences with grieving over the loss of his wife seem to corroborate Carverhill's (1997) and Campbell and Silverman's (1996) findings that widowers experienced their wives as central to their lives as well as to their sense of identity. Frank seems to be working on redefining himself when he speaks of becoming more mature, "having to deal with the hard stuff," which he allowed his wife to handle when she was living. Frank is becoming more responsible for both himself and his daughter. His story illustrates Campbell and Silverman's (1996) belief that men must relearn their sense of themselves and renegotiate a relationship with themselves. Frank speaks of "trying to be true to himself" more than he did prior to Sarah's death and says that widowhood has provided him with an "opportunity to find my own adultness."

Frank's story supports research finding that widowers who care for dependent children struggle with grieving while having to develop new parenting skills. In Frank's case, his wife stayed at home to raise their daughter, so that he has also struggled with learning new household chores. During the initial phone contact with Frank, when scheduling the interview, he mentioned having to get used to all of the "morning chores" before being able to plan his day. According to Worden and Silverman (1993), Frank is more at risk for depression as a newly widowed parent with a school-age child. However, Frank has been wise to continue to use the support of his therapist, his widow/widower support group, and his friends to cope with taking care of his daughter and himself. With regard to gender issues, Frank seems to be able to cope with his feelings and his thoughts. He does not fit the typical "male pattern" of responding cognitively to the loss of his wife, since he has been able to share his feelings with his support group.

Frank is working hard to hold on to the good memories without going back to "the dark place" that immoblizes him. He is attempting to integrate the real loss of Sarah with a different, continuing form of the relationship. As Frank begins to consider dating, he realizes that, although his memories are still involved with Sarah, he thinks "there's room for somebody else." However, he believes that he still needs a bit more time before making a committed relationship because of the degree to which "Sarah is still in there."

Frank is also aware that he has become a different person in many ways because of Sarah's death. He is reconstructing his relationship with Sarah, which provides him with the strength to begin his new life as a single man. He believes that he has grown more mature because he can't be as "light-hearted" as he once was, and he is now "the captain of my own ship." Frank, like many bereaved partners, lives more in the here and now and cares less about what others think of his behavior.

BEREAVED OLDER SPOUSES

Findings from Lund, Caserta, and Dimond (1993) reveal considerable diversity in the course of bereavement among older bereaved spouses and within an individual. Every outcome measure used by these researchers revealed a broad range of responses at each time period among the research participants (Lund et al. 1993). Some bereaved spouses were devastated by their loss and had great difficulty managing their personal lives for many years, while others described themselves as socially active, independent, and motivated to make the best of a difficult situation. Diversity in bereavement reactions was also found within individuals. "It was not unusual for the bereaved to feel angry, guilty, and lonely, yet at the same time feel personal strength and pride in how he or she was coping" (Lund et al. 1993:245). Flora and Jack both report this in their stories below.

The strongest predictors of well-being in older adults during bereavement were "personal resources unique to each person." "Experiencing the death of a spouse in later life requires a wide range of adjustments to meet the demands of a radically different social environment and life style" (Lund et al. 1993:252). Research evidence supports the need for older bereaved adults to preserve and enhance their well-being by taking charge of their lifestyles and situations. "Taking control requires motivation, pride, skill, flexibility, some help from others, and the passage of time" (Lund et al. 1993:252). Positive self-esteem and personal competencies in managing the daily tasks of life had the strongest impact upon every aspect of well-being that was measured by these researchers (Lund et al. 1993). The importance of social relationships was found to be a moderately consistent predictor of the well-being of older adults during bereavement (Lund et al. 1993). Those older bereaved adults who fared the best had supportive relationships with others, participated actively in their religion, and had remarried. Although these researchers do not suggest remarriage as a coping strategy for those who are reluctant, they did find that remarried persons had a "greater reduction in their stress levels and greater improvement in the measures of life satisfaction and resolution of grief" (1999:251). More important were the qualitative aspects of a support network in contributing to life satisfaction. These qualitative aspects include perceived closeness, self-expression, contact, shared confidence, and mutual helping.

Flora

Flora is an eighty-nine-year-old widow who lost her husband, Jim, when he was eighty-seven. Jim died of massive heart failure when Flora was eighty-three. Flora and Jim had been married for almost sixty years at the time of his death. About one month following the death of her husband, Flora suffered the loss of her adult son, who was thirty-one at the time. Flora is quite mobile but suffers from some respiratory and heart difficulties. These health problems do not prevent Flora from having an active, interesting life. She has been a social worker all of her adult life and continues to practice in her home, not only seeing clients but providing supervision to other social workers. Flora has always had a particular gift for relating to and working with children and teens and enjoys her work with them. She continues to live in the house that she and Jim bought more than forty years ago and has two adult daughters, who live nearby and help her with doctor visits. She has four grandchildren, who range in age from twenty-four to six. Flora sees her grandchildren regularly and enjoys their visits.

Flora was very surprised when Jim died, despite his multiple sclerosis and deteriorating condition. "Jim was supposedly getting better. Of course, as I look at it now, I know he never could have gotten better, but he was getting better from this particular episode. He had fallen and broken his hip, and I felt rather responsible about that because I hadn't been able to sleep downstairs with him. He had some trouble going up and down the steps, so we didn't want him going up and down at night. I had been sleeping downstairs with him but he had been so restless and got up at night, and I couldn't sleep. He would go back to sleep, but I couldn't. One night, when I went upstairs, he went to the bathroom by himself; he slipped, fell, and broke his hip. That was some time in the night, and he did push himself off the cold floor. So when I came down early in the morning, I found him on the floor. I'm sorry now that I called 911, because they took him to a local hospital and we really wanted him down at University Hospital. That's where his doctors were. So, he had to stay all day on one of those darn, not very comfortable, things in the emergency room. I was unhappy about it and also felt some guilt. If I had been down there, or if I hadn't called 911, or if I just called to find an ambulance or something.

"So that was the beginning of the last round, really, because he had been in the hospital before for a fall. He had been all through rehab, which he hated. He was better, and then this happened. He was supposed to go to rehab the day he died. . . . I had been in on Thursday night, and I continued to take the class on Russian history and would go and talk to him about it. He liked that. I don't think I called him planning not to go in, but he encouraged me not to come in because he said he was fine, and I should get my rest and come in the next day. So, I didn't go in. And nobody else did from the family either. . . . In the middle of the night, I heard the telephone ring, and I said, 'Oh, there's something wrong with Jim.' I thought, 'I can't cope with it,' so I went back to sleep again and a little bit later, the phone rang again, and I said, 'This is it.' So I went to the phone, and sure enough, they told me that Jim had died some time in the middle of the night. It was a great surprise to them. The doctor had seen him and had thought he was fine. In other words, I had no preparation for this. The nurse had seen him—she thought he was fine. He told me he was fine.

"They asked me if they could do an autopsy, because they couldn't understand it, and I said, 'Sure.' The autopsy was not real clear as to what it was. You know, I always had in the back of my mind, 'Did he just give up?' But he wasn't a giver-upper, although he did hate going to the rehab. . . . What they put down was a massive heart failure, but they said his arteries were unbelievably clear and his lungs were okay. So, we really don't know what it was." It still haunts Flora that she didn't realize Jim was going to die. She didn't talk to him much because there was so much difficulty with his speech. "One time he looked at me so fiercely, and I figured what he was really trying to tell me was that he cared about me." Flora and her family made plans for a memorial service to honor Jim's life.

Following Jim's death, Flora remembers how wonderful friends were toward her. Flora had been involved in an art group, and they made delicious dinners and brought them over. "I think it's very important that people have friends who can help you at that time, because your children can't.

And I realized they couldn't help because they're dealing with their own feelings. If I hadn't had all these kind friends, I would have been much worse off than I was." Flora clearly believes that her friends were what helped her cope most with Jim's death. Flora said that she had a discussion with a friend who had lost a son and she and her friend decided that several months following a death, friends tend not to call as much. "I think that they feel that you're better, now, and you're not, but they don't know it. This idea was so helpful to me, because when people began not to come to dinner and not to call me up, I thought, 'It isn't because they don't like me, it's because they think I should be on my own now, which I'm not.' But my very good friends stood by. My next-door neighbor brought food—I had so much food I didn't know what to do with it. So I froze it."

Flora compares this experience of support to the lack of support she received when her son, Jed, died. Jed had suffered from a disability for years and lived in a group home several miles away. With her husband's death, support was a big help "because they all knew him. The thing that was so hard about Jed was that there was nobody close except the young man that had gone up with me all the time to visit him—that made my healing for him (Jed) much, much harder. Besides, I think it's really harder to lose a son than it is to lose a husband."

Flora later spoke of the ongoing support she received from her adult daughters. One daughter "picked me up on a Sunday and took me out to her house and we had lunch, and then I stayed for dinner. We saw a movie, and then she brought me home. That was nice. They both call me every day now. They didn't do that before." When Flora needs to go to the doctor, one of her daughters takes her.

Flora spoke of how difficult it is to lose a spouse because you lose part of yourself. "You have put so much in . . . and the other is like part of you dying too. I'm such a feisty individual that it was hard for me to even accept that. One thing that became very clear to me was that there were friends that we had that were for the both of us. I'm thinking of two people in particular, and they just could not be friends with me alone. One was a couple that we'd met on a wonderful tour we went on. They're exceedingly wealthy, but Jim enjoyed talking with them so much, and we'd have dinner together. After he died, we went out to dinner once, but we never did it again. I thought, 'Isn't that funny.' I thought I knew why. Then there was a woman who used to come and talk to both of us, and I enjoyed her very much. Now she'll say, to me, 'We must go to New York together. . . . Oh, you know, I want to have lunch with you.' But she never does, and I thought about that, and I thought, 'It's just the same thing.' One time after she had left from a visit, Jim got really angry at me. He said, 'You just butted in, and we weren't able to talk at all.' I didn't feel that, but he and she had a lot of interesting discussions around religion, and I was more interested in the social part of her." In reaction to these people that knew Flora and Jim as a couple, Flora said, "I feel deserted and angry at the people and at Jim."

Flora spoke of her angry reactions toward Jim after he died when "three weeks after he died my furnace went out, and he had been nursing this furnace for years . . . and it just went bad—so I had to replace it. Something else blew up right after . . . I think it was the dishwasher. Those were the things he always fixed, and he wasn't here." The other thing that I missed him so . . . he always would twist the tops off things, and I can't twist anything. I never could, not much. Any little thing that needed fixing, he'd fix, and I am absolutely no good in that area at all." Flora is also angry at Jim for not sharing philosophical thoughts, which he had written down, that she found after he died. She felt left out of an important part of Jim's life. "He often shut me out about some of the things he talked to his friends. But he didn't talk to me. He was a very 'into himself' person. He was not a sharing person at all. I remember when we were first married. There would be something wrong with him—so I used to get him and go out for walks. I would walk and walk and try to get it out of him and finally did. Then, after I had children, I didn't have time for that. He was still the same way, so we didn't communicate as much." Flora also shared that she was angry at Jim before he died because he got angry at her for not understanding him. Flora believes that these experiences enabled her to acknowledge her anger toward Jim after he died.

Flora reported that she was most affected by Jim's death by not being able to go on trips together. "I went on one overnight trip with a group to look at gardens, and I took my granddaughter with me. I missed him very much on that trip because he always was the one who found the house where we were going to stay, the restaurant where we were going to eat. . . . My granddaughter did none of that, so I had to do all that, and I missed him very much. I was glad I went, but it wasn't nearly as enjoyable. The times when we really had fun together were on those trips. Other times, at home, he fussed at me about my kitchen all the time and I have to laugh, because you see couples all the time together, and they're always fussing about their kitchen."

Flora was clear about a gradual transition that occurred for her, from feeling very angry at Jim for not being with her and remembering negative experiences and thoughts, to the present time when she tends to remember the more pleasant experiences she had with Jim. "I know I was angrier in the first year than I am now. I'm sure I was angrier because I would think of the things that were awful about him, and there were plenty of things that were awful. After he died, I found all these papers that he had written about a whole lot of things that he never discussed with me, and I would have been interested. I can chuckle over some things now. "I can think about nice things now. For example, he used to rub my feet. He was so proud of me that he'd almost embarrass me. I was on the board of an agency and they made me the subject of their annual meeting and gave me this pretty bowl. He was so proud of me. And that happened about the time he was in the hospital, because when I went in to see Jim, the nurses said, 'Oh, yes, we know about you.' Also, unlike some people's husbands, he never objected to my getting an advanced degree—in fact he typed my thesis."

Flora has always been an independent woman and earned an income of her own. Jim, unlike some of her friends' husbands, supported her in having a career. "The wife of one of his colleagues from graduate school said, 'Well, Dave wouldn't let me work.' I didn't say anything at the time, but I said to Jim later, 'You'd have had a hard time with me.' He laughed and said yes, he would have. I had a college debt and I wanted to pay it off. I always want-ed to have money of my own. I didn't like being dependent on him."

With regard to the comforting thoughts that Flora has now about Jim, she said, "I think sometimes it's one way and sometimes the other. Some-times it's very comforting and sometimes it's very zapping. I didn't know very much about multiple sclerosis when he had it. . . . I did look it up, but there was not much—there's been a lot since then." Flora also remembers how Jim always took care of all the bills. "I hate to get the bills ready." She also thinks about how Jim would have thought about certain things. "Jim loved his young granddaughter and would have worried about her not doing as well in school."

Although Flora believes that she has lost part of herself and some of the social relationships that she and Jim shared together, she spoke about find-ing a new part of herself and building upon that. "I get very discouraged with my health and my inability to do things because of my wobbliness. But I try. I keep my practice going, which I like."

Flora believes that she has changed since Jim's death. "Well, I think one thing is that people think that within a year they're going to be the way they were before. And I think that you're never the way you were. You're a dif-ferent person, and you've changed—that's all. I realized that I was not the outgoing person that I thought I was. When we went on trips, he was the one who talked to people. I would come along with him, but I realized that it wasn't easy for me to relate to new people. I can relate in a professional way, but with new people and new situations, it's hard for me. I've realized that I'm much more comfortable with myself than I thought I'd be. And being alone has certain advantages—I had no idea about that. You can get up in the middle of the night and turn on the light and do something, and no one says, 'What are you doing, for heaven's sakes?' You can leave your kitchen dirty till the next morning without any worry. . . . You can eat when and what you want. I've learned to read in the middle of the day, which I never did—it wasn't that he prevented me, but that did change in me. I did change by being alone. I used to think it was a sin almost (being alone)."

"Anyway, there's lots of places I don't go that I would like to go. I look at workshops at the university and I just don't go—now it's funny, because he didn't go to all the places with me—it's that I've changed. Of course part of my not going is my physical disabilities, too. It's hard to separate one from the other. But I can go to a fancy restaurant by myself. He always wanted to go to the local buffet—which I hate. I haven't been to that buffet since he died. I said to him one time, 'I'd rather stay home and try to get something together here than go to an inferior restaurant.' He thought I was a snob about that. I suppose I could be looked on that way, but that was the way it was. I do go to some nice restaurants around here alone and I don't feel uncomfortable by myself in most of them—none of them have ever made me feel uncomfortable."

Analysis

Flora's behavior demonstrates the importance of taking control of one's life following the loss of a spouse (Lund et al. 1993). Her story also illustrates how the kind of support she received from others, both from her family and friends, is so important to the older adult in coping with the loss of their partner (Lund et al. 1993). For Flora, the large home that she and Jim shared for more than forty years carries multiple symbols of past associations and interactions that Flora has had with Jim and her children. Moss and Moss speak of how the home "may evoke and represent a continued sense of being cared for" (Moss and Moss 1985:203). It is clear that having a large home to care for can be a heavy responsibility for an older adult like Flora, but familiar surroundings bring her a sense of comfort and security and provide a sense of continuity. Although the older adult may have increasing health difficulties, which can represent threats to the self, the home may be an "unchanging refuge, a retreat" (1985:203). In addition, the older adult has a sense of control over her home. Her home offers a place in which she can recall a cherished past.

Flora's story illustrates again how grief is intensified by loss of the spouse as well as by loss of the part of her that was connected to him. Flora spoke of "how difficult it is to lose a spouse because you lose part of yourself. You have put so much in . . . and the other is like part of you dying too." At eighty-nine, Flora is working on a redefinition of herself to include understanding that part of herself is not as outgoing as she believed when she was married to Jim. She is becoming more content with being by herself and enjoying "the new part of herself" that is emerging. This behavior corroborates the work of Lopata (1996) and Silverman (1986), who refer to the reconstruction of the self-concept as one of the most important tasks of the grieving process. This same reconstruction process was demonstrated in the stories provided by Kristen, Marion, and Frank.

Flora's memories of Jim have shifted over time. She has more pleasant memories than the angry ones that first emerged. Several years after his death, Flora is able to balance the positive and negative aspects of her relationship with Jim. Although she can still feel angry that he "shut her out" of some of his life and his thoughts, she is also pleased that he was so proud of her professional achievements. Flora's experiences illustrate Rubin's 1999 findings that the relationship with the deceased is transformed over time. As the bereaved achieves a new organization in her life, she is able to balance her feelings about the relationship with the deceased. Like the narratives provided by Marion, John, and Frank, Flora's story shows that when the memories and thoughts of the bereaved are available in a balanced way, they provide a measure of strength, warmth, and solidarity (Rubin 1999).

George

George is an eighty-one-year-old retired man whose wife, Barbara, died of a cerebral hemorrhage after the couple had celebrated their fifty-second wedding anniversary. She died just before they would have left on a trip to visit their daughter and their grandchildren on the West Coast. George was seventy-eight when his wife died at age seventy-three. He has two adult children and four grandchildren, ranging in age from twelve to twenty-six. George's son and his family live about twenty miles away, so he sees them quite a bit, and they go on trips together. George is in fairly good health except for macular degeneration in the right eye, which eventually causes blindness. Despite his problem, George is able to drive and "can read as long as I have good light." George and his wife met in college, where he studied merchandising. They married when George was in the Army and had a Catholic service that Barbara's parents did not attend. "Barbara was a wonderful, wonderful person. We celebrated our fiftieth wedding anniversary and had a big bash."

Barbara was ill for three years with myelodysplasia. "It's a condition where your bone marrow doesn't produce the proper number of red blood cells. Consequently, your blood count goes down. This is over a gradual period. She was transfused two or three times. . . . She had problems with bruising terribly. Never knew what caused it, and she lost a lot of weight, and she knew she was dying." Barbara and George planned a trip to the West Coast to visit their daughter. "I told her she wasn't well enough to go. She says, 'I'm going.' I made all the arrangements. I arranged for a wheelchair at the airport. That afternoon we came home, and she took a nap. And she rarely slept a half-hour if she took a nap. She slept three hours, and I thought it was kind of strange, but then she got up, and we got a pizza and brought it home. We were in front of the fireplace and I fell asleep. I woke up suddenly, and the TV was blaring. Barbara had a hearing problem. . . . She'd turned the TV up, and it was blaring. And I looked over, and she was slumped over on the couch . . . only about three feet from me, and I said something, . . . 'Barbara, what's wrong? She said, 'I can't see,' and that's the last word she uttered. I called 911 and had an ambulance there in no time and got her to the hospital, and the doctor said, 'Well, her life signs are good. She may be all right.' But of course, he didn't know anything about what her conditions were. I could see that she was breathing with difficulty. I knew she was dying. I finally got hold of my son, and he got there, and we called my daughter on the phone, and the neurologist came. It was almost midnight, and she explained the whole thing to me." Barbara became brain dead from the blood that had entered her brain, and "they hospitalized her and called me in the middle of the night and she was dead."

George was devastated for months following Barbara's death but commented, "I'm gradually getting over the trauma . . . but I still find myself weeping a lot." In fact, George cried several times during the interview but said he had cried only with his children before this. Following Barbara's death, George sold the townhouse they lived in and bought a more comfortable, "easy-to-care-for" condominium. He is trying to make a new life here, although it is located in a town in which the couple had lived together for many years of their marriage. George says, "I find myself very lonely." One of the resources that George has found helpful in his healing process is joining and actively participating in the local church. Joining the church is also a way for George to keep a continuing bond with Barbara, because prior to her death, she was a member of this same church. Although he used to attend services with her occasionally, "I was agnostic—I didn't believe in formalized religion. And when I moved back, I decided I would . . . I sort of promised Barbara I would go to her church and I went." George has now been appointed a deacon.

George is not active in community affairs. "I'm sort of withdrawn except for the church. And that's nearby." He enjoys the people, the music, the camaraderie, and the minister. George keeps himself in good physical shape by playing golf at least twice a week. George says that golf has helped him cope with his grief. "It's been three years now, and I seem to get better each year. I don't like to talk about it. It's . . . because I break down whenever I do. Even in front of my children." At this point George shared his tears with me, and we talked about how much it helps to cry. I asked George if other men have helped him with his grief. He said, "My son helps, but other men don't . . . they just go about their own lives. I have a friend in New York . . . he's probably been more helpful than any of my friends around here. He comes to visit me, sometimes, and brings his wife. We talk on the phone." Yet the male friends who live near George, whom he sees on a regular basis, don't provide any emotional support to him. Instead, George and these friends "do things together." George says that he thinks "women are more sensitive to something like that (talking about and sharing grief) than men are."

George keeps memories of Barbara present through regular visits to the cemetery where she is buried. George doesn't talk to Barbara, there, but sometimes, around the house, he'll say, "Barbara, why aren't you here?" He really misses Barbara in many ways, but especially because she was so handy around the house. "She was a plumber, a carpenter, a banker—she did all those things that I never found time to do." George also stays in touch with Barbara by talking with her brother on the telephone once a month and by visiting him when he visits his daughter on the West Coast. "Tom talks about Barbara a lot." This seems comforting to George.

George has begun to have a social life to help with the loneliness of his life and particularly the dinner hour. He belongs to a country club and often eats dinner there. George says, "I eat dinner with two friends of Barbara's . . . friends for forty-five years . . . so I eat dinner with one of them about twice a week." George also enjoys the company of one woman "who

comes up from Maryland and stays with me for four or five days at a time."
When I asked George about this arrangement, he said, "But I don't like it
too much. A couple of days is all I can stand." This woman was a very close
friend of his wife. George admits that this relationship is not "romantic,"
but rather companionship. "It's something to do. And [laughing] I don't
have to cook." While George was talking about his new social life, he began
to reflect on his feelings about Barbara. One of the other women George
sees "is very outspoken. The same way Barbara is. She called a spade a
spade." This is one of the characteristics George most liked about Barbara.
"I like the way she always had something to say. She was very, very enter-
taining. . . . I guess I liked everything about her. We got along beautifully.
We had our spats, like everybody, but nothing would ever last." George has
no intention of ever marrying again. "I live a bachelor life. I do see these
two gals. The one who lives close by comes over here, and we go out to a
little deli in the country and to the museum. She's added a lot to my life.
The woman who comes up from Maryland "thinks she owns the place because she designed it."

   George seems to have the most difficulty with "having to do everything
myself, now, and I can't sit down and have a cocktail and have my dinner served. . . ." George began crying at this point and apologized, saying
that he has only ever cried with his children about the loss of Barbara. Life
is getting easier for George now. He has been feeling better each year but
still does not like to discuss Barbara's death. When he does "break down,"
it is only with his children. When I asked George how the children responded to his "breaking down," he said they were OK with it. Near the
end of the interview, George began to cry and shared with me, "I'm
angry at Barbara, angry at the doctors. Why, why, Barbara did you do this
to me? And I said to myself, 'You never prepared me for this.' She never
taught me how to use the washing machine, dryer, or cook, or anything.
She always wanted to do it herself. I never even made coffee." Just six
days before Barbara's death she was preparing for a Superbowl party, and
George says, "I tried to take over the Superbowl party. Barbara said she
was going to do it."

Analysis

   From George's story we can see the difficulty he has had in managing his personal life and how intertwined his identity was with his wife,
Barbara. George's comments about his relationship with Barbara are similar

to those made by the widowers in Carverhill's 1997 study, who reported that their wives were central to their lives and perceived that their identity as a spouse had been critical to their sense of themselves. Just as George expressed his loss of Barbara as a companion, lover, friend, and traveling partner, the widowers in Carverhill's study believed that they had lost not only a partner but the "mirror image of the many roles that their spouse played" (1997:14). However, we can also see George's resiliency as he tries to learn how to take care of himself by doing the daily tasks that his wife had performed. Although he strongly believes he will never be romantically involved again, we can see his attempts to socialize with some women who were his wife's closest friends. This seems to be his way of integrating the relationship and the continuing the bond with his deceased wife as he moves on with his new life.

As Lund, Caserta, and Dimond (1993) have reported, resiliency is a common pattern of adjustment in the older bereaved adult. These researchers found that "many bereaved persons were resourceful enough to find effective ways of managing their grief and making satisfying adjustments" (1993:247). Similar to George's mood swings with gradual improvement over time, Lund et al. report from the transcripts of their interviews with older adults that a typical comment made by a seventy-year-old widower was, "It comes on gradual and reaches a peak until you break down and cry. You get a little better for a while and it goes up again" (1993:247). Lund et al. found that, for some older adults, the "roller coaster" of ups and downs never ends, but they learn to "live with it or adjust to it. Others are more active in meeting challenges and find ways to manage the ups and downs of the process" (1993:248). Both Flora and George were meeting the challenges of this process—possibly Flora in a more active way, as she still maintained her professional career and was involved with her grandchildren.

George's experiences reflect some of the gender differences that Lund et al. (1993) reported in their findings, in that males and females differed in their lack of specific skills for daily living. We also see differences in patterns of grieving mentioned in chapter 3, in which men, like George, are more active in coping with the grief process. George reported that he plays golf with his male friends on a regular basis to cope with his grief. Yet George is also experiencing his grief on an emotional level, albeit in a "private way," like the men described by Golden and Miller (1998). Some of this private grieving may be related to the fact that men are less comfortable in sharing feelings with other men. As Golden (1996) reports, when examining men's grief from their perspective, valuing autonomy, independence, and action, "it is easier to see why men tend to grieve in a private and quiet manner. They don't want to be a burden to others, they want to maintain their independence, and they want to use their strength of action in dealing with a very powerful force such as grief (1996:82). George also finds that talking about his late wife with her brother, her friends (whom he sees regularly), and his children help him to cope with his loss.

Moss and Moss (1985) argue that "the widow(er) who generally does not remarry has a particularly potent tie with the deceased spouse formed out of many years of being together" (1985:196). These researchers contend that the conscious awareness of the marital bond has "the potential for enhancing the widow(er)'s identity and well-being" (1985:196). In the narratives of Flora and George, we can see the persistence of the tie to the memory of their spouses, with whom they have shared more than fifty years of marriage. With Flora, although she openly discusses some of the negative aspects of her relationship with Jim, "there tends to be a theme of acceptance and forgiveness, combined with affirmation of the marriage" (1985:197). With George, it is clear that, although he is enjoying the companionship of other women, these women sustain his memory of Barbara because they were Barbara's good friends. Furthermore, George is insistent that he will not remarry and only wants companionship. For both Flora and George, "memory revitalizes the past in the present" (1985:197).

A long-term marriage that has spanned several decades, as in the cases of Flora and George, develops unique qualities central to this close, interdependent relationship. Themes that tend to be central to this relationship are caring, intimacy, family, commitment, and reciprocal identity support (Moss and Moss 1985). George still sees Barbara as caring for him and watching out for him. Flora, who has a more independent lifestyle, still finds herself thinking about what Jim would think of her grandchild or how he would handle some of the financial aspects of her life. Both Flora and George hold on to an image of their spouse, which helps to stabilize them in their current lives. Moss and Moss (1985) speak of a continuing interaction with the image of the deceased that moves from "initially talking to the deceased, to consciously considering what the deceased would think or do, to finally having the deceased become an internal referee who is ground for the widow(er)'s behavior" (1985:202–203). Both George and Flora clearly speak about internal conversations they have with their late spouses. This behavior illustrates the description of grief provided by the postmodern thinkers (Klass et al. 1996; Neimeyer 1998, 2001; Rubin 1999) provided in chapter 2.

Family relationships, particularly with the couples' adult children, are paramount in the lives of both George and Flora. Both of these older adults see their children and grandchildren on a regular basis and believe them to be critical supports to their lives. George cries only with his children about the loss of Barbara. He is unable to do this with most of his peers. The persistence of the bond with the deceased partner can generally be viewed as a nourishing link to the past. This tie can enhance rather than interfere with the widow(er)'s ability to establish new roles and relationships and can become a part of the older adult's new assumptive world (Moss and Moss 1985; Klass et al. 1996; Rubin 1999).

CHAPTER SUMMARY

Flora and George's experiences, as well as the other narratives presented in this chapter, corroborate the postmodern view of grief regarding the importance of reconstructing the relationship with the deceased partner. In a recent interview with Phyllis Silverman, Zucker provides the following quote by Silverman:

> While we can't live in the past, we can't act as if we had no past. . . . what we are dealing with is reconstructing a relationship. In many ways we are maintaining a connection with the deceased and by necessity building a different kind of relationship to him or her. The relationship changes with time, and it grows as we grow. As we get older we understand different aspects of the person who has died and we 'know' that person in different ways.

> (2000:1)

One of the themes dominating the narratives of the widows and widowers who shared their narratives in this book is that the loss of a spouse involves not only the loss itself but also a loss of that part of the bereaved that was connected to the deceased spouse. Marion's identity was intertwined with that of her husband, so that she felt she had "lost herself" after Sam's death. Marion has been able to reconstruct a new identity as a single woman by incorporating some of the strengths of her relationship with Sam, as well as by changing the direction of her life. Marion believed that she, her children, and her husband were more of an "isolated unit" prior to Sam's death and is now working on expanding her social network because she wants and

needs other people in her life. For the first time in her life, she is leaving
the children with babysitters, so that she can have an occasional weekend
away from home. Frank is also working on redefining himself when he
speaks of having to become more mature and "deal with the hard stuff" that
he allowed his wife to handle when she was alive. Even Flora, age eighty-
nine at her husband's death, spoke of "how difficult it is to lose a spouse because you lose part of yourself . . . it is like part of you dying too." Flora is
working on redefining herself so that she can enjoy the "new part of herself" that is emerging. This behavior corroborates the work of Lopata (1996)
and Silverman (1986), who refer to the reconstruction of the self-concept as
one of the most important tasks of grieving over the loss of a spouse.

As the literature (Carverhill 1997; Shaffer 1993; Lopata 1996; Silverman
1986) suggests, following the death of a spouse, both the widows and widowers who shared their narratives in this text reexamined and changed values and priorities, as well as the meaning of work in their lives. For the
youngest widow, Kristen, the changes in both her professional and personal life were dramatic, as she moved from work in animal research to ob-
taining a degree in counseling, so that she might help others who are grieving. As Shaffer (1993) has suggested in her work with young widows, loss
at an earlier time may enable the younger widow to remake her life and start
over in a way that may seem unrealistic to an older widow who loses a
spouse later in life. Both Frank and John's narratives illustrate Carverhill's
(1997) findings that men are often forced to examine the meaning of work
in their lives following the death of their wife, because they have experienced their wives as central to their lives as well as to their identity. Before
his wife's death, John was not very involved in parenting his three daughters. Following her death, John changed his priorities dramatically, because
he recognized how important it is to spend time with his children. Instead
of considering work as his reason for being, "getting my daughter to music
lessons became a reason for being at that point." Following the death of his
wife, Frank took a sabbatical from his work in order to set new priorities
for his life with his young daughter.

The narratives of both Frank and John support research that suggests that
widowers who care for dependent children struggle with grieving while
having to develop new parenting skills. In both narratives it is clear that each
of their deceased wives had been the primary caregiver to their children and
manager of the household. Becoming a widower meant learning to "do
household chores" while taking on the role of single parent and working
full-time outside the home. Both men spoke of how difficult this was at

first, but given time and support from family and friends, they were able to manage the transition.

All of the narratives suggest that widows and widowers experience the inherent dynamic of the grieving process in which the bereaved spouse oscillates between experiencing the pain of the loss and moving away from the pain, so that they can move forward in their lives. John spoke of how he can go for "long periods without feeling connected to Bobbie" and yet he can be driving a car and "puddle up" with tears for no reason. For John, as for most of the widows and widowers who shared their narratives, "Things get better, but they never get totally better." This is significant, because John has been widowed for almost sixteen years. Marion speaks of her worry about "forgetting Sam" if she doesn't stay with the pain and yet recognizes her need to move away from the pain so that she can manage her new life. Frank reveals his dilemma by stating that, "Sometimes I don't want to remember because it makes me so sad. So who wants to be back there? But I don't want to avoid the conflict—there's that remembrance that you do want to hold on to." This theme corroborates the belief that the continuing dilemma of the bereaved spouse is whether to be comforted by these reminders or to avoid them (Simos 1979; Bowlby 1980; Schuchter 1986; Stroebe and Stroebe 1987).

Chapter Four

Loss of an Opposite-Sex Partner

DISENFRANCHISED GRIEF

Other than the groundbreaking work of Kenneth Doka (1989, 2002b), little literature exists on the loss of a heterosexual partner in a relationship in which the couple has been cohabiting. Doka, a prominent writer in the field of disenfranchised grief, defines it as "the grief that persons experience when they incur a loss that is not or cannot be openly acknowledged, publicly mourned, or socially supported" (1989:4). This concept of grief emphasizes the fact that societies have norms or rules of grieving that "specify who, when, where, how, how long, and for whom people should grieve" (1989:4). These rules often translate into personnel policies, which allow workers who have lost a spouse to take a week off following the death. These policies indicate that each society defines who has a legitimate right to grieve and define *legitimate* as corresponding to familial relationships that are socially sanctioned and recognized. These grieving rules do not always correspond to the nature of attachments or the feelings of the bereaved partner. For example, society grants no official legitimacy to the status of couples who have been cohabiting in either heterosexual or homosexual relationships. Thus, when a partner dies, the grief of the survivor is disenfranchised. In fact, there are usually no expectations for the disenfranchised griever. "It is as if society says, not only do we not recognize your need to grieve, we also do not recognize your relationship in the first place" (Pine 1989:18).

In our society, more attention is placed upon kin-based relationships and roles. When the relationship between the bereaved and the deceased partner is not based on recognizable kin ties, the grief may be disenfranchised. Doka notes that although research tells us that the intensity of a grief reaction corresponds to the closeness of the relationship with the deceased (1987), the underlying societal assumption is that "closeness of relationship exists only among spouses and/or immediate kin" (1987:456). The closeness of nonkin relationships is often not understood or appreciated.

The emotions experienced by the bereaved in a traditional relationship (anger, guilt, sadness, depression, loneliness, hopelessness, and numbness) are often intensified in nontraditional relationships. Because these nontraditional relationships are "negatively" sanctioned, feelings of guilt may be especially intensified (Doka 1987, 2002b).

In addition to intense anger, bereaved partners in nontraditional relationships are also inhibited from behaviors that can be therapeutic. Some studies (Hamovitch 1964) have shown that care of the dying person can help with the grief adjustment of the bereaved. Those involved in nontraditional relationships may be excluded from an active role in the care of the dying. This exclusion can be physical, as in the rule often invoked by intensive care units, when visiting is limited to the immediate family. Two researchers (Kimmel 1978; Kelly 1977) found that male homosexuals complained that restrictions in visiting the sick partner, as well as negative attitudes of medical staff, inhibited their anticipatory grief.

Although one of the critical factors in the healing process is the presence of social support (Grothe and McKusick 1992; Sowell et al. 1991), those partners involved in nontraditional relationships are less likely to have support, either during the time of death or for some time after the death. When a spouse dies, the surviving partner undergoes a transition into the role of widow or widower. This role carries with it a certain status that is recognized by the larger community. This status carries legal and social rights, which allow the spouse time off from work and permission for a wider range of emotional expression. Partners in nontraditional relationships lose significant roles when their mates die, "but there is no defined transitional role for them to assume" (Doka 1987:462). Thus, there is no formal recognition that they are bereaved, no personnel policies to support time off from work, and little support or sympathy for their emotional reactions. One bereaved woman who was involved in an opposite-sex partnership reported,

"I don't even know who I am. How will I explain this to my future husband or kids? He was more than a boyfriend, less than a husband. What am I now?" (1987:462).

Partners in nontraditional relationships may also be denied any role in planning or participating in funeral rituals. Sometimes the exclusion can be unintentional because nonfamily members can be easily forgotten (Doka 1989, 2002b). The funeral helps to reinforce appropriate attitudes of members of society to one another and, as a ritual, the funeral provides some closure. At the same time, the funeral underscores the value of the services of the living. It is here where the disenfranchised griever is at a great disadvantage because, in most instances, the services of the living are acknowledged only for those who are thought of as "legitimate" or "sanctioned" by society (Pine 1989).

Practical and legal difficulties are frequently an issue for bereaved partners who have been in nontraditional relationships. When the surviving partner has joint ownership but no legal status, there may be problems of inheritance, legal battles with relatives, and problems of ownership. Practical difficulties that can impede the resolution of grief include situations in which nontraditional couples are not carried under each other's medical insurance or have not shared financial resources that can provide emergency services (Doka 1987).

Disenfranchisement is most obvious in the social realm, but as Kauffman suggests, "there is also an intrapsychic dimension of disenfranchisement"(1989:25). An individual in a nontraditional relationship can also "disenfranchise himself" by his or her own failure to acknowledge and recognize the grief. In Kauffman's new work (2002), he clarifies this self-disenfranchised grief, calling it a "psychological symptom" when the griever "disallows the recognition of grief without any actual outside input" (2002:61). He further states that the self is *always* involved in disenfranchised grief. According to Kauffman (1989), shame is the operative process, as the individual may be embarrassed over his or her own grief. Such embarrassment may inhibit the expression of grief. Kauffman (2002) makes it clear that self-initiated disenfranchisement may "merge into socially disenfranchised grief, or it may occur entirely on its own in an act of self-disenfranchising or as an implicit exposure of the anxiety that permeates grief" (2002:71). Because shame and guilt may be inhibiting, this may lead to complications in the mourning process.

Because of a lack of social sanctioning and social support, the bereaved who were partnered in nontraditional relationships may become alienated from their community (Kauffman 1989, 2002). One's basic sense of identity and belonging are realized in the space of family, friends, church, neighbors, and colleagues. When bereavement needs are not recognized by one's community, the part of one's identity that is tied into this community can be negated (Kauffman 1989:29). The value of a person's bond to the community can be damaged because this pain defines who one really is.

Implications for Grief Resolution

When a partner in a nontraditional relationship experiences the loss of his or her significant other, it is more difficult to complete the tasks outlined by Worden (1991, 2002) in chapter 1 that lead toward the resolution of grief. Worden lists these tasks as (1) accepting the reality of loss, (2) experiencing the pain of grief, (3) adjusting to an environment in which the partner is gone, and (4) withdrawing emotional energy from the deceased and reinvesting it in others. First, it is more difficult to accept the reality of the loss if the bereaved partner is excluded from the dying process, restricted from the funeral rituals, and/or inhibited from acknowledging the loss (Doka 1987, 2002b). Furthermore, formal and informal systems of support may be neither helpful nor available.

It is important to examine the meaning that the relationship had for the bereaved partner, as every relationship supports some sense of self. In attempting to understand the grieving process, it is also important to consider what aspects of the self are supported by the relationship and how they will be maintained in the absence of the relationship (Doka 1987). Resolution of grief is more problematic in situations in which there is more energy invested in the relationship and/or when there is more ambivalence about the relationship (1987). In addition, the degree to which the nontraditional relationship is accepted or rejected by others influences the experience of the bereaved. When the relationship is accepted, there is greater possibility for social support from both family and friends, which facilitates the resolution of grief.

Doka (1987) views nontraditional relationships as being part of a series of continuums. At one end might be relationships that are open and accepted and that involve heavy degrees of commitment and affect. In modern American society, many cohabiting heterosexual relationships fall closer to this end. In these cases, grief may be similar to that experienced by many spouses, although, in many cases, without available sources of traditional support. Homosexual relationships may be at other points on the continuum.

The following narrative represents the grief reactions of a woman who lost her male partner after they had been separated for a period of time.

Marie

Marie is a forty-six-year-old woman who lost her partner of twenty years when she was forty-four. Marie currently owns her own business, in which she trains physical and occupational therapists who provide their services to clients in the community. Bert was forty-two at the time of his death from congestive heart failure, having been seriously ill with diabetes and heart disease for a ten-year period. During this period Marie was the main caregiver to Bert. "I was doing IVs every day and putting medications through the IV three times per day—I was giving a lot of physical care. The doctors said they never had anyone live longer than one year with a patient as sick as Bert."

Ten years before Bert's death, before his diagnosis with serious heart problems, "I told Bert I wanted to end the relationship, and he said, 'Please don't leave me.' About eight months before Bert died, Marie brought him to the hospital, where the doctors agreed to place Bert on a list for a heart and kidney transplant. Marie said, "At that point, I had to be honest with myself—it was such a horrible, horrible time for me because I realized that the only reason that I had stayed with him for all those years was my own guilt. When the doctors told Bert that he was eligible for a transplant, Marie became seriously depressed. "It was a terrible thing to have to admit, but that's how I felt. I talked to the social worker at the hospital and told her, 'If I end this relationship I don't want that to affect him going on a transplant list.' She said that it wouldn't affect this decision, and I said, 'I need to get this person out of my life.'" Marie stayed with Bert for a few more months because he kept begging her to stay. "I finally said to him, 'I need my own life. You have hope, you have a chance to live, but I can't be a part of it. I need to have my own life.' It was like a weight lifted off my shoulders after all those years." Marie wasn't trying to add additional emotional pain to Bert's life, but after twenty years of living with a negative and very controlling man, she finally found the strength to say, "I don't want to be with you."

Although Marie and Bert hadn't spoken for a few months prior to his death, she will always be grateful that he tried to call her the night before he died. Bert's sister contacted her and said, "He wants to see you." Marie was very glad that she went to see Bert, because he had finally come to terms with their relationship. Bert told Marie, "I know you did a lot for me. I can't make you love me if you don't. You were supportive. I appreciate all you did. I hope we can still be friends." Marie could hardly believe what she was hearing but was happy for the closure that it helped to provide for her about their relationship, since Bert's heart stopped the next day. When Marie was notified about Bert's death by his family she began crying and was very upset. "It's not fair—I didn't want him to die. I just wanted him out of my life. I was happy that he had another chance at life. When the doctors said he was eligible for two transplants and he had a chance, that's when I knew I had to tell him I wanted out." Marie was experiencing guilt for the anger she had felt toward Bert and repeated to me, "I really believed he was going to make it—I was so upset to hear that he had died. They (Bert's family) let me go to the funeral, but no one else in my family was allowed to go."

Marie has developed some understanding of why she chose to live so long with a partner like Bert. Marie became involved with Bert when she was twenty-three and realizes that he reminded her of her mother, who had been so demanding of her, requiring her to care for her brain-injured brother. "I wasn't allowed to have my own life." Marie believes that Bert's controlling behavior was a comfort to her on some level, "because that's what I was used to handling." Marie reports that she "knew from the beginning this wasn't someone I wanted to spend my life with, but after the first ten years, when I got the courage to get out of it, he got sick. Then I felt like I couldn't get out of it."

Marie discussed some of the financial and legal issues that were difficult for this couple because they were not married. Marie said, "He [Bert] never thought that since I was his significant other that he should be financially responsible for me at all. We split everything—that enabled me to maintain my independence and to feel that I had some control." When Marie decided that she wanted to end the relationship, she planned to "buy out his lifetime rights to the house." Marie had been paying all of the expenses for the house during the last three years of their relationship, because Bert had lost all of his money in gambling debts. "He didn't want to be responsible for the upkeep of the house and turned over (ownership of) his half of the house to me." However, although Bert died before Marie had signed any agreement to that effect, the state real estate laws protected her. Marie considered giving his family some money following his death but decided that she didn't owe them anything for the house. Consequently, Bert's family sued Marie for his lifetime half of the house. They lost in court, and she has not spoken to them since. Marie feels bad that she has no contact with his three nieces, because they had a very close relationship. At first she continued the tradition of sending gifts to his nieces at birthdays and holidays but has stopped since one niece returned a gift to her.

Occasionally, Marie thinks about Bert now and said, "I do—sometimes I even have dreams about him. There is very little good I can remember, so I don't know why I dream about him—probably to get him out of my life. The bad things were bad." Bert had told Marie to keep all of the birthday and Christmas cards she had given him. Marie made a ritual out of dealing with the cards she had given and had received from Bert. "One night I gathered up all of these cards and wanted to purge him from my life. I read each one of them, and I was crying—kind of purging him. I put them all together and threw them out. I didn't want to remember him as some love of my life—that's what he wanted me to feel but I wasn't. This was a very positive step for me—getting rid of twenty years of cards . . . looking at all those words of love that I put in there because I was trying to make myself believe it. He did love me in his own way, but he only knew how to be controlling—that was his way of loving, but to me that wasn't love." At the same time that Marie was talking about needing to purge the "bad" things about Bert from her life, she said, "I would often talk to the sky and say, 'I know you think this means I never loved you, but I did.'" Marie said, "I don't need bad memories to drag me down. Bert's family's relationship with him was different—they have no idea how difficult he was. He was so possessive—I could never have my own friends—only his friends."

Marie reported a very spiritual experience that occurred the evening of Bert's death. "The Sunday night that he died I had the sense that somebody's spirit was in the house. My dog started barking in anger, which is not ordinary for him. So, I thought it was my father or grandmother. I didn't know, but I said, 'Whoever it is, Hello.' I do believe in life after death. I believe that our loved ones are there to guide us through difficult things. But the next day, I realized that it had to be Bert because he was afraid of dogs—he was never allowed to have dogs. That's the other thing I did as a result of Bert's death—as soon as he died, I got a dog." During the interview with Marie, her two dogs, of whom she is very fond, sat next to her on the sofa as we talked about Bert.

Marie believes that the community reacted differently to her relationship, and to her as his caregiver, because they were not married. "Marriage has a certain position that recognizes a certain level of respect. If you're not married, you don't get that same level of recognition. When nursing services come into your house and ask, 'What's your relationship with Bert?' and I told them that we were partners, they were being judgmental when they found out I wasn't married." Marie was also upset that Bert left her nothing in his will after she took care of him for all of those years. Friendships were also difficult for this couple. Marie says, "My best friend stopped going out to dinner with us—Bert always insisted on going out with us and she couldn't stand him."

As a result of Bert's death, Marie believes that she's become "self-actualized." "Now that he's finally out of my life I feel like I have a life of my own. I am my own person. I know that I'm a good person and have valuable things to give to society. I'm happy for the first time in twenty years. When I was living with Bert I was always worried about being yelled at for something. I now have a remarkable sense of freedom. If I had to do it all over again, I would have found the strength to leave when he got sick the first time and not stayed with him because of guilt." Marie also believes that she's become more assertive. "I'm more aware of my own feelings and have a sense that my feelings count. I was never allowed to have my own feelings count before. I have a remarkable sense of freedom and it's wonderful. Bert died, and I know that he's in a better place—probably feeling a lot better, but I'm free to go on and live my own life and make my own choices. It feels good!"

As a result of her own personal growth, Marie has decided to return to the practice of social work and is working on a per diem basis at a local hospice. Marie had left the profession of social work several years before Bert's death because of burnout. She started her own business, which has allowed her to pay for her house and to have more control over her life. "I needed to be in a field with bonuses, where I could tuck some money away for a retirement account, which I could never have done as a social worker. Having done that and earned the money I need, I can retire early. I can work in a field like social work that makes me feel good. It gives me satisfaction that I'm helping people to help themselves." Marie has used her experience as a caregiver for Bert to focus on the needs of a caregiver when a loved one is dying. Marie says, "I truly have so much empathy for the caregiver in the case of someone who is dying. Obviously the needs have to focus on the dying, but the needs of the caregiver are often not addressed. I can actually pick up on that and let the caregiver see how valuable they are and that they need to look out for themselves as well. I often tell them, 'I had a loved one who was sick and died—I know what you're going through.' They can really relate to that because I know it is a burden. They feel guilty about feeling burdened. I tell them, 'It's not that you don't love them.'" Marie is using her own experiences to help caregivers with their guilt about wanting to meet their own needs while taking care of a loved one. Marie says that caregivers rarely get credit or get recognized for the work they do.

After Marie left Bert, she grieved a bit for their relationship for a few months but then she decided to rebuild her life. She contacted old friends and met someone whom she has been dating for two years. "He's such a nice person—such a difference—we were together for almost a year before we had a fight." Marie believes that she has learned a great deal from her relationship with Bert that will enable her to have the kind of long-term relationship that she has always wanted. "I know that I will never allow myself to be in the kind of relationship where someone controls or harasses me." Marie would like either to live with someone in a long-term relationship or be married. "I like that way of living—to truly share my life with someone and not just be a convenience for that person."

Analysis

Marie's story provides an example of how the care provided by the bereaved partner in a nontraditional relationship may be questioned by medical professionals involved with the sick partner. Marie reported that when the visiting nurses came to the house while she was Bert's caregiver, they questioned her role and were judgmental when they discovered that she and Bert were not married. Marie states, "Marriage has a certain position that recognizes a level of respect. If you're not married, you don't get that same level of recognition." This seems to occur because society does not give legitimacy to those relationships in which the couple has remained unmarried (Doka 1989, 2002b). Marie also experienced difficulty with financial and legal issues because she and Bert were not married. Following Bert's death, Marie had to take Bert's family to court in order to obtain rights to the home that was clearly hers. This can be so difficult during the time that a partner is grieving for the loss of a significant other and can contribute to complicated mourning (Doka 1989).

Marie's story illustrates how a partner in a nontraditional relationship can "disenfranchise herself" by her own lack of acknowledgment and recognition of her grief. Kauffman describes such partners as "being ashamed of one's own guilt" (1989:25). Marie experienced much guilt following Bert's death due to her hostile feelings toward him and her move to separate from him. Additionally, Marie seemed embarrassed about staying in the relationship with Bert and allowing him to abuse her emotionally. Her self-esteem was negatively affected by this long-term relationship in which she received little, if any, support from family, friends, and the community at large. When bereavement needs are unrecognized by one's family and friends, the parts of oneself where the unrecognized pain exists are negated (Doka 1989:29).

Marie still thinks about Bert, but her memories are negative ones, and her dreams are nightmares. Marie created a ritual of "purging" Bert from her thoughts by throwing out all of the greeting cards the couple had sent to one another over the twenty years they lived together. According to the postmodern grief theorists (Rubin 1999; Klass et al. 1996; Neimeyer 1998), Marie is not able to develop a continuing bond with her deceased partner, which may lead to complicated mourning. However, Marie has transformed her relationship with Bert into one in which she feels separate from him and can allow herself to experience freedom for the first time in her adult life.

Marie had a very ambivalent relationship with Bert, which ended negatively. Doka (1989, 2002b) points out that the meaning the relationship has for the bereaved greatly influences the grieving experience. Marie's negativity and anger have prevented her from feeling "entitled" to appropriate grieving for a long-term relationship. In addition, she received little recognition and few supports from family, friends, or medical personnel for her relationship and her care of Bert. She is now dedicating her life to helping other caregivers focus on their own needs. Despite a negative relationship with her partner, Marie has been able to derive meaning from her experience of loss. She believes that she has become "self-actualized" and has "become her own person." In letting go of her relationship with Bert, Marie has achieved a new sense of freedom and an ability to make her own choices. Neimeyer (1998) speaks to the importance of reconstructing a personal meaning of the world following the loss of a significant other. Marie has been able to do this both professionally and personally.

Barry

Barry is a seventy-six-year-old retiree who worked in real estate and sales for most of his life. Barry was seventy-five when Julie, his fiancée, died of cancer at age fifty-seven. Barry and Julie had both been widowed for about three years when they met at a dance for widows and widowers. "It took me quite a time to get to dance with her because she was such a good dancer and such a nice person and dressed very sharp. I took one look at

her and said, 'I've got to meet that girl.'" That was the beginning of a relationship that deepened each day. Barry recognized the large age difference
and was concerned about it. "I tried to break things off before it got too serious. And she would have no part of it. Julie said, 'I'm very happy with
you and I'm very satisfied. You don't act your age—just forget about it.'
She said, 'age is only numbers.' So we did. We continued to go out."

"She was working as a school teacher in Wilmington and lived in a sub-
urb south of the city with her single adult son. It took her one and one-half
hours to commute on a crazy interstate where she had a couple of bad experiences. She almost got into a couple of accidents, and she was out there
in all kinds of weather and all kinds of traffic. So she started spending the
weekend here with me. I said, 'Why don't you just try leaving from here
to school?' She'd get to work in anywhere from fifteen to twenty minutes. . . . So we fell into a pattern of her staying here a little longer every
week. It sort of just blended right in and she was here seven days a week.
Every other week we'd go to her house for a weekend so that we could
take her son out to dinner and do what she had to do around the house.
Eventually, she had all her clothes here and she was moved permanently.
We used to go to Florida on spring break to my condo." Julie was diagnosed with breast cancer four months after her husband died. "Julie was all
by herself and she took care of herself. She went and had her chemo treatment and she was cancer-free." Barry tells the story of her recurrence.

"We went on spring break last year . . . we went to Florida. Then just as
we got to Florida she was in such pain that she went right to bed, and I
went out and got some food. The next morning she was in such agony that
I had to take her to the emergency room in the hospital in Florida. The
doctor said she had a slipped disk. He made her lay down . . . he made her
stay in bed for four days. Then she got up. We came home on a Friday
night . . . we no sooner got in the house and I had to rush her to the ER.
They gave her some pain medicine and did x-rays and didn't find anything.
They said that she probably had something wrong with her back . . . her
disk. We went to my family doctor, and he was on vacation, and he
couldn't really give her a thorough examination, but he suspected something . . . he said, 'I think she should have some sophisticated tests done of
her liver and get some blood work.' We went back to her oncologist, and
he said, 'I don't want to hurt you or anything, but you've got a recurrence
of your breast cancer, and I'm going to put you in the hospital immediately.' She definitely had cancer, and she also had a tumor at the end of her
spine, and that was why she was getting all the pain."

Barry wasn't satisfied with Julie's care and took her to a doctor who was recommended by a friend of his. "Julie had radiation treatments and it was starting to affect her, so we took her off of radiation, did all kinds of tests, and put her in the hospital. Because her blood count was so low, they had to give her several transfusions. So they decided to do the chemotherapy, and she was doing real well. Then, about two weeks before she died, she just started getting pain—she could hardly walk. So we took her to the doctor and he had some more tests done. The doctor told us, 'The tumor is gone, but she has it in her liver.' He put her in the hospital immediately. She stayed in the hospital for about ten days and she passed away in the hospital."

"She was having terrible, terrible pain and they called me on the morning that she died and said, 'You better get here immediately.' When I got to her room, the bed was empty. I kind of panicked. I said 'Oh, my God.' I prayed that she would stay alive till I got there so I could see her. The nurse saw me and said, 'Don't get upset, we took her to intensive care. . . . She took me there. I saw her in there and I was able to talk to her. . . . They had a big mask on her face because she was having difficulty breathing. And she was so swollen from fluids. Her whole right side . . . I couldn't believe it was her. She was retaining fluids because I guess things were starting to break down. She was trying to tear the mask off, but she had to have it on because she had to breathe. I said, 'If you understand who I am, squeeze my hand', and she squeezed my hand. That's how I talked to her. And then, by that time, all my family came in, and all her family came in, and there were about fifteen of us in the room. My daughter, my son-in-law, my son, my grandson, my granddaughter, my brother, my sister—they all got there. They were all able to talk to her. My granddaughter and my daughter were next to her. Julie loved them both, and she knew they were both nurses.

Then the doctor came in, and this is the part that is really heartbreaking. . . . She was lying there and he said, 'Do you know who I am,' and she shook her head, and he said, 'Do you know how serious you are?' I think she shook her head, and he said, 'There's nothing I can do for you. I can make you comfortable with morphine.' I could have killed him. I didn't know why he had to tell her that she was dying. I think she sensed it, but why did he have to tell Julie that? I asked my niece, the one that's a doctor, and she said, 'Uncle Barry, they're duty-bound to tell the patient.' I said, 'I don't believe in that. Tell the people that are surviving her, that are with her, the loved ones, but don't tell the patient.' I don't know, I can't tell you whether she was upset or not. But he said, 'Do you understand what I'm saying,' and she nodded her head yes. . . . By that time her daughter had arrived, and her daughter was never close to her."

Barry is angry about how Julie's adult children reacted. "Her family didn't react at all. Her son acted like nothing was going on . . . he was oblivious to the whole thing. . . . Her daughter would call us up and tell us, 'We're going to make meals for you because we know how busy you are going back and forth to the hospital all day, and we'll bring them over and put them in the freezer and you can eat.' I never got one of them! I thought that was a nice gesture, but it was just a gesture, just to hear herself talk. Even Julie was a little concerned about it, but she never said anything, because lots of times, we'd be so tired from being in the hospital all day, and her treatment, and all, and she'd go right to bed. It would have been nice if we had the food there."

Barry experienced some difficulty with Julie's family because he and Julie were living together, despite the fact that the couple had become engaged and were to be married the June after Julie died. Julie's adult daughter "always objected to her mother living with me. She wanted her mother to move into her house. They were going to make a room for her down in the basement. She wanted her mother to be there because Julie loved the children and she had been a great babysitter. She would have been able to, more or less, control her mother. Her mother was very independent, and she didn't want that. I said to Julie, 'You're not going to go there.' She said, 'No, I'm not. I have my own home here.' One time, her daughter said to her mom, 'What am I going to say to my children if they should ask if Barry and . . . grandmom . . . they're not married, how do I explain it?' Julie said, 'We're going to get married.' Julie's daughter objected to us living together because she was a turn-around Catholic. She had been Presbyterian all her life."

Later, when Julie died in the hospital and then funeral arrangements needed to be made, this religious attitude about living together became a heated issue. Although Barry himself was a Catholic, he was upset about the following events: "She [Julie's daughter] took control that last day in the hospital. Everyday that I went to the hospital, the doctor would talk to me. I would take Julie to the hospital, and he would explain to Julie and I together what was going on. Her daughter was in the room when I was in there with Julie when she was dying. He never approached me. . . . He never looked at me. He did all the talking to the daughter. Now I don't know for sure whether she said to him, 'Anything that concerns my mother, you'll talk to me.' Julie had appointed her daughter executor of the estate, and she said, 'I'm her daughter and they're not married.' She must have said that, because he ignored me completely and that hurt me. Everything that was said was said to her.

"She brought in a priest from her parish and I didn't know this. Julie is dying, and she's going to convert her into a Catholic. The priest is talking to her, and he said he couldn't give Julie her last rights unless she became a Catholic. I just didn't know what to do. My daughter and my granddaughter were there. I don't know if she understood him or not, but she was on her deathbed. And he said, 'Now you're a Catholic,' and he gave her her last rights and left her, and her daughter was very happy. She said, 'Mom, you're going right to heaven and you're so good.' All at once she became the loving daughter, and this was all missing when Julie was alive. We'd go to the babies' parties and she made more fuss over her husband's family than she did her own mother. Her mother, Julie, would have a new outfit on and never once would she ever say, 'Gee, mom, you look pretty or . . . or spend some time with her. We were like two people who were like strangers. We would stay close together because we were kind of ignored. I used to notice that, and Julie noticed it too. But we never discussed it because I didn't want to make her feel bad. But she was ignored, and all at once, at her deathbed, she loved her mother . . . to me it was a phony act. It was an act to give the impression that she was that loving, caring daughter, which she wasn't. But I had to bite my tongue. I couldn't say anything because I'm not legally her husband, and I didn't have any say in anything, as much as I wanted to. If I had had a say, I would have thrown them all out. There's a priest coming in, doesn't even know her, and he's a young priest, and I think he was browbeaten by Julie's daughter.

"We were there all day, and everybody went outside to just relax for a few minutes. I stayed with Julie. I was the only one in the room with her, and I was talking to her and holding her hand, but she was so full of morphine that she was out of it, which was good. I was watching the monitor [Barry was crying at this point], and I can see her blood pressure dropping. I was holding her hand, telling her how much I loved her. She gave a sigh and she just passed away. I was grateful that I was the one that was with her when she died."

Although Julie's daughter wanted to make all the final funeral arrangements, Barry asserted himself because he felt he knew what Julie would have wanted.

"I got a little ticked off, and I figured I'm going to take control, here, a little bit. I'm not going to let people think I'm just a piece of scenery, here.

I said to her daughter, her brother, and her son, 'Julie loved Greenwood, where she lived, and she loved the Presbyterian church on the corner.' Across the street is an undertaker, and I said, 'She's going to be laid out in Greenwood. That's where all her friends are, and anybody else that wants to see her, they're going to come to Greenwood to see her. I'm going to call the undertaker and have him get Julie and bring her over there.' Her daughter didn't know what to say, but she agreed to it."

Barry was very hurt by the funeral service, in which his relationship with Julie was not mentioned. The priest mentioned Julie's love for her grand-child, her daughter, her son-in-law, her son, and her brother, but not for Barry. "So I felt like I didn't exist. There was not one word about how happy she was with me." Since Julie's death, Barry has mentioned his anger to Julie's daughter, and although she has apologized, it has not helped Barry with his feelings about it. In fact, Barry admits, "I cried so many tears over that . . . it's like her family didn't want the world to know that we lived to-gether and we were happy together. I think her daughter resented the fact that we were living together, and she wanted us to be married, just to sat-isfy friends. We weren't going to rush into it. We just lost our spouses and we were taking our time. We wanted to have a lasting romance and a mar-riage, and we took our time because we were going to care for each other."

Barry has little desire to keep in touch with Julie's daughter but does keep in touch with her son, who "calls me and talks to me and I try to help him out. He feels like I'm a relative because we always said, 'If your mom had lived, I would have been your stepfather,' and he said, 'That would have been great.'" Barry has also stayed in touch with Julie's brother and plans to see him and Julie's son for a "guys' night out."

Barry is concerned that he is still having so much trouble with his sad-ness. "I talk to my daughter and my granddaughter, no one else. I just stay here and cry and wait for the day that I'll stop. I know I will." Talking with his daughter and granddaughter helps him get through most days. Barry also engages in a regular exercise routine each day, followed by a game of pool. Music is another source of comfort to him in his grief—he plays his stereo all day when he is home.

Barry keeps Julie's memory close to him by talking to her and by staying in touch with her son and her brother, with whom he can share memories. "I kind of talk to her every night. . . . If I have a problem, if something's bothering me, I talk to her. I just have feelings in my heart that she's lis-tening and that I'm communicating with her." Recently, when his grand-son applied for a big promotion, Barry "said prayers to Julie and Marie (his deceased wife) every night, and I asked them both, especially Julie, to help him get his promotion." Barry also keeps memories of Marie close to him. In fact, after Julie died, when Julie's daughter was packing up things in his house that belonged to her mother's family, Barry told her, 'I don't want their things. I have my own things from Marie. In his home, Barry has prominently displayed photos of both Julie and Marie on his living room wall. Barry says, "Marie was a great girl too. I'm very fortunate. God gave me two great ladies. But He took them away from me too soon." Barry expressed his fear of getting involved with another woman because of the two deaths he has experienced.

Barry also finds that Julie's dog provides comfort to him and is a way for him to remember Julie. Before Julie's death, right after the cancer was discovered, Julie said to Barry, "If anything ever happens to me, please don't let anybody take the dog. He loves it here." "I said, 'Julie, don't worry, nothing's going to happen to the dog because the dog stays here.'" As Barry spoke with me about Julie, he was holding her dog in his arms. Barry says he feels the same "grief and hurt" over the loss of his wife and Julie "whether I was married to Julie or not. I don't know why I'm taking Julie's death harder than I did with Marie. I guess it's just that Marie lived her life and Julie was really starting to experience the good life. . . . She was going to retire early, and we had so many plans of what to do when she retired. And her death just changed everything. With Marie, I enjoyed life with her after she retired." Barry is currently helping to plan a special memorial dinner in honor of Julie, during which he will be the featured speaker.

Barry is trying to figure out how to begin his life again. Friends have asked him to come to visit them in Florida, and other friends and family have suggested that he return to the dance group he belonged to with Julie. He told his daughter, "I can't go there." He is considering a trip to Italy with his sister, about which he seems excited. Barry is also taking a computer course as a new venture as well as a sewing class. He chose a sewing class because of his relationship with Julie. "Julie was a great sewer. She made all the costumes for her grandchildren . . . she used to do a lot of work for me, too . . . my cuffs, my trousers, my sport shirts. And there's a couple that she started and didn't finish. I figured . . . it's a beautiful sewing machine, and it's sitting here, and somebody's got to learn to use it. . . . I'm the only male who shows up for the course." Barry believes that the new people he is meeting in the courses he is taking and his relationship with Julie's dog are helping him cope with his grief. Barry also is an active gardener and loves sports. He believes he'll return to dancing because "you can meet a lot of nice people dancing."

Following my interview with Barry, he contacted me—just prior to the memorial dinner in honor of Julie. He asked if he could send me the following poem, which has been a comfort to him and which he plans to use at the dinner:

> You never said, "I'm leaving."
> You never said, "Goodbye."
> You were gone before I knew it and
> God only knows why.
> A million times I've cried.
> If love alone could have saved you,
> You never would have died.
> In life I loved you dearly.
> In death I love you still.
> In my heart you hold a special place
> No one can ever fill.
> It broke my heart to lose you.
> But you didn't go alone, for a part of me
> Went with you the day God called you home.

Barry felt that perhaps this poem might help others who have lost a partner.

Analysis

Barry is demonstrating his ongoing relationship with Julie in many different ways—through caring for Julie's dog, through photographs, by talking with Julie's son and brother, and by taking a sewing class to help him carry on some of the tasks that Julie performed for him in their relationship. Additionally, Barry talks to Julie when he has a problem or when something is bothering him. Barry has reached a point where his memories and thoughts of Julie are available in a balanced way, so that he finds a measure of strength and warmth from his reconstructed relationship with Julie (Rubin 1999). Perhaps Barry's age, seventy-six, is helping him to "build a different kind of relationship" with his deceased partner, one that allows him to start to move on just one year after his partner's death. His responses mirror those of the older spouses, Flora and George, whose stories are presented in Chapter 3, rather than those of Frank, who was much younger and was interviewed more than three years after the loss of his wife. Age may well be a factor in allowing bereaved partners to find comfort in the reconstructed relationship with their deceased partners.

As Rubin (1999) has noted, it is helpful for the bereaved partner to begin to transfer his or her relationship into a memorial. In a very concrete way, Barry is doing this by helping to plan a memorial dinner in Julie's honor. This form of memorializing the relationship is one of the more masculine forms of grieving described by Golden and Miller (1998). Of the interviewees, the only other partner who planned a similar memorial was John, in his creation of a permanent Girl Scout memorial for his wife, Bobbie.

Although Barry was not excluded from an active role in the care of Julie while she was dying, as nontraditional partners often can be, he certainly reveals his pain about the planning of the funeral. Julie's family and the priest made him feel as though he didn't exist. The family's reactions to Barry's grief as a nonmarried partner reflect society's tendency to pay more attention to kin-based relationships and roles. For couples like Barry and Julie, who have been emotionally involved in a relationship but for whom there is no official status, when a partner dies, the grief can go unrecognized. Doka (1987) notes that the emotions experienced by the bereaved partner in a traditional relationship, such as anger, sadness, loneliness, depression, and guilt, are often intensified in a nontraditional relationship. Barry was clear that his grief for Julie was much more difficult for him than his grief for Marie, his wife of over thirty years. Perhaps it was not only Julie's age but the reactions of her daughter and the priest during the funeral that made it more difficult for Barry to work through his feelings—feelings that were ignored by part of the community of grievers. Barry's reactions seem similar to those expressed by the participants in Sklar and Hartley's study of survivor-friends, who did not feel that they had been acknowledged by others as "truly grieving to the same degree that a family member might" (Sklar and Hartley 1990:110). Sklar and Hartley also found that the participants who consciously attempted to grieve, as did Barry by being active in planning Julie's funeral service, "discovered they were not permitted to do so by the family" (1990:110).

Just as with George, the older widower in chapter 3, Barry is able to cry only with his children, although he also cried with the author of this text during the interview. Men of this generation have particular difficulty allowing themselves the luxury of ventilating their sad feeling to others in their network. Just as Miller and Golden (1998) have pointed out, although men may be grieving, they often do not express their emotions. They sense that a public display of their emotions can cause discomfort for others in their lives, who are not used to seeing them behave in this way.

The following narrative is that of an older woman who lost her partner.

Ida

Ida was eighty-nine when her partner, Henry, died at age eighty-seven. Ida and Henry were "together" for twelve years, although they maintained their own households throughout the relationship. Ida and Henry knew each other long before they became partners, having met through their children in the community they shared. Ida had been widowed for seventeen years before she and Henry began sharing their lives. "We didn't live together except when he had surgery, and then he stayed here. We had meals together, we'd go shopping to the store, and he'd go home at night. My girlfriends here in town teased me, 'My goodness, Ida, that's not what I'd do. When I want company is at night.' But I was glad to have company all day and was sort of ready to relax at night." Ida has one adult daughter, who lives in a nearby state and visits her regularly, and three adult grandchildren whom she sees less often. Henry had several adult children whom Ida knew because she had taught them in school.

Ida began to notice changes in Henry's behavior but didn't realize that it was the beginning of Alzheimer's disease. "He became real helpless, but he would not give up driving. He also had a heart problem—the oxygen didn't get to his brain." Henry's heart problem made it difficult for him to be as active as he would have liked. Ida also has had heart problems, which led to the installation of a pacemaker following several fainting episodes. Shortly after Ida had her surgery for the installation of her pacemaker, Henry died in his room at a retirement home.

Ida was not involved in planning the funeral service for Henry. "He had three girls, and as I said, I taught two of them in school, so I didn't want anything to do with it. And of course, they didn't ask me. If they had asked, I would have been willing to." Ida isn't certain how Henry's daughters felt about her relationship with their father. "His youngest daughter, who used to come here and visit some while he was here, has only been here a few times, but not as much. I think they've made it one time since he passed away and that's all."

Ida has many fond memories of her relationship with Henry. "We had a lot of good times together. We shopped together and he was great for "going." The miles that he rode every day really put miles on the car." Following Henry's death, Ida finds that she misses him very much. "I feel lonely because he was here every day, even though at the last he had changed so much. Yes, I was losing him a little all along, but I didn't quite realize it even though I knew his condition. But I'd never been around a person like that, and when you see them every day, you don't recognize it like you would otherwise. I had never been entirely by myself, because I was so occupied with the farm when my husband passed away. My brother lived just right across the field in the other house, and he was here every day, just about. I was still working at the bank. I worked there part-time about twenty years. I was always very busy. So this is the first time I've really been alone. My brother moved over to an apartment in another part of the state, so I don't see him at all. My husband's nephew has been a lot of company this summer, so that helps, the company." The other person who has helped Ida cope with her loneliness is her adult daughter, with whom she speaks daily. "I call one day and she calls the next. She is a blessing, a guardian angel. She's got a life of her own, too." Some of Ida's neighbors have also helped her out. Once, when Ida fell and was knocked unconscious, she asked a neighbor to "come and stay with me an hour or two . . . but I've always been independent and always wanted to be."

Ida had been married to her husband for thirty-four years, and she describes the home she still lives in as "My husband's and mine, and Henry's and mine." She believes that there was a difference in the way people responded to the loss of her husband versus the loss of her partner. Although she had quite a few calls and letters following Henry's death, "they'd say, 'Well, he's not your husband.' That's what you'd hear most of the time. It sort of put a little dent into the way I felt, to a certain degree. You think about marriage at our age, and each one of us was established, so why would we want to marry? Sometimes it made me wonder if I was doing the wrong thing. But then you stop and think, why spend day in and day out by yourself when you can have company or somebody to talk to and share things with?"

Thinking about the loss of Henry, Ida said, "You feel like you've lost a part of yourself. You feel like you've lost quite a bit. And the older you are, the more you feel you've lost, because you're not as active. He called me every morning and every night, to see if I was all right and to let me know he was all right. Now there's nothing that interrupts you. I'm asked about getting out in the car, and I've said I could if I was younger, but I don't feel like doing it now. I don't feel like getting the car out of the garage. It all seems like a burden."

Although Ida is a very independent woman, she still feels that one of the most difficult things about Henry's death is "being alone—just not having anybody to say 'Hi' or anything." When she thinks about her memories of Henry, she says, "I just think about the good things. I did the same when my husband died. You think about the good times you had. I think about the road trips we took. It helps me." However, Ida admits that shortly following Henry's death as well as that of her husband, "you grieve first. You think about how much you miss him. You do think about your good times then, too, but you think about how they're gone and not coming back. Gone for good. And then you think, when you're ninety years old, what companionship are you going to have now?"

Analysis

Ida's story reflects how an elderly couple chose to be partners in the later stages of life. Ida and Henry were the only couple interviewed who did not share the same house. They considered themselves to be lifetime partners, however, because they spent all of their time together except for sleeping together at night. Ida's story reflects some aspects of disenfranchised grief, when she discusses how, although her friends called to support her following Henry's death, they would say, "Well, he's not your husband." Ida was quite aware of the difference between her friends' reactions following the death of her husband, seventeen years before she and Henry began to share their lives, and felt that their reaction to Henry's death "put a little dent" into the way she was able to express her own sadness and grief.

Ida's story also reflects the recurrent theme of "losing a part of yourself" described in other narratives throughout this book. Ida believes that "the older you are, the more you feel you've lost, because you are not as active." Henry provided Ida with a source of support by contacting her every day and every night when they did not spend time together. At Ida's age, many of her older friends and relatives have died, so that the loss of Henry has deeply invaded her sense of self.

Ida keeps Henry's memory alive by remembering the "good times together." She misses Henry very much, and these memories have helped her in her grieving process. Ida readily differentiates the loneliness that has come from losing Henry from the loneliness following the loss of her husband. Because Ida was "so preoccupied with the farm" when her husband died, she felt that she had "never been entirely" by herself. Ida was also working at a bank and enjoyed the company of her colleagues, as well as that of her brother, who lived across the street. Ida says very poignantly, "This is the first time I've really been alone." However, just as in the narratives of two elderly widowed partners, Flora and George, in chapter 3, Ida's close relationship with her adult daughter, with whom she talks regularly, provides critical support to her life.

Peter

Peter is a retired school teacher who was fifty-nine when his partner, Marilyn, died from a severe viral infection at age fifty-seven. Before meeting Marilyn, Peter had been divorced twice, but has maintained positive relationships with both of his ex-wives. Peter has two adult children, ages twenty-nine and thirty-one, with whom he shares very close relationships. Marilyn was a talented artist who had been divorced before meeting Peter in their neighborhood. Marilyn had two adult children—a daughter and a son. Peter and Marilyn had shared a relationship for six years before Marilyn's death. They began living together about a year before Marilyn's death and had considered marriage. Peter "never loved anyone as I loved Marilyn."

"One of the nicest compliments in my life was when Marilyn said to me, 'I wish we could have had children together.' Before she died, we were talking about getting married. Neither of us wanted to get married when we first met. Our real commitment was to the relationship . . . marriage, it somehow evolved to that point. I knew I didn't want anyone else in my life and I knew there'd never be anyone else in my life as long as we both lived." At the time of Marilyn's death, Peter had his house up for sale. They had decided to make Marilyn's home their permanent residence. Peter was very sad when he shared the story of Marilyn's illness.

Marilyn's illness was a lengthy one; she was in the hospital for nine months. "For the first six months, I went to the hospital every day. My sabbatical was over, and I had to get back to school. Once I was back at school, I went every other day. Marilyn became hydrocephalic as a result of her illness, but the doctors were unable to put shunts in because of the fear of spread of infection. Dealing with her was like dealing with an elementary-school child or even an infant. She knew my name, but there were a couple of occasions where she didn't even know who I was. She was paralyzed on the left side as a result of a stroke from the brain infection." Peter cared for many of Marilyn's personal needs while she was in the hospital. At first the nurses resisted his involvement but finally agreed to allow Peter to change her bedsheets. During Marilyn's hospitalization, Marilyn's son took a leave of absence and was "there everyday along with me. I don't think that was easy for him—my being there. I don't know that he knew what she meant to me. He didn't know me very well, and it was kind of awkward at times." When Marilyn needed at-home care, there was some disagreement with Marilyn's son about who would take her home. It was resolved without too much difficulty, and after Marilyn's nine-month stay in the hospital, Peter brought her home to care for her. "Then, out of the clear blue sky, she became ill again. We were supposed to leave for Europe, and on the weekend, she was hospitalized. She died two weeks later."

Peter's children were very supportive during Marilyn's illness, and his daughter helped him change Marilyn's soiled clothing. Following Marilyn's death, Peter's daughter wrote a letter in which she shared her strong feelings for Marilyn. In the letter she wrote, "I want to be sure to let all of you know how much I loved Marilyn. She was more than my Dad's girlfriend. She was my stepmom. I had even started referring to her and Dad as my parents. She became part of my ever-increasing extended family. I will miss Marilyn and I will never forget her."

As a result of Marilyn's death, Peter believes that one of the "biggest changes I see in myself is that I am a much more giving person than I've ever been in my life. Through all this time, other people saw me in a different light. It goes back to the fact that I gave. I have a nephew that I did not get along with real well, and I think shortly after I was taking care of Marilyn, I just felt a sense of peace, like there was a softening in our relationship." Peter remembers Marilyn as one of the most loving, generous people he has ever met, which he believes influenced his own personal growth. Marilyn's interest in the arts helped to enhance Peter's interest in cultural activities, which he still maintains. Peter also believes that Marilyn saw strengths in him, such as his creativity, which he had not recognized.

Peter keeps memories of Marilyn close to him. "People talk about growing older—I love being where I am right now. The contentment I have, even with Marilyn gone, it doesn't change who I am. Marilyn will be with me as long as I live." Although Peter is slightly allergic to dogs, he has kept Marilyn's dog with him and feels very close to him. Peter also believes that his relationship with Marilyn has heavily influenced his new relationship with Nancy. "One of the things that I take away from her [Marilyn], which has really made a big influence in my life, is that I had a tremendous respect for her—an admiration. I guess if you have that, everything else seems to fall into place. . . . Another thing that I bring to my relationship with Nancy is a dedication. If you want to have a special relationship, you cannot take someone for granted. . . . That relationship continually needs to be fed or cared for. That's something I did naturally with Marilyn." Peter believes that he brings this capacity to his relationship with Nancy. He says that at times Nancy is jealous of Marilyn. "I have a tremendous love for Marilyn. I have it as well for Nancy, but it is not the same. When Nancy would tell me that I was comparing her with Marilyn, I would say, 'You're really different and I certainly love both of you.'"

Analysis

Peter's story reflects an attempt by the bereaved to maintain a continuing relationship with his deceased partner by keeping memories of Marilyn close to him as he develops a new relationship with Nancy. As he says, "Marilyn will be with me as long as I live." Peter learned, from his relationship with Marilyn, the true meaning of respect and commitment, which were not present in his first two marriages. He has incorporated what he has learned into his relationship with Nancy, for whom he has tremendous love. Peter's grief experiences reflect Rubin's 1999 work, which suggests that the ability to incorporate the memory of the deceased "into the fabric of the bereaved's life" (Rubin 1999:687) allows for a greater opportunity to expand one's social relationships.

Peter has reconstructed his self-identity as a result of his relationship with Marilyn. He believes that he has become a "much more giving person than I've ever been in my life," and attributes this personal change directly to his association with and love for Marilyn, who was "one of the most loving, generous people" he has met. He has also incorporated Marilyn's love for cultural activities into his new life as a single man. Peter has reconstructed his personal world so that it again "makes sense" and has restored a sense of meaning and direction to his life, which has been forever transformed (Neimeyer 1998:94).

Because Peter's relationship was accepted by Marilyn's family as well as their peers, Peter seems to have experienced less disenfranchisement of his grief than did Marie or Barry. Doka (1989, 2002b) reports that when the relationship is accepted there is a greater possibility for social support from family and friends. This facilitates the resolution of grief. Furthermore, both Peter's children and Marilyn's had the joint medical authority to make decisions about Marilyn's care once she was incapacitated. This contrasts with the experiences of Marie and Barry, who had to relinquish all decisions to the partner's family. The letter that Peter's daughter wrote to him and his family, in which she stated that Marilyn was "more than my Dad's girl-friend—she was my stepmom" indicates the degree of acceptance from his family. Peter also spoke of the support he received from both of Marilyn's children following her death. However, Peter does allude to the difficulty Marilyn's son experienced when he and Peter spent so much time togeth-er in the hospital. Peter said, "I don't know that he knew what she [Mari-lyn] meant to me—it was kind of awkward."

Peter felt that he "won more points with others because I wasn't married to her." When Marilyn became ill and Peter took care of her, "there were people that praised me for taking care of her and the way I took care of her, particularly because I wasn't married to her." Peter's positive experience, in which he was respected as a caregiver, provides a direct contrast to Marie's experience, which made her feel that neither friends, family, nor medical personnel respected the caregiving that she provided for Bert. As a conse-quence, Marie is still struggling with many negative feelings about her ex-perience, while Peter feels honored that he had the experience of caring for Marilyn. Unmarried people who suffer the loss of a partner experience a greater amount of disenfranchised grief when their relationships are reject-ed by others, and their grief is affected as well by the meaning that the re-lationship had for the bereaved partner (Doka 1989).

Francine

Francine was fifty years old when her "life partner," Steven, died at fifty-five in a plane crash. Francine was married in the early 1970s and di-vorced in the early 1980s, when her daughter was very young. When Francine met Steven, Francine's daughter was ten years old, and "he helped to raise her—he did homework with her." Steven had two college-aged children when the couple met. Before meeting Francine Steven had lived with another woman for eleven years, and "he wasn't close to his kids. Steven's former partner didn't let him bring the kids to the house. One of the things that I did for Steven was to bring him and his children closer to-gether. Once we became a couple, they came for holidays and other times of the year."

"I called him 'my honey' when he was living, but when he died, I had to come up with a term that fit our relationship. 'Life partner' seemed best, and it's what I used in the obituary." Francine and Steven were together for nine years, and she felt that she was married. "Since he has died I do refer to him as my husband, because it's too complicated to explain the situation."

Francine was an interior designer when she met Steven but began substitute teaching and taught full-time for a few years before Steven died. Steven had a financial relationship with an ad agency for a radio station but had significant financial difficulties. "I was the one who didn't want to marry him because I couldn't accept his economic woes as a part of my life."

Francine and Steven met on Valentine's Day. "Mutual friends introduced us at dinner, and I liked him right away. It was a strange evening, because in the middle of the dinner he had to go get his daughter and bring her to dinner with us. He didn't call me after the dinner, but I felt so positive about him I called him and invited him to dinner. At the time we met, he was six months away from a painful separation, and his father had just died. After that we just enjoyed each other until Steven's death."

"Steven left on a business trip and said he'd be gone for two days. He called the first night and said he was fine. The second night he called from the airport and said he would catch a later flight because his meeting had gone on longer than he thought. He told me to wait up for him. He missed his original flight and the flight he got on crashed. "He shouldn't have been on that plane."

Five and one half years following the crash, the airlines have finally recovered some of Steven's remains and "his children and I have selected a date to spread his ashes over the sea." Francine believes that when she and Steven's adult children have an opportunity to scatter his ashes at sea, this may give her some closure. Although Francine is looking forward to the opportunity of sharing memories about Steven with his children, she is ambivalent about facing the pain that this experience may bring her. In addition, Steven's ex-wife will be present at this family ceremony. "This will be very hard for me. His ex-wife has become very inclusive of everyone and thinks Steven was her best friend." Steven's ex-wife took care of Steven's mother when she was dying. Francine and Steven's mother were estranged. After Steven died, "She called me and said, 'You weren't married to him. You don't deserve to get anything.' I was devastated, since I always felt like I was Steven's lifelong partner. I never contacted her after that."

When asked about the differences between being married and not being married when your partner dies, Francine said, "Yes, there are differences, and most of them are negative. If I'd been married I'd be wealthy right now. Aviation law doesn't recognize common-law marriage, so I didn't receive the death benefits after the crash. Because the children were emancipated, they didn't get anything either. His kids signed so that I could get anything that they would get. Since he didn't have any income coming in or money in the bank, there wasn't any money. After his death it was hard to prove he was worth any money. I became obsessed with proving his worth. I had to get letters from everyone—including the company he visited just prior to his death." Francine contacted this company and asked why they hadn't even called her after his death. The company told her they were sorry. Francine never discussed life insurance with Steven. "Right after he died, his daughter showed up at the house and wrote a check for all the money in his checking account. I had to pay for everything that we had both been paying for. I did everything he did. He didn't have a will or insurance like you would if you were married. I saw myself as his lifelong partner, not a significant other. Society is not so kind to partners who aren't married."

"I came out of my mourning about eleven months after Steven died, and I wanted to date. After his death my primary focus was to meet someone. I've made my peace with that. I have an interesting life. I've met and dated more than thirty men, and no one comes close to Steven. Steven was a unique person—a good listener, nonjudgmental, interesting, and very kind. He was a rare combination of all of those traits, and I consider myself lucky to have found him, although he was in economic difficulties. We both loved to cook. We traveled all over the world together and traveled on weekends. The memory that comes most often to me is of Steven coming home at night after work and giving me a big hug. He would make his martini and we both understood what a peaceful life we had together. We made each day count. It was wonderful."

Although Francine cherishes the relationship she had with Steven, she recognizes that their partnership limited her personal growth and her independence. Since Steven's death Francine has become more independent. "My friends who have lost partners all talk about who we've become—we've become independent and have grown tremendously. We'll never be who we are with our mates—you decide who you want to be on your own. I'm a strong force, and I'm a lot more proud of who I am now. When I was with Steven, there was part of me that didn't want to be as successful as my husband. I held back. I didn't want to be the provider."

"Steven was an artist before he met me, and I was too. But we didn't do it while we were together. We didn't make our artwork flourish. I didn't read when I was with Steven, but I read a lot now." For Francine, another negative factor about cohabitation was that "my daughter had to go through the teen years with knowing that I was living with a man." Francine and her daughter had a difficult relationship while she was living with Steven because "she would have liked my attention more—Steven and I were such a strong, loving couple. Since Steven's death I have put together a better relationship with my daughter. I've put my daughter through college—I paid her tuition, and I'm proud of it."

In order to cope with her grief, Francine joined a bereavement group. "It was helpful. I cried and I listened." She met women in this group whom she still sees. In fact, some from this group and others she has met travel together regularly—they are "soul mates." Francine believes that she has "grown more from this relationship and the loss of it than people could grow in a lifetime. I started a book club—I put a studio in my house—I got into my art. I took up horseback riding one year ago. I went to Spain and looked up a family I lived with when I was in college. I've reconnected with this family. I take my daughter all over the world. I'm a strong person. I can land anywhere in the world and can pick up and drive. Before Steven's death, I had to be on a man's arm. It seemed traditional not to take care of yourself. Steven would be thrilled with who I am now. I ironed out a lot of things about myself and he'd be proud of me. You make your own life—you don't have others make it for you."

In creating a new life for herself, Francine has been reflecting upon relationships and societal rules. "I have been meeting people on the Internet—I've met some lovely people. So many have been divorced and remarried several times. Where do you pull the new rules for a new society with the growing numbers of couples who are choosing lifelong partners instead of spouses? A lot of old categories don't hold about who we are anymore. In a partnered relationship the old rules don't work. We don't have a way to state what we had [meaning the relationship]. I know that my relationship with Steven was better than a lot of marriages. Maybe living together takes the pressure off—the together till death do us part. We were there because we wanted to be there." Although Francine believes that people may lose part of their identity when they marry, which may lead to so many divorces, she said, "I did lose myself—even in a partnership."

Francine has found many ways to continue her relationship with Steven. "In the time that I was healing from his loss, I must take what I learned from this spectacular human being. I try to be nonjudgmental like he was. I learn from what that person was. I started a scholarship in his name. One year after his death I had a party for him with our friends. I see his good friends now, and we talk about him." Francine is also learning Spanish as a way to reconnect with Steven, who was fluent in the language. "Steven had a dog, which died, but I now have the son of his dog. The daily habits are there—I still wind his clock. If I burn a pot I'll say, 'He'll kill me.' I have kept the house much the same. I have learned to do things in ways that he did things. You think people don't want to hear about him—it's been so long. But some people like to talk about him with fond memories."

On the other hand, Francine is ambivalent about the pain that certain memories will bring for her. "Steven's daughter thinks that when we scatter his ashes we'll talk about Steven. I'm concerned about that, because I'm not sure what she means. The things in my mind are private thoughts—between Steven and me. There is tension between Steven's daughter and me. I think she was jealous of the relationship I had with her father, because she was just coming back into his life when my relationship with him was deepening. However, I'm very close to his son." Francine still hears from families of the air crash victims; most of them visit the site regularly and have purchased land to improve. "I've never gone to the site—I've never wanted to go there. A lot of the other survivors have gone. However, as a group, we have also been involved in helping to change the way the airlines handle survivors after a crash—we were handled very badly. We weren't given information we needed."

Francine offered some advice for other adults who have lost partners. "Grieving is very important, and I did do it. It's so fulfilling—to come out of that—you can repair and have such a rich life. I feel sorry for people who stay stuck in their grief. In my group, one woman is living with a man and two are scared of having relationships. You hope for someone to be able to grow from the grief experience—to take good things from the person who died. I'm healthy, happy, and have an interesting life. You make your own life—you don't wait for someone to make it for you."

Analysis

Francine believed that her partnership with Steven was not given full recognition by society, particularly by Steven's daughter, his mother, and the airlines. Doka (1987) notes that emotions experienced during grief in a traditional relationship are intensified, but that with nontraditional relationships, "because these relationships are negatively sanctioned, feelings of guilt may be particularly evident" (p. 457). Following Steven's death, Francine's obsession to "prove Steven's worth" may have been a reaction to guilt over having been involved in a nonsanctioned relationship. Another symptom of Francine's guilt may be that she now refers to Steven as her husband "because it's too complicated to explain the situation." Before his death, Francine called Steven her "honey" and, more formally, her "life partner."

Francine seems to be struggling with how others and perhaps she herself can accept the loss of a relationship unsanctioned by society. At one point she says, "We (society) don't have a way to state what we had."

Although she loved her relationship with Steven, Francine was very vocal about the difficulties of cohabitation. She experienced discrimination from the airline, which did not grant her a settlement for Steven's death. Doka (1989) speaks of the policies in society that define who has a "legitimate" right to receive financial compensation, regardless of the nature of the relationship. Francine was angry that she was not covered under life insurance policies or a will, as she might have been had she and Steven been married. She was also furious that Steven's daughter assumed the right to his bank account, which the couple used to pay some of their joint expenses. According to Doka (1989), these practical difficulties can "impede the resolution of grief."

Although Francine received support from their friends following Steven's death, Steven's mother was hostile to her, saying, "You weren't married to him. You don't deserve to get anything." This felt unfair to Francine, who felt like a lifelong partner and, in many ways, a wife to Steven. Perhaps this demonstrates Doka's point that those partners involved in nontraditional relationships "are less likely to have support both during the immediate time of death as well as some time after the death" (Doka 1989:462). Part of the difficulty is that, following the loss of a partner, not only do the bereaved partners lose significant roles, "but there is no defined transitional role for them to assume" (1989:462). In contrast, when a spouse dies, the surviving partner undergoes a transition into the role of widow or widower, which carries certain legal and social rights.

Despite all the difficulties following Steven's death, Francine was able to move forward with her life and grow in ways she never thought possible. In fact, she feels that she has become more independent and no longer feels the need to be protected by a man. She has returned to her artwork and has developed wonderful relationships with her daughter and her female friends—relationships she did not have when she was living with Steven. However, it is significant that Francine has found ways to continue her bonds with Steven through incorporating his nonjudgmental attitude into her identity and by performing daily, habitual tasks that the couple had enjoyed together. It seems that although Francine has a new and interesting life, she is staying connected to Steven and keeping a part of him within herself. This behavior corroborates the work of Rubin (1999), Neimeyer (1998), and Klass et al.(1996), who believe that the most important work of grief is the reconstruction of the relationship with the deceased partner. Silverman is quoted in an interview by Zucker as saying, "As we go on with our life, we honor our loved ones by continuing to recognize the connections to them and recognizing that the connections change as we do" (Zucker 2000:1).

In Francine's story about spreading Steven's ashes at sea and sharing memories with his children, we see her ambivalence about becoming involved with memories of Steven that will bring her back to the pain of his death over five years ago. This behavior demonstrates the challenge to all bereaved persons, which is to reconcile incompatible urges of yearning to be in touch with the pain as a way of connecting with the deceased, but wanting to avoid the pain (Stroebe et al. 1998; Simos 1979; Marris 1986; Bowlby 1980).

Laura

Laura had just celebrated her forty-second birthday when her partner, Jake, died of cancer at forty-six. Laura was separated from her husband for several years before living with Jake and was able to obtain a divorce only after Jake became very ill. Jake had been divorced for many years and had two children, a twenty-one-year-old son and a sixteen-year-old daughter. Laura has no children of her own. Laura and Jake shared a life together for two years before his death. They had worked at the same hospital for fifteen years, so that their relationship really began as "colleagues, in a wonderful way." They had "a very long history of being colleagues and eventually becoming friends before becoming involved with each other." At the time they began their partnership, Laura knew that Jake was ill. Laura says, "For me it was difficult because I was in the process of separation and divorce, and it was just not something I expected to happen. Part of the reason it happened was that we were already close. We had gone through a number of really awful things at work that made us spend a lot of time together, and I think it was a very natural outgrowth of that when it eventually happened."

Laura believes that although she knew about Jake's illness from the beginning and knew that "any kind of remission or cure was almost impossible, . . . what you can imagine can never be the same as what you live through. But I can also say that, knowing we only had a certain amount of time together—once that became much more clear as the prognosis got worse and worse—we really appreciated every day we had together. I'm sure people would think this is so hokey, but you do truly realize how precious every moment is. You have a remarkable awareness of what's valuable and what's not—what's important and what's not."

Jake worked until the time of his death. He was committed to his profession as professor of medicine. At the end of the summer, Jake's health deteriorated rapidly, and Laura was uncomfortable taking him to the hospital over the Memorial Day holiday because of the poor treatment he had received one year earlier over the July 4 holiday. "I knew what would happen—nothing would get done, he wouldn't get seen, and he'd be uncomfortable because he loathed lying in the hospital. So I kept an eye on him and would have taken him at any time had I felt he was in imminent danger. On Tuesday I called his doctor and told him I wanted to bring Jake in. It took me two hours to get him up and dressed and downstairs. He didn't want me to call an ambulance. I finally reached a friend of mine who was a doctor, and he came over. It took forever to get to the hospital, and by the time we arrived, Jake was not breathing. The hospital asked me what I wanted them to do. The problem was that I had no legal authority to tell them what to do. They took him in and I had to contact his brother, who was his closest living relative. By the time he got to the hospital, Jake was breathing because they had put him on a respirator. The doctors came in and asked me if I were his spouse and when I said 'No,' they told me I couldn't make any of the decisions—that they needed to talk to the closest living relative. So I had to wait for his brother to come. After he arrived, they realized they still needed the paperwork, the Living Will, to see what his wishes were. Now, I had no authority to do anything, but I'm the one who had to come back home and find the paperwork and take it back to the hospital. I knew Jake didn't want any extreme measures or machinery used. . . .The doctor finally told us they were going to take him off the respirator. I have to say, his brother and sister-in-law were very good about asking me what I wanted to do, but the doctors saw that I had no legal standing. That was really horrible, really horrible." Once Jake was taken off the respirator, he kept breathing for a few hours. Laura kept telling Jake that it was OK, "he had fought really hard but that it was time and that I would take care of the kids. When I finally let go, he died within minutes."

The time following Jake's death was extremely difficult for Laura because she knew Jake's wishes better than anyone else, but "I had no rights. After everything we had been through, I felt that I wanted to do everything. I felt like no one knew him as well as I did. Nobody was as close to him as I was. Yet everything that had to be done I had to do with his brother and sister-in-law. When we went to the mortuary, I had no rights—it was only that they were very decent about it that allowed me to be involved. Choosing the casket was a real problem, because his sister-in-law wanted a metal casket and I knew that Jake loved wood—that he would want wood. I wasn't willing to give in. Again, they were really good about it, but it started to get a little tense."

Jake had arranged to be buried in a local cemetery, "but because we had originally planned to get married, we had arranged to have joint plots. At one point the owner of the mortuary came in after calling the cemetery and said, 'They say there's a wife.' The indignity of being the nonspouse . . . it was so humiliating to have to explain. I shouldn't have had to explain this because it's nobody's business. Yet here's this person who represents the mortuary and his brother and sister-in-law and I have to explain. I can't just say, 'There's no wife' and leave it at that." After Jake's death, all of his "worldly goods that he had when he left the hospital" were given to Jake's sister-in-law. Although Laura understood their legal obligation to do this, she believed that "it was ridiculously obvious who I was. When the doctors came in to talk, they addressed their remarks to his brother."

The worst part for Laura occurred after Jake's hospitalization and death. "I was just constantly reminded that I had no worldly tie to this person other than the fact that I had lived with him and taken care of him and loved him. It seemed as if nobody recognized this. Although his brother and sister-in-law "tried to be very inclusive, they started calling my workplace, they started making arrangements, they started taking care of all the legal things that had to be done, because I had no standing to do that. They had to ask me where things were. I was in the position of being the repository of all the information needed, but I couldn't do anything about it. On one hand, you might think this was good, because that was one less thing I had to take care of, but part of the process when somebody dies is that it's help-ful to know that certain things are taken care of, and I couldn't do any of those things." Laura was glad that she made the decisions about the memo-rial service and his family respected her decision. However, "when the will was read, when there were legal matters about what happened to the house," it was painful for Laura. "Since we weren't married and because of the way the law is structured, I actually had no place to live. Also, all of Jake's stuff was here. I didn't want anyone to touch his stuff but me. Tak-ing care of all that stuff—it's very hard to do that. The way I coped with it, partly because I didn't have the ability to go through all the steps I was sup-posed to go through, was that I went at it like a banshee. Some people wait

and can't deal with it and leave everything. I started cleaning out closets—
I went through everything."Laura felt that others perceived her as a
"friend" when she was sorting all of Jake's possessions. The hospital where
both Laura and Jake worked "was very good to me, very supportive. I took
the one week off because I just couldn't go back there. I stayed with a colleague because I couldn't come back to our home. The hospital offered to
do anything I wanted with regard to a memorial service. It was awkward,
because I don't think most people at the hospital knew that we were involved. We had been very careful because it's a very private thing, and
Jake's a very private person. I didn't care, but he did. Close friends knew,
and eventually, everyone knew, because we were living together and that
was known. The hospital was very good about things, but legally they were
obligated to deal only with his brother. So I couldn't deal with any of the
legal aspects of his ending with the hospital. The personnel department
would contact his brother, but every once in a while I'd hear from someone that they were having trouble with things, and because I worked there
it then became my responsibility to deal with it. There was this kind of
awkwardness about that which I think was distinctive to my situation. I
don't think that would have been such a problem had it all been mine to
take care of. There was a way in which I wasn't fully involved and was only
involved when it was absolutely mandatory for me to be called. At a certain point I just removed myself. It was just too difficult. I couldn't bear
being in Jake's office—it was too hard."

Laura also faced some other difficult losses concerning her relationship to
Jake's children. Jake had joint custody of his children and had dinner with
them every week. In addition, Jake brought his children to Laura and Jake's
home every other weekend. Laura became very attached to the children and
has been devastated by their reactions to her since Jake's death. "When he
died, there was no question of his daughter coming for the weekends—I
knew that wouldn't happen—but I called her every week to set something
up. Initially she was very, very responsive. We would go out once a week and
spent at least a couple of hours together. That went on for a considerable period of time. I also went to all of her games, since Jake and I had done that
for all of the sports she played. When Jake died, I thought it was important
that I keep going. That was hideously awkward. All of these people who were
on her teams, all of these parents who'd seen me with Jake—they must have
known who I was, and nobody would talk to me. His ex-wife would often
be there and say hello, but then kept on going and sat with other people.
There was one woman out of the entire group who eventually introduced

herself to me. Although we had clearly been a couple, nobody said they were sorry to hear of my loss. After the game, Jake's daughter would always come over to me, and sometimes I would sit there for about twenty minutes after the game was over, just to wait to say hello to her. Eventually, it became clear that she was uncomfortable—that she didn't want to come over—she started making excuses about having too much work."

Laura continued to call Jake's daughter but found that she spent the entire week worrying about her response. "I didn't know how she was doing at school, I didn't know what she was doing. It was excruciating." Laura also found it difficult to stay in touch with Jake's son, who "was never in his room when I called him" and visited so briefly over the holidays "he might as well not have bothered. I wanted the contact with them, but clearly, they didn't want it with me. At a certain point, despite the promise I had made to their father, I had to stop trying to see them and had to let them be the ones to contact me. I had to find a way of negotiating this so it wasn't killing me. I love those kids. Not seeing them is just horrible. But I had a choice to make. I don't get to see them anymore, although I do get e-mails once in awhile. I think one of the worst parts of this is that I think if I had some so-ciety-sanctioned relationship with them, I think they would behave differ-ently. I think if they could somehow rationalize in their minds that I was their stepmother, it might make a difference."

"In terms of my grieving, in addition to losing Jake, this makes it a loss two or three times over, because of the kids. If there weren't kids, I think the whole situation would feel different to me. It's almost prolonging the healing process for me. I hope sometime we can talk about it. I've asked them countless times if they wanted to go to the cemetery. I didn't even call them on the anniversary of their father's death. I just couldn't do it. Re-jection on that particular day would have been just devastating to me." Laura was very tearful when she spoke about the loss of a family. "It's just that we weren't officially sanctioned by some sort of legal document, but we were a family. We had vacations together—we spent time together. Friends of mine told me that at the funeral they could see that I was the one the kids were looking at and looking to. "

Laura believes that our society is awkward, not only in dealing with the issue of death, but also with two adults who are partners without the sanc-tion of marriage. "We (partners) live in a very small segment of society that sanctions a lot of things, but this isn't the rest of the world. We have a tendency to forget that. What I was doing was crossing a boundary. As long as I was within that little circle it was fine, but every time I had to cross that boundary it was one of the great difficulties. Losing a partner is an experience that brings home in a very fundamental way how different our lives are. I have friends who are gay and have lost partners. They have a community that supports them and gives them sustenance. It's funny, but I think they have more in the sense of an understanding community than I did. People who were around me—my friends and colleagues— were really great. But the difficulty is that when you negotiate death and all of its ramifications, you end up making that leap out of that immediate community. It makes it much harder. I couldn't have anticipated some of what occurred because it wouldn't have dawned on me that those things would happen."

Laura has found it difficult to access support systems to cope with her grief. "Think about how all those survivors' organizations are organized. They're organized for spouses, for parents, for gay men, although not for lesbian women, but we (partners) fall through the cracks. We're not quantifiable. We're in pockets. We're not part of any identity group. I don't think our grief is more or less or anything like that. I just don't think we have the same systems of support. I did go to a grief counselor. I felt I really needed to see someone to deal with this stuff, and it was enormously helpful. But it's still a different dynamic than having other people who've gone through the same kind of thing." Laura was very clear that joining a support group for cohabiting couples who have lost a partner might be helpful, but would never consider joining a group for bereaved spouses. "God, no. Can you imagine? Talk about isolating. I can't imagine anything more isolating than going to a survivors' group that was for spouses." Even dealing with her family about the death of Jake was awkward. "My family didn't know what to do. It wasn't a spouse, after all. They had never met him. By the time we were involved, he was sick and couldn't travel. One of my sisters even told me she didn't know what to say to me."

Laura has used a suggestion that her grief counselor provided to help keep Jake's memory alive. "She suggested that I spend some time every night, at the same time every night, creating kind of a ritual space where I would just sit and think about Jake. This would somehow mitigate my grief so that I wasn't falling apart during the day, but I would have time at night to just sit and reflect—this was very helpful. Although I've come a long way in the year that Jake's been gone, I still think about him and the fact that he's not here anymore. In some respects it gets much easier, despite these tears, and in some respects, as it gets farther away and certain things become less tangible and less fresh in my mind, it becomes almost . . . but I wish I could kind of hold on to it. I know this is natural, and that it's part of the process that I'm moving away from it. But I'm the kind of person who has a tendency to want things to be done yesterday, so I want to be through this already, and it still is very painful."

Laura believes that Jake's death has changed her life by making her realize that "there is nothing I could ever go through again that would ever be this horrible, unless I went through the same thing again. I think the death of a child would be worse, but I just can't imagine anything being this bad again. In a way, that has been liberating—I know there is nothing I can't cope with now. I also know that there are a heck of a lot of things that aren't worth getting upset about or getting worried about. Things just aren't that important. I'd like to say that it's made me appreciate every day, although I find it difficult to appreciate a lot of days because of how I still feel. I always believed in the importance of friends and the love I have for my work. The things that were important are even more important to me now, and the things that are inconsequential seem to fall away." Laura also finds that her appreciation for the "connection that can be made with human beings" has become intensified. "Being kind to people and trying to help other people because you never know what somebody's going through has also become more meaningful to me. We are only here for a short time, and if we can't make the best use of it, what's the point? What else is there? I'd love to believe there's an afterlife, but I don't want to live my life thinking about the other end. I want to live my life thinking about now. I think this experience has intensified that feeling too."

Analysis

Laura's story provides a vivid picture of how disenfranchisement of grief of the bereaved partner in an unmarried couple can complicate the process of mourning. From the time that she took Jake to the hospital, Laura was confronted with the fact that being unmarried was a clear disadvantage in negotiating with others who were involved in handling Jake's death. Once doctors discovered that she was not married, they informed her that she could not make any decisions about what would happen to Jake. This was particularly difficult because Laura had taken care of Jake during his entire illness and knew "that he didn't want any extreme measures or machinery." Laura found the "indignity of being the nonspouse humiliating" when the owner of the mortuary assumed that she and Jake were married because they had arranged to have joint plots.

Laura speaks of the difficulties in accessing support systems other than her immediate family and closest friends and colleagues. In fact, even her sister had problems in offering support. Laura is aware that survivor organizations exist for spouses, parents, and gay men, but "partners fall through the cracks." She believes this is so because "we're not quantifiable. . . we're not part of an identity group." For Laura, "losing a partner is an experience that brings home in a very fundamental way how different our lives are." Laura's remarks are similar to those of Francine in the preceding narrative, who claims that the "old rules" of our society do not hold true for couples who have chosen to live together without the sanction of marriage. Laura states, "We don't have a way of stating what kind of relationship we had."

Laura believes that her friends who are gay "have a community that supports them and gives them sustenance. When you negotiate death and all of its ramifications you end up making that leap out of that immediate community." Laura's reactions seem to demonstrate the work of Doka (1987), who found that partners involved in nontraditional relationships are less likely to have support both during the immediate time of death and some time after the death. When a spouse dies, the surviving partner undergoes a transition into the role of widow or widower. This role carries with it a certain status that is recognized by the larger community. Partners in nontraditional relationships lose significant roles when their partner dies, "But there is no defined transitional role for them to assume" (Doka 1989:462). Because one's basic sense of identity and belonging are actualized among relationships with family, friends, church, neighbors, and colleagues, one's sense of identity is deeply affected when the pain of grief is negated by others (Kauffman 1989, 2002).

Laura has used her therapist's suggestion for keeping Jake's memory alive for herself. Each night, at about the same time, Laura creates a space where she sits and thinks about Jake. Laura finds this process very painful, although she believes that she has come a long way in the year since Jake died.

Laura believes that Jake's death has changed her life by helping her to realize what is important in her life. As with many of the survivors who have provided their stories for this book, Laura is able to let go of the inconsequential things in her life and focus on her appreciation for the "connection that can be made with human beings." She, like other survivors, believes that we are here for only a short time and must make the best use of the time we have. Laura wants to live in the moment as much as she can.

Unlike the stories of other bereaved nonmarried partners, Alisa's story is of a very young woman who lost her partner while she was engaged to be married.

Alisa

Alisa was twenty-three years old when Brian, only twenty-five, died suddenly while jogging near the neighborhood in which the couple lived. Alisa and Brian had become engaged four months before Brian's death. Alisa was a teacher and Brian was a computer consultant. They had been dating since Alisa's senior year in college and began sharing an apartment when their engagement was formalized. "He died suddenly and unexpectedly while he was jogging one day. It was the Fourth of July weekend, a long holiday weekend. He went out jogging and died. It's still very unclear to me how he died. There was an autopsy, and it showed no trauma in the body such as heart trauma. Basically, the death certificate said he died of heart arrhythmia combined with dehydration—it was extremely hot, and he didn't have enough fluids in his body. They explained it to me as one of those freaky things where the heart happened to skip, didn't get the electric impulse, and, combined with the effects of the dehydration and the heat, it just stopped and didn't come back on."

"The morning he died we had gotten up and played tennis, but it was too hot. After we played half an hour or so, I said I couldn't take the heat and suggested that we go swimming. He said he wanted to go jogging, and I asked him if he was sure he wanted to do that because it was way too hot. I'm very heat sensitive and just about pass out if I get overheated. So he went jogging, and I went back to the apartment to get into my bathing suit. I walked in the door at 12:00 on the nose. I knew the run and how long it took; it was a three-mile run, and he usually did it in fifteen minutes. At 12:20 I looked out the window but couldn't see him running as I usually did, so I knew something was wrong. I thought that he had become overheated or something and, in the worst-case scenario, had passed out. I even started getting angry at him for not listening to me. I decided to check with a friend of ours who lived in the same neighborhood, to see if maybe he stopped there. As I was walking toward our friend's house, Glen pulled up in his car and told me to get in, that Brian had collapsed. It turned out that Glen had been driving down the road and saw Brian lying on the side of the road and stopped. He called 911 on his cell phone. I think Brian basically died in Glen's arms. Glen tried to give CPR but wasn't trained in it,

and he just was too late. I remember Glen asking me at a crossroads if I
wanted to drive down to where Brian and the ambulance were or if I wanted to go straight to the hospital because I didn't think I could see him lying
there. That was how he died."

Unlike other partners whose stories are included in this chapter, Alisa was
included in all facets of planning the funeral. Alisa and her mother-in-law
shared a very close relationship in which "she practically accepted me as her
own daughter. She included me in every step of the way. She wasn't looking at our relationship as losing a son, but as gaining a daughter. I kind of
took over because I'm very good in a crisis, always have been. She included me in everything, every step of the way. In a lot of ways she was so distraught. So we planned together. Each of us did our own thing with the
florist. I had my own floral arrangement and she had hers, and we went together to pick out his clothing for the funeral. There was no question about
what we would do, because Brian had said, 'If I die I want to be cremated.'
I know it's unusual, but I distinctly remember having this conversation with
him. He would talk about it with his mom, and she'd say, 'Oh, Brian, stop
talking about dying,' but he'd tell her anyway."

Alisa also felt very fortunate because Brian's mother gave her half of his
life insurance. "It was amazing. Of course she got everything, that's the way
it goes. But it was bizarre, because after we were engaged and discussed getting our beneficiaries in order, he didn't have time to do it before his death.
So everything went to her, but she did share it with me. That's why I feel
very fortunate, because I do know other people who did not have that kind
of experience when they were not legally married. So I do think things were
a little different with me. I was recognized by his family as his true partner."

Alisa also received support from her own family, whom she described as
"very nontraditional. My aunt, who practically raised me, is a lesbian and is
so very sensitive to that kind of partnership not being recognized. In fact,
her partner had died just a couple of months before Brian. They hadn't been
together for a few years, but before that, they had been together for a very
long time. She was grieving too. Although she hid it in many ways, she did
talk to me about it. She is not open about her lesbianism, so when she talks
to me, she doesn't talk to me in terms of her "partner" or her lover, as if I
still must not know she's a lesbian. I think she knows that I know, but it's
not acknowledged. She knows that when she talks to me about her partner
and that kind of loss and what she felt, she knows in some ways that I understand what she's saying and what she's talking about, and that I acknowledge how important her partner was to her."

Following Brian's death, one of Alisa's sisters came to stay with her for three weeks and helped her find a place to live. Alisa was very comforted by this sister, who had lost a boyfriend when she was a teenager with a small child to raise on her own.

Following Brian's death, Alisa was also supported by her workplace, which had been founded by a gay and lesbian health advocacy group. "So the people I worked with were very diverse people and they were very, very supportive of me in recognizing what Brian meant to me and acknowledging him. They gave me whatever time I needed, telling me not to worry about it—it was completely recognized as the death of my life partner." Alisa was named as the fiancée in the obituary of Brian's death. She believed that this recognition and her engagement ring helped her to receive the acknowledgement that she needed from others at the time of Brian's death. Alisa knew that if "I shared my experience with somebody who wasn't of my background, I could use 'fiancée' to really get my story across in a way they could resonate with and understand."

For a brief time Alisa joined a support group for young widowed adults. "When I called the facilitator of that support group and told her that I hadn't been married but only engaged, she said not to worry about that. Yet when I went to attend the support group, everybody clearly had been married, except the facilitator, who had lost her fiancée about twenty-five years previously. I didn't find the group especially helpful, but only because I didn't seem to connect with anybody in there. Most of the people who were in that particular group had not lost anybody to a sudden, unexpected death, but to long-term illnesses. The other thing was that they were married, most of them had children, or they were older and had grown children. At least they were not young in my mind." Ideally, Alisa would like to have joined a support group for engaged couples but realizes this type of group does not exist.

"Something I still crave and desire is a young women's support group— young women who are alone. I find that more now than at the time of Brian's death, but even then it would have been around other young women who had lost a partner. Alisa began to find some support that she needed by reading books on loss and death, especially ones written by survivors. Alisa's aunt was also helpful because she understood what Alisa had lost on an emotional level. Alisa felt that she "had lost the one person who understood me the most. I felt I had lost the one constant in my life. . . .It's the sense of a home feeling that you lose. When you come home it's no longer the same home. What's strange is that at the same time I lost him and I felt lost, I was so able to recognize and see myself in a positive way for the first time, because I had lost the one thing that was reflecting that for me. I started to miss all that support and encouragement he would give me, but when I saw it disappear, I could somehow start to recognize my own worth."

Alisa's personal growth following the loss of Brian also included "the spirituality I was starting to uncover in myself." Alisa lived on her own for the first time in her life following Brian's death, as she had "gone from my home to the home with Brian." Alisa believes that although she experienced the loss of companionship, she also felt "he gave me a gift because I truly felt loved by him. I felt loveable and felt I would find someone again." However, Alisa's first relationship after Brian's death ended after a year, and she "started experiencing loss more deeply. I think in some ways I put my loss of Brian on hold, and only in the last year or so have I really, really experienced loss." Alisa believes that she is now "revisiting the trauma of Brian's death." Through a therapeutic relationship, she is just beginning to start healing. "I now realize that my loss was so sudden and unexpected that I was in shock for a really long time. I had never experienced death before, and I was totally blown over by how one day your life is like this, and the next day it's completely changed."

At first Alisa did not really miss Brian. In the beginning "I was able to talk about him with his mother and keep his memory alive. That's the only way I would talk about him. Except for the occasional time when someone would bring him up and want to ask me about him—I was putting him behind me in some ways." Now, a few years later, Alisa has "been trying to remember Brian. I know he loved me and cared about me and wanted to marry me. I have to remember that to keep myself from descending into that pit of self doubt." Alisa finds that connecting to Brian's memory is healing for her, although she does "experience pain about it. But it's a pain you need to feel and that has to come out and surface."

Before Alisa's interview for the book, she took out her photo album "because it had been so long since I even looked at his picture—it seems like another world, another time. Looking at me with him, I feel I'm looking at another person. Looking at him, he almost looks like a stranger to me now." Just as other spouses and partners have discovered, "it's uncomfortable. We all struggle in life, it's a human condition to need to feel connected somehow. In this day and age, when I find it even more difficult, it is important to remind myself to feel connected. So even if it's a painful memory, it at least makes me feel alive." Alisa also keeps Brian's memory alive by staying in touch with one of his close friends who lives nearby. "I know I could call Bob up anytime and he would be there in seconds."

Alisa believes that her life has been greatly altered by Brian's death. "I felt as if I had been catapulted into adulthood. I'm twenty-seven, but let me tell you, there aren't many twenty-seven-year-olds I can connect with. In some ways, I just feel old. It's a unique experience. I really felt independent after that. I felt stronger. It opened up so much for me to discover who I was. Women in general tend to live their lives through their partners. Brian was the one who did all the exploring, and I just kind of tagged along with him." In some ways, Alisa views Brian's death as a major learning opportunity. "He was a great, wonderful person, but in some ways, maybe marriage itself seemed very stifling to me. Following his death I began to feel more in touch with who I was. I grew spiritually and thought for the first time that I could take care of myself." Although Alisa does not subscribe to a religion, she believes in a higher power. "I believe in energy and in karma. If you're putting positive energy out there, it will somehow recirculate itself to you, and likewise with negative energy." Alisa is trying to discover new parts of herself and is feeling as if "I need a sense of community, a sense of belonging, so I'm actually looking at churches." Alisa has also begun a graduate program in counseling as part of her new journey.

Analysis

Alisa's story is quite different from the stories of other partners whose narratives are included in this chapter. Alisa's relationship with Brian was more socially and legally sanctioned because she was viewed as a fiancée, with the rights and privileges that this status brings to a partner in our society. Alisa and her future mother-in-law planned the funeral together, using most of Alisa's ideas. Contrary to the literature, which indicates that partners in nontraditional relationships are often denied a role in planning and participating in funeral rituals (Pine, 1989), and unlike other bereaved partners whose stories are included in this chapter, Alisa was actively involved in this ritual. She believes that she received support from her workplace after Brian's death because her colleagues recognized the meaning of the relationship between her and Brian and because she was wearing an engagement ring. She believes that the role of fiancée helped to "get her story across in a way that others could resonate with." However, it was still impossible for Alisa to find a support group that was appropriate for her grief. The support group for young widows and widowers that Alisa joined for a brief time was not helpful to her, since she could not connect with the experiences of its members, who had been married.

Soon after Brian's death, Alisa kept Brian's memory alive by talking with his mother—in fact that is the only way that she would talk about him. During that first year, Alisa felt as though she "was putting him (Brian) behind me." Now, four years later, Alisa has been working on remembering Brian, and has found that "connecting to Brian's memory" has been healing for her. Alisa's experience corroborates the work of Klass et al. (1996) and Rubin (1999), who suggest that connecting with memories of the deceased can enhance current functioning of the bereaved partner. Alisa believes that the connection she experiences when she remembers Brian, although painful, "helps to make me feel alive." This is similar to the experiences of other bereaved spouses and partners whose narratives are shared in this book, as well as experiences of bereaved partners seen in the literature. People will do whatever it takes to sustain a relationship with their deceased partners. Yet the evidence of the partner's existence can trigger very painful feelings (Bowlby 1980; Marris 1986; Schuchter 1986).

Alisa believes that the loss of her partner has changed her life in profound ways. She feels as though she has been "catapulted into adulthood." She feels much older than twenty-seven, yet more independent and stronger." She believes that Brian's death gave her an opportunity to "discover who I was. I grew spiritually and thought for the first time that I could take care of myself." Alisa's changes resemble those of Kristen, a young widow, whose life was profoundly changed by the loss of her spouse at a young age (see chapter 3). Shaffer (1993) found that all of the young widows in her study experienced "positive shifts in life perspective . . . rebirth." Shaffer (1993) believes that loss at an earlier time in their development allowed these widows to remake their lives, to start over in a way that might seem unrealistic to an older widow who loses a spouse later in life. Both of these stories, as do others throughout this book, reflect Neimeyer's belief that "the attempt to reconstruct a world of meaning is the central process in the experience of grieving" (Neimeyer 1998:83). He believes that the bereaved are faced with the task of transforming their identities following a severe loss in which one must "relearn the self as well" (1998:90).

CHAPTER SUMMARY

Most of the narratives in this chapter illustrate Doka's work (1989), which suggests that the bereaved partner experiences a sense of disenfranchisement when the loss is not or cannot be openly acknowledged, publicly mourned, or socially supported. Alisa, who was young and engaged to be married at the time of Brian's death, was the only one who did not express this sense of disenfranchisement. Her more positive experiences are directly related to her socially sanctioned role of fiancée, to which family and colleagues could respond, thereby validating the meaning of the relationship. All of the other bereaved partners experienced some negation of the importance of their relationships by family members, friends, colleagues, or medical professionals. Even Peter, who received support from Marilyn's family at the time of her death, felt that the nurses were reluctant to have him involved in Marilyn's care. It was also awkward for him and Marilyn's son to be at the hospital together, especially since they disagreed about who would care for Marilyn after she was discharged from the hospital. Barry was very upset at Julie's daughter's lack of respect for his relationship with Julie, even though he and Julie were engaged. Although Julie's daughter wanted to plan the funeral without his input, Barry asserted himself and planned a service that he knew Julie would have wanted.

The narratives of both Laura and Francine provide a clear picture of society's discomfort in dealing with the death of a partner in a relationship other than marriage. Francine was extremely vocal about the lack of support from her partner's family as well as the lack of societal support. Society failed to recognize her relationship with Steven as more than that of a friend. Francine stated that the "old rules" of our society don't apply to couples who have chosen to live together without the sanction of marriage. She is concerned that there are no new rules for this growing segment of our population. Laura experienced discrimination in negotiating funeral plans, in dealing with Jake's children following his death, and with the personnel department at their joint workplace. Laura was also ignored by some of the friends the couple had made during their partnership and poignantly states that "although we had clearly been a couple, nobody said that they were sorry to hear of my loss." Laura's narrative may provide some insight for all of us in understanding what happens when partners in nontraditional relationships, who live in a small but growing segment of our society, cross "a boundary" when a death occurs in a society with rules and sanctions for coping with life's transitions. It seems significant that, except for Ida (who was eighty-nine) and Marie (who had been in an unhappy partnership), all of the bereaved partners expressed a wish that they had been married at the time of their partner's death. The narratives in this chapter seem to corroborate Doka's (1989, 2002b) suggestion that those partners involved in nontraditional relationships are less likely to receive support, because there is no role transition that occurs for them that is similar to that of widow or widower. The role of widow or widower carries with it a certain status that is recognized by the larger community. Although partners in nontraditional relationships lose a significant role when their mates die, "there is no defined transitional role for them to assume" (Doka 1987:462). Furthermore, in a society that has difficulty coping with death and the feelings of any bereaved partner, having "no defined transitional role" intensifies the sense of lack of support felt by the bereaved, unmarried partner. Death brings with it confusion and intense emotion, which heighten the lack of recognition and respect for a nonkin relationship at death.

Chapter Five

Loss of a Gay Partner

ISSUES FACED BY A BEREAVED GAY PARTNER

Issues that face men who have lost a male partner through death can be related to the literature on disenfranchised grief discussed in chapter 4. According to Shernoff, when a gay man loses his partner, his grief is intensified by the lack of "mainstream culture's recognition of his relationship, his loss and his becoming a widower" (1998:27). However, some gay partners do not experience disenfranchised grief. Shernoff (1998) found that when a gay partner has not hidden his sexual orientation, he is more likely to have a network of supportive friends and family who will help him during the mourning process. The gay partner who claims that his lover was a room-mate is much more susceptible to experiencing disenfranchised grief than a partner who has gained support from his family and/or his community.

Richmond and Ross (1995) report that in the case of a death caused by AIDS, additional stresses are experienced by the bereaved partner. This partner may be infected himself and may face the demands of coping with his own illness and possible death as well as the burden of losing his loved one through the same illness. Consequently, a number of problems may arise within the relationship that will probably complicate the bereavement. These concerns include the following: "(1) the source of infection in the couple, (2) the needs for care of the more severely ill person, (3) alteration in the quality of the relationship, and (4) a sense of watching what they will be going through or a rehearsal of their own death" (1995:162).

Other factors that may affect the bereavement process of death from AIDS include friends becoming infected, loss of employment due to increasing illness, and the stigma of AIDS. Furthermore, Richmond and Ross (1995) concur with other researchers (Shernoff 1998; Doka 1989) that the relationship of gay partners "may not be recognized by others as having the status of a primary attachment and therefore the recognition and acknowledgment of the partner's or family's grief may be diminished" (Richmond and Ross 1995:162).

For family members, the loss of an adult child may be complicated by ambivalent reactions to the infected adult's sexuality or drug use. Since death from AIDS often occurs in early adulthood, this untimely loss may result in excessive guilt and secrecy about the disease for fear of societal stigma. Family members may also fear or actually experience isolation and the loss of social support if members of their own social network become aware of their adult child's diagnosis. This makes it difficult for family members to provide support to the bereaved partner. Bereavement in a gay partner may be increased by the coexisting issues of both gay identity and AIDS, grief induced by communal losses, exclusion from involvement in funeral arrangements, and lack of acknowledgment of the relationship between the bereaved and the deceased (Richmond and Ross 1995). Several themes that emerged from a review of research on AIDS-related bereavement include (1) lack of support because of a lack of community resources and support from friends and family, (2) lack of closure through being excluded from funeral or memorial services, (3) conflict with the deceased partner's family or executor, (4) survivor isolation stemming from fear of sharing their loss with others for fear of exposure or rejection, (5) lack of preparation for the death, (6) the impact of multiple losses in the community, creating a "bereavement overload," and (7) fatigue and emotional and physical distress from caring for the dying partner (Richmond and Ross 1995).

Richmond and Ross (1995) also reported on themes that emerged from the experiences of bereaved partners of AIDS patients and their memories of the deceased. Surviving partners reminisced about times they had shared with the deceased as well as "feelings and emotional strains and gains that they had experienced throughout their relationship" (1995:170). Other partners described characteristics and attitudes typical of the type of person the deceased represented. The most common themes to emerge were "holding on to memories and experiences; the feelings they had for each other; and the way they were treated by family and friends" (1995:170). The bereaved partner may initially dream that the partner who has died is vividly alive and feels that each awakening is a painful renewal of grief.

Other studies (Boykin 1991; Sanders 1989; Murphy and Perry 1988) identify "survivor guilt" as an important issue for gay men who have lost partners. According to Boykin (1991), there was a trend toward a high degree of guilt in the HIV and/or AIDS population that participated in his study. This issue present in the case of Jim.

Jim

Jim had just turned forty-seven when his partner, Matt, died at thirty-eight of an HIV-related illness. Jim and Matt had lived together for more than eight years at the time of Matt's death. Matt had been married, with two children, and was divorced two years before Jim met him. Matt was an architect and Jim is a counselor.

Jim was raised as a Catholic and was able to "deny being gay the whole time—it really didn't come out until I was twenty-six." Jim met Matt when he was in his early thirties. Jim said coming out at this time was "the worst time in the world, but I did it with a vengeance. These were the days that you weren't being tested and there wasn't a whole lot you could do even if you had been exposed to the HIV virus." Just before his relationship with Matt, Jim had ended a relationship with David, who died within a year of the time Matt and Jim started being together. "Denial, work, love—we were able to pretty much deny it the whole time until Matt got ill." Jim first noticed things weren't right when he and Matt were on vacation in Canada. Matt had always had a lot of energy, but on this trip "he just wasn't right. There were times when he just wasn't there and I was just beginning to see something. So we got home from vacation and I told him that he needed to do something for me—and that was going to see my doctor."

Jim reported that Matt's HIV-related illness "was a very unusual cancer of the brain that was really very devastating, but very fluid. There were times when he literally didn't know who I was, who he was. With some minor adjustments with meds, he would be clear and overworked for another two months and then it would return. The end stages were completely debilitating. It was very difficult for a while. I had to keep him at home and work with him and be able to maintain a job. I did have some health aides come in. There wasn't a lot known at that time in terms of how to treat that particular kind of brain cancer. There were never answers. I remember at least two or three times when I was told, 'He's not going to make it through the night,' and the next day he was fine and two weeks later he was back to work. It was about a nine-month period of time that was very hellish, like a roller coaster—numbing, numbing, numbing."

At the same time that Matt was dying, Jim was experiencing the loss of many other friends. "Within a three-year time there was a group of about twelve of us, my peers, my friends, not former lovers, but close friends. During that time a vast majority of everyone had died—this was all AIDS related. At the same point Matt was dying, my closest friend, Larry, was also dying. In terms of surviving a loss, this is certainly the larger picture. I've had some issues in terms of 'Why me of all the people to survive?' Within the year after Matt died, I lost the last friend in that group of twelve.

"It's been difficult trying to get past the point of seeing the illness and death and the calamity of so much loss at such a young age. It's difficult not to be caught up with the anger and hopelessness of some of it. Our relationship was really the only significant relationship for both of us, other than Matt's marriage. There were some ups and downs, but he was the only real love of my life—the only real connection besides friends and things of that sort. He had been very healthy up until about a year before he died. We had lost enough friends to have gone through the awareness, the process. It was there, but not really a part of us. But it's always a part, because there were just too many deaths within the first two years that we were together. I guess that was the wake-up call. It wasn't just out there. It was very much a part of our existence.

"It's so hard not to idealize the relationship at this point. I think that is part of the process—to own the good times and to value what was there. But living without Matt has been the hardest thing to deal with. I know the first two years, I certainly was depressed. I also tried to be positive, but I didn't expect to live much longer myself. I did have a consciousness of taking care of Matt and then suddenly going away to die. Within that period of time, a close friend, George, had lost his lover. George and I were the two survivors out of the group of a dozen or so. I had loved George as a friend years before I met Matt. George and I had decided to move to Arizona and just die in peace and quiet. For me it was certainly not putting anyone else through what I had gone through. Sometimes that was so hard, the consciousness of living with this. It will never be the same—a sense of never being whole. There is a part of you that is just gone. It made sense to me to just pick up and go. I very much did not want any of the people that I cared for to watch this go on any further.

"So it seemed to be, 'This is it, this is closing.' I knew at the time that George was not necessarily healthy, but there was nothing going on. So we moved to Arizona, and I found work, and it really was a nice existence. Unfortunately, within six months after moving there, George started getting yellow, and medical care was horrendous. To make a long story short, we did move back, and I cared for him during the last three or four months. I was very glad to do it. Soon afterward, we learned that our friend Peter, in Arizona, had died. So there was a point where I felt everything was done. I did certainly withdraw from friends. I did not want people to deal with these horrible messy deaths, and apparently my style of grief is to do it on my own. Things that seemed to have made a difference used to be my work. I stopped counseling. I certainly didn't feel I was in any capacity to be a good counselor." Jim found it was easier to focus on administration within an agency and believed that the "management, budgeting, the staffing, the training, and the supervision piece didn't have an emotional pull on me. Throwing myself into work made all the difference. Work was probably the only remaining stable piece in my life. I certainly did not lose all my friends to AIDS, that's not a fair statement, but honestly that's what it felt like.

"In my distorted way of thinking, it was better to end it now. The move to Arizona made a lot of sense. I was very much aware of a kind of emotional closing down. I was preparing to move on. I don't believe I was suicidal. There wasn't a need to be suicidal, because I saw the end kind of right there. It wasn't too hard to believe it. I very much owned it, although I was never sick. Living with the knowledge that I had the same infection that I had watched devastate healthy young men of my own age was awful. My parents were dead, and an aunt of mine had died of cancer. It was an awful lot of loss within a ten-year time period. Living with an infection at that point certainly was considered a death sentence. It's manageable now, and I've been extremely lucky I've never been ill. It may have been part of the hopelessness and the giving up. In some strange way it felt like a legacy— this is what happened to everyone and this is what's in store for me. I certainly didn't dwell on it. I was able to use enough techniques to get my mind away from that, because that would make life crazy."

Jim believed that "the mix of guilt with survivorship was a point in time when I knew very much that Matt did not want to have this kind of death. We had certainly talked that he didn't want to go there, he didn't want to get that bad. Unfortunately, the way the brain disease came back and forth, there was no way I was going to use the pills to help him die. I couldn't do it—I was too much of a coward. Afterwards, I did feel guilty. It ended up with him dying in a hospital, and I wasn't there at the time. I have a lot of guilt about that. There were times I should have done more; there were times I should have done less. There was one specific time when Matt was at home and he was failing. It looked like end stages—it really did. His mother had come that day and we talked a little bit. I had the doctor on the phone, who said, 'You need to make a decision—do you want him to die at home or do you want to go through this again?' Part of me felt this is the best we could do. I could not tell his mother 'no,' so we went to the hospital, and we probably gained another three or four weeks." This constant questioning of himself on this issue was very difficult for Jim.

Jim found that having "the two people I cared about most in my life and watching them both go down simultaneously and the constant feeling of needing to be with both" was the most difficult part of the experience. George had been the closest friend to Jim when he came out, and Jim struggled with his loyalty to both George and Matt. "It culminated to the point where Matt was in hospice, and they wanted to do the morphine drip, and that's pulling at me. The message to you is that 'We want to help you let go, we want to move this along.' I did say, 'Just let me bury George and I'll be here to do this.'"

Although Jim was not with Matt when he died, he "just knew that Matt was gone, knew that this was it. One of the hard parts of the illness was the knowledge of knowing there wasn't a hell of a lot you can do in any circumstance. You could care, you could love, you could bathe them, you could do tons of physical things, but the realization that nothing is going to turn this around is devastating. There was no question that his type of illness was irreversible." Friends constantly asked Jim if he was angry, but he replied, "I've never been able to muster much anger about it, though I've always been afraid of finding there were some of the things that should have been done differently. Watching the struggle of people who fought and the powerlessness of knowing that there was nothing else that could be done was awful." Jim also found that the level of physical fatigue was very high. "There were days when I really didn't think that I could take much more. It got to the point where he needed total care a whole lot more than I could give. It was emotionally and physically draining, in that nothing is going to change, and then not being able to communicate with him towards the end. It was so hard losing George and Matt at the same time."

Following Matt's death, Jim found that Matt's eldest daughter, "who happens to be a lesbian, was wonderfully supportive and involved as much as she could be." Matt's younger daughter had some conflicts with both her dad and Jim. "Jane pretty much distanced herself from everyone in her family after her mother died. Matt's mother and father were very supportive, even though they learned one year before Matt died that he was gay and dying of AIDS." Jim was not directly involved in planning the funeral because Matt's mother wanted a Catholic mass and funeral, and Matt had never said that he wanted anything different. Although Jim was invited to be with the family, he drove to the funeral with three of his friends and went out with them afterward. Jim and Matt's eldest daughter "stood at the casket together and said good-bye."

Jim still has vivid memories of Matt, and "to this day I can remember his voice, his smile, his laugh, and his ability to disregard things. I also remember our visit to England and our drive along the coast—it was gorgeous. It was kind of a lifelong dream of someplace I wanted to see and that sense of just being us. For a period of time we were able to just be okay and not worry about the job, AIDS, and friends dying. So a sense of just being us and being fine in a healthy environment and needing to take care of nothing, other than each other, for awhile. I remember very clearly those kind of days. I can't put into words why I loved him so much and why this made perfect sense, but I did. It was the only time in my life that I remember feeling that I wanted to be with someone—wanting him in my life. Those moments of clarity where everything makes sense, where you know this is right, yet it was infuriating at times. It was hard. He needed to keep things quiet. There was this struggle with me feeling he needed to be with his daughter more and not really wanting it and her not wanting it." Jim vividly remembers "the initial pain, that emptiness—that hollowing—that literally your heart is ripped out. I remember having dreams, and in that moment of drifting out of the dream, when there was that sense again of having to let go, and at that moment you know it was a dream and not wanting to wake up, not wanting to give it sight." Jim had this type of dream for a number of years following Matt's death, but now the dreams are "more pleasant, and it's not this painful letting go again." Jim believes that the memories and dreams have kept his connection with Matt.

For Jim, making sense out of "the person's life more than the illness is one of the hardest things for me. That took me a long time. It was important for me for there to be more than the last nine months with Matt—that the illness was not to be the defining feature of these wonderful people's lives. So, in my heart and my existence, I knew that there was more to it. The reason it was so painful in the end was the letting go of all that—I saw some wonderfully creative, good people die a horrible death. People that don't deserve to get ill, but that madness, the horribly debilitating illness that took all kinds of crazy forms and took the brightest people that I knew to be the best. But there was more to it, and maybe that's just a particular part of my healthy side that was not going to let AIDS be the defining factor. The illness was only part of it. There was a period of time when you knew someone was dying and it was just a day-to-day fact. Life becomes more precious. There was almost a sense of hyperawareness that your friends who are dying are getting their pleasure from enjoying the music, the books, or the sunshine." For Jim, reading "was a solace. I've always thanked God I could read—that was something that was a help to me. There would be a time that there would be nothing better than to crawl in bed with a good book and block everything else out." Jim believed that it was the "holding on that made any sense at all, just perpetuating that—there are still clear lessons and laughs. Once you get past that initial point of that person you see who you enjoyed being with, eventually you can kind of share it in a strange sense—the sense of preserving the life, the love, the brilliance—that ability to maintain that. So in some ways, I have become the keeper of a number of flames—that has eased the grief.

"I have gotten some strengths from that experience. There are moments when I think, 'Is there some reason I'm still here?' I have gained so much from those individuals, and I do have the sense of needing to do something important or something worthwhile—or not to feel sorry or not waste time. Maybe that's been a bigger problem of mine, trying not to waste time over grieving and trying to push through it. That may have caused grief to pop up at different other times. But in terms of what to do and how to live with loss, there were many lessons that were learned from these friends."

Following Matt's death, Jim began to face his own issues of mortality openly. He felt that he "didn't have the time to grieve because I needed to use the little bit of time I had left to live. I had been through enough and was going to try and find pleasure. Initially I turned myself into taking care of George. Then that was settled, and I had about three years when I started realizing that I needed to take care of myself and I wasn't going to die. At this point in my life, my statistics indicate that I'm a long-term survivor. I've never been ill, and my numbers are very good, so there's every reason to believe that I have many good years left. So I shifted my feelings, I moved around, and I met someone. But that relationship ended because we both "got into it for the wrong reasons. I wanted a partner, but I was not going to take care of somebody else emotionally. I moved out, got my own place. In a lot of ways, it feels good to be pretty much focused on myself. At this point I do not have any friends that are (HIV) positive or gay—so that's another experience."

Jim believes that "one of the damages that the amount of losses from AIDS has created is a decreased ability to invest in being a partner in the future. I've pretty much come to terms with that. I could not duplicate what I had with Matt. This was the love of my life—this is what made sense, and trying anything else feels less than, or feels forced." Jim tried having a new relationship but believes that "I've gotten to a point where I'm whole and fine as it is. I think I'm much better with friendships than trying to make a go of a partnership. I really wonder if I would do that again. I'm not sure emotionally whether that is there."

For Jim, "work has made the biggest difference—having something that meant something. Some days I got out of bed for the dog, and there were some days I didn't get out of bed, but having the work, the pressure of doing something, helped me cope." Jim has also found that "self-pity is very unattractive and doesn't allow me to make use of valuable time. If you focus on it, it will rip you apart." However, Jim still "maintains aspects of the lives of Matt and others I was close to—there is still a connectedness." Jim has taken with him "that spark of life that at some point we were connected—needing to value them, to hold on to the good stuff."

The hardest part for Jim is the loss of so many friends in such a short time. "This was my peer group, and I think that's been the hardest part—that I don't have a gay male peer group." However, I still have some connections with friends of friends. The life force, there was something that was there that does go on, and I can hear it, feel it, see it, and live it. Just that sense of honoring those people who have lost so much and that it would be wrong to be stuck in some level of self-pity, although there is some pain and some regret." Jim finds himself dipping back into the pain at times, but is "trying to go forward to maintain myself and not hit that point of loss." Jim says to himself, "No, I just won't go there. Since there has been so much pain, what I need to do is to hold on, to keep the good. I can do that without feeling as much loss with it because there is that level of love that continues." Jim believes that he has lost the person, but that the love of that relationship goes on in time. "It's that life source—that spark—it's that connection that was there. It's what worked, that spark of life, and that's why we grieve so badly, because it's lost. That ability to see past the pain, to see past the horrible loss, and to carry that spark with you is what I do now."

Jim believes that he has changed in several ways since the death of Matt and other friends that he loved. "I do feel amazingly strong and capable of doing anything. I lost my lover and my best friend in the same week. What the hell are you going to do to me—there is not much else you could do. If it doesn't kill you, it makes you stronger. I've learned to live with the demons and have a newfound ability to channel my emotions." Jim believes that this experience has made him a better counselor, especially when working with a client that has come to accept that the love of her life is not going to be the man she is living with and she is going to have to live without him. "You live with it because the other choices are just worse. The hardest part is knowing that you will survive—that you're going to have to get on with this. I'm much more compassionate and much more willing to listen to the mood shift of people's pain. My experience has made me value the human experience—the ability of the mind and body to cope and to survive. Out of a group of twelve people, many great wonderful people, I am the one that is still here. I need to get something out of these days and to do something that makes sense to me. I do like my work. It does support me emotionally, and there is that ability to feel like it's worthwhile."

When Jim speaks about the grieving process, he states that, "loving Matt is the thing that did make me whole, made me a man, and made me clear about everything. It took a long time not to feel everything was lost." Sometimes, even now, Jim feels that "I can give everything up—give up the future for one more hour and try to negotiate for a week. If given the opportunity, I would give the future up to spend another hour with him. That may contradict a lot of what I just said. You don't just get over it— you live with it in some ways. Denial is needed until you've reached that point where you can deal with it a little bit more at times. I certainly dealt with it in pieces after a period of time."

With regard to his own health and mortality, Jim is no longer hopeless. "I live with HIV every day—I take the meds and have heard about the numbers, but have stopped listening to them." Jim believes that a positive attitude makes a difference in mortality. "The friends that fought it and did not cave in and lived with the horrible stuff and a couple of others that said, 'I'm out of here,' gave up, and literally died quickly." Jim also found that HIV support groups have been helpful to him following the loss of both Matt and George. "I went to an HIV-positive support group that was more for me, but many people were dealing with losses and that was helpful. That was the first time I talked about the guilt of not being able to assist Matt in ending his life because it wasn't assisting him—it would have been me doing it, and that was something that was untenable. It was the first time I really dealt with all the losses and in a safe place. Everyone in the group was living with it, but had lost friends, and there were a number of people who lost partners." Jim stayed with this group until he moved. Currently, Jim is considering a move back to the city where he met Matt and will become involved in a support group there. Eventually, Jim became a "buddy" to other men who were HIV positive and had lost friends and/or partners.

Analysis

Jim's story demonstrates the reactions of a gay partner who has faced the loss of his partner, as well as other devastating losses, to AIDS. He speaks of the isolation that he felt when he was the only one left alive in a group of twelve friends. Superimposed upon his losses of his partner and close friends is the realization that having an HIV-positive diagnosis makes you confront your own mortality. At one point, Jim moved with a sick friend to Arizona and believed that he himself would die. Jim says very poignantly, "In some strange ways it felt like a legacy—this is what happened to everyone and this is what's in store for me." Jim's story corroborates the research done by Richmond and Ross (1995) stating that, in the case of death caused by AIDS, additional stresses are experienced by the bereaved partner. Richmond and Ross speak of how watching one's partner die of AIDS is a "rehearsal of their own death" (1995:162).

Jim also speaks of the survivor guilt he experienced, which is noted in the literature (Sanders 1989) and which can complicate the relationship between the dying partner and the survivor. Jim struggled very hard to be supportive to both his partner and a close friend, who were both dying at the same time. Jim may have wondered if his HIV-positive status was responsible for Matt's infection. Some researchers (Boykin 1991; Murphy and Perry 1998) have suggested that survivor guilt is directly related to the bereaved partner's being absent at the time of their partner's death from AIDS. Jim certainly expressed this guilt in his story. He was unable to be present when Matt died because he was supporting another friend with AIDS. Jim said, "It ended up with him dying in a hospital, and I wasn't there at the time. I have a lot of guilt about that." Perhaps this has contributed to Jim's difficulty in handling the grief process.

Jim's experience in managing Matt's care during the year that he was very ill was stressful and difficult, in part because of the roller-coaster quality of the disease. As mentioned in chapter 2 of this text, Ferrell (1992) found that managing the care of the partner with AIDS greatly impacts bereavement outcomes. Jim clearly states that he is glad that he participated in Matt's care, as difficult as it was for him. Just as Ferrell's (1992) surviving partners found, Jim acknowledged a positive experience in his own psychosocial growth as a result of managing Matt's care, as well as the care of others in his network of friends. Through caring for Matt and suffering through his death, as well as that of many other friends, Jim says, "I do feel amazingly strong and capable of doing anything. I've learned to live with the demons and have a newfound ability to channel my emotions." Jim believes he has learned many lessons from the friends for whom he cared during their illness.

Jim has vivid memories of some of the good times with Matt, especially their trip to England together. Jim reported, "To this day I can remember his voice, his smile, his laugh and his ability to disregard things." These reactions are similar to the findings of Richmond and Ross (1995), who found that partners of AIDS patients "reminisced of times they had shared together as well as gains they had experienced throughout their relationship" (1995:170).

Jim's experiences following Matt's death are clearly representative of the postmodern view that partners remain connected to their deceased loved ones while they move on with their new lives. Jim still "maintains aspects of the lives of Matt and others I was close to—there is still connectedness." Jim speaks of "that spark of life that at some point we were connected—needing to value them, to hold on to the good stuff." Jim believes that he can "go forward to maintain himself" but can remain connected to "that level of love that continues." Jim can carry that "spark" with him in his current life.

The following case study is similar to Jim's story of Matt, in that Tom's partner died of an AIDS-related illness. However, Tom did not lose an entire community of friends at the same time.

Tom

Tom was forty-two and worked as a manager when his partner, Rob, died at age forty from an AIDS-related illness. Rob had been in the field of merchandising most of his life. "At first, we were together in a nontraditional relationship . . . we didn't live together. We had been sexually involved before we became romantically involved. Then one day we realized that we really cared deeply about each other. We fell madly in love and stayed that way until the day he died. We were together emotionally, romantically, and physically, but we never lived together until eight years later." Tom and Rob shared living quarters for four years, until Rob's death. Soon after they moved in together, Rob decided to move to New England during the summers to pursue a business interest, which involved opening a small retail gift shop. Tom was not happy with this arrangement because "I knew I would miss him deeply, and I did. He would go for the spring, summer, and early fall and return to Baltimore for the winter. I would travel up to see Rob a couple of times, which I learned really to love quite a bit. It's a beautiful place.

"We had not been monogamous sexually, although I was quite a careerist, so I hardly had time for sexual activity very often. I had no inkling as to Rob's sex-life activity, although I assumed he was engaged in some form of recreational sex with other people and that was okay. I had my own philosophy that two people may not be destined to satisfy each other's sexual needs forever or solely forever, and that's probably true in the straight as well as the gay community. Somewhere along the way, and there's still mystery about the incubation period of the HIV virus, he became infected. There had been, in retrospect, symptoms several years prior to his diagnosis, in the form of shingles of the face and chest. The shingles occurred about four years after I met Rob, and there was really no serious testing effort under way at that point. It was not standard procedure to be tested. It was often done by the brave, by the informed, but certainly not by the average person. I was afraid the test results would be recorded and influence my employment and my insurability. People shied away from testing, and they also didn't want to know, because in those days it was truly a death sentence to be HIV positive. There were questions of how people would treat you. There were none of the support structures that exist now, some fifteen years later. Rob wasn't tested, nor was I, and our lives continued as described.

"I had just left a consulting firm and was taking some time off while deciding what I wanted to do next. I had had a long, fairly glorious corporate career. I left the consulting firm and decided to travel up to New England to spend some time with Rob . . . now I was a free agent, thinking lots about money and jobs and stuff, but not up against the wall financially. When I arrived—the day that will forever be marked in my history—Rob said, 'I didn't want to concern you while you were at a distance—I just want you to know I haven't been feeling well.' I said, 'Oh, well, I guess you have a cold or the flu or something. We'll go see the doctor tomorrow.' We went to the doctor the next day. A couple days went by, and Rob got sicker and sicker, with fever and difficulty breathing. . . . Still, it had not really crossed my mind that he had AIDS . . . although there was an inkling, there was a quiet little drumbeat. Finally, as he found it more difficult to climb steps because of his respiratory problems, we went to the local hospital. A young physician saw Rob and called me into his room, at Rob's request, and said to Rob, 'Are you a homosexual?' Rob turned to me and said 'Honey,' . . . I said, 'Tell him the truth' . . . and Rob said, 'Yes.' The doctor said, 'I think you have a compromised immune system. You can only have that if you have what is known as Acquired Immune Deficiency Syndrome. I think you should go back to Baltimore. We aren't prepared to handle this here. We don't really know how to treat it here. Twenty-four hours later Rob was in a Baltimore hospital with an AIDS-related pneumonia. He nearly died."

The doctor told Tom that they couldn't do any more for Rob. He believed that Rob had "given up, and with that attitude, very little could be done." Tom confronted Rob with this news, and "three hours later he had recovered from pneumonia and was released from the hospital five days later." Tom and Rob made "every effort to continue our lives," which were in turmoil because of the illness and Tom's career change. At this point, Tom moved in with Rob and rented out his own home. "I took care of most of his day-to-day needs. He was fine and functional most of the time for about eighteen months. I tried to give him the very best life. With some help from friends, I cooked, cleaned, took care of Rob, and did some work. In the background for me were the questions of my own health status. Maybe I was engaging in some denial, but I was quite confident along with my own good health that I was not infected. I was just not ready to get tested and face that, because if I was infected it would have been just enormous pressure on what we were trying to maintain."

"I knew Rob was going to die. I looked for every piece of good news about drugs, went to a support group, and I also continued to drink heavily. I went back to my traditional roots in Catholicism and went to church every day. Rob spent a lot of time reading the Bible." Tom's drinking problems escalated to the point where Rob "arranged for an intervention by a counselor who had been working with the two of us on illness and death issues. He was at the front door, sat me down, and Rob announced that I either did something about the drinking or he was leaving. This is a moment one doesn't forget. When one's dying partner says he will walk out the door if you don't do something, you do it. I hadn't been arrested, I hadn't lost everything, but I was about to lose Rob. I decided to do something. I decided I would detox myself. I called my doctor and he said he'd prescribe some drugs, but I didn't want to go that route. So I detoxed myself over six-teen days by cutting the number of ounces of alcohol out by one ounce every other day." Tom found a gay and lesbian recovery clubhouse as a sup-port for himself and has never had a drop of alcohol since then. "It probably saved my life. I had enough support through AA and a few other people that I knew this was not a simple process."

Rob's illness continued to progress and they found a wonderful lesbian doctor to care for Rob while they lived in New England. "This doctor stood tall against forces that thought that faggots and AIDS were not nice neighbors. The hospital system was not supportive of this. They were scared to death of getting blood on them. At one point, the doctor took Tom aside and told him, 'Look, you have to prepare yourself. He is going to die. You are not. You have got to start taking care of yourself.' I realized she was right. Everything in my life had been geared toward Rob's care. So I start-ed to create some distance. I would not sleep in the same room with Rob because of his snoring, and I wasn't getting enough sleep. He didn't like that. I knew I needed to have some distance from the event. I still loved Rob and cared about him deeply, but I needed to feel some independence."

Rob was finally hospitalized in New England. Tom has vivid memories of the way he was treated by doctors at the hospital. "I went to enter his room and the nurse said, 'He does not want you in here.'" There was a new doctor and this was her first residency assignment. She was clearly not happy to have a dying AIDS patient on her hands. I remember standing at the nurses' station and she looked up at me, as if to tell me that my table was ready at a restaurant, and said, 'You know, he's probably going to die tonight.' I said, 'Well I didn't know that but I certainly thank you for telling me.' I couldn't get into his room, so I went into the waiting room and made a bed for myself. Then this nurse came out and told me that Rob was gone. I never saw the doctor. Then someone said, 'You must go look at the body because partners are in a strange status in these circumstances.' I'm on the papers as the executor, but I'm not legally his partner. So they took me, along with Rob's business partner, to see Rob's body. I feel kind of like I missed something, but life doesn't deal an even hand."

Rob's family arrived the next morning, and they took his body. "They had the legal rights to his body and I did not. His parents announced when the service would be." When Tom spoke with his own family, they were not surprised but devastated." "He was not your average guy. He really left huge footprints. He was very charismatic. I never knew anyone who didn't love him. I went home to my family for a few days and then came back for the service. This was his family's service, where I was treated as if I wasn't there. His family had his business partner stand in the receiving line at the funeral. I didn't want to be near those people, but not so much as thank you. I used to change his diapers. At the service, my family and I sat at the back." Following the service, Tom realized there were a few things he wanted that had belonged to Rob. "I asked the family politely and they said, 'We want what we're supposed to get.' I said, 'I'll give you some pictures of his grandmother that I don't want.' But, no, they got the stuff."

Until recently Tom continued to live in the apartment in Baltimore that he and Rob had shared. Since Rob's death, ten years ago, Tom does find ways to stay connected to Rob. "I thought about him for a long time every day, and he's with me like the grain in wood. He's there as a spirit with me. I don't have to work at it. I kept a lot of pictures until recently. There's one or two of them in the bedroom. I must have had twenty of them all over that huge apartment we shared." Rob was a big collector, but when Tom moved out of their apartment, "I wanted a different, simpler life. I wanted something free of clutter and maybe free of a certain degree of emotional attachment to Rob." About one year after Rob's death, Tom began a new business venture, which is thriving today. This business "sits in the middle of what's thought of as a gay neighborhood. We have to be politically involved. We donate to many causes." For Tom, Rob and he were "the dearest, loving, protective friends. I mean, we still are. He just isn't here."

Tom believes that Rob's death has changed him in many ways. "It has made me vastly and dramatically more aware of the scarcity of time and the precious nature of life—especially life with advantages I enjoy. I really try to stay in the present moment. I think the value of time, staying in the present moment . . . it's taught me to be more gentle. I am more aware of the fragility of people." Tom also believes that he has learned "to live with a certain amount of uncertainty. I took a lot from that experience, but it's taken me ten years to translate it into a right philosophy. Knowing what to overlook . . . being less quick to judge others. On the negative side, it's taught me that people go away and nothing is forever. Yet, adversity has taught me about my capacity to love and to care about someone, I mean really care. I think it's increased my capacity to give and take affection."

Tom believes that involving himself "with others through a support group and Action AIDS, . . . knowing that my pain was not just my pain, but respecting the fact that it is my pain, yet there are others that join me in the universe with that challenge, helped me to cope." Tom has had HIV testing and is fine.

Analysis

Although Tom lost his partner to AIDS, he did not lose his whole group of friends at the same time. Tom's story seems to illustrate the disenfranchised grief described by Doka (1989, 2002b), which is experienced through the loss of a partner in a relationship that is not legally sanctioned. Tom spoke of how poorly he was treated by the doctor at the hospital where Rob was dying. He was not allowed access to his partner during those last hours, after having cared for him for several years. Studies done by Kimmel (1978) and Kelly (1977) indicated that male homosexuals complained that restrictions in visiting the sick partner, as well as the negative attitudes of the medical staff, inhibited their anticipatory grief.

Following Rob's death, Tom states that, although he was designated as the executor, he did not have "legal" rights to Rob's body. Instead, Rob's parents planned the funeral service, "where I was treated as if I wasn't there." Tom and his own family sat in the back of the church. Tom was deeply hurt that Rob's business partner was chosen by Rob's family to stand in the receiving line at the funeral, when Tom had been the one to take care of Rob throughout his illness. Rob's family refused to recognize the importance of his relationship with Tom as well as Tom's need to grieve. Participation in the funeral service as a ritual provides some closure for the loss of a partner, an involvement that Tom was denied. One can only suspect that this has contributed to a complicated mourning process for Tom.

Tom has remained connected to the memory of Rob through pictures in his home. Tom doesn't have to work at remembering Rob, who died ten years ago, because "he's there as a spirit with me." Tom continues to support Action AIDS in memory of Rob as well as other friends who have died. Like many bereaved partners and spouses, Tom has been made aware of the "precious nature of life" and "stays in the present moment" as much as he can.

Unlike Jim and Tom, David's partner did not die of AIDS, but his story provides another glimpse of disenfranchised grief.

David

David was forty-five and had been partnered with Brent for eighteen years when Brent committed suicide. David and Brent were longtime lovers but did not share the same apartment. "We spent all of our free time together." David is a salesman and Brent worked as a contractor until his death. Brent suffered from depression, which surfaced more intensely every two or three years. The summer before his death Brent quit his job, and over the holidays, his depression "got the best of him" and he hanged himself. David, who found him in his apartment, said, "I was glad I found him rather than a family member because we were not 'out' to his family." The weekend before his death Brent came out to his parents. During this same period he told David that he was having an affair with another man. David "understood that Brent's affair was part of his depression. The day that Brent died, he admitted it to me, and we talked about the man he had been seeing, as well as the pain he felt after telling his parents that he was gay."

David believed that Brent's refusal to tell his parents about their relationship had been a problem from the beginning. "Shortly after we were together, his parents suspected something, but it was never confirmed because we didn't live together. He didn't want to cause his parents grief." David was never included in any of Brent's family's gatherings. However, David and Brent had told David's family about their relationship, and they were very accepting. When Brent died, David called 911, as well as Brent's sister, with whom David continues to have a relationship. She contacted Brent's father, who lived nearby. Until Brent's father arrived at the apartment "the police and everyone involved directed everything to me, but as soon as Mr. Bloom arrived, the police only spoke to him. It was quite bothersome to me. The neighbors knew me and were coming with coffee and donuts."

The funeral experience was very difficult for David because "his family made all the arrangements. Brent and I didn't cover ourselves in terms of life insurance policies—which was stupid. Both Brent and I listed our parents as beneficiaries. My name was not mentioned in the obituary, although I asked that it be. On the other hand, my family was incredibly supportive. All my family, including my six brothers and sisters, my aunts and uncles, and our friends came to the funeral. Brent's parents were overwhelmed by the support of the gay community, here, because they really stood behind us. They were with me for two and one-half days in the funeral home and a Catholic mass—all arranged by Brent's family." David felt fortunate that "a few gay people I knew worked at the funeral home, and they were nice to me. They got me a copy of the visitors' book and thank-you cards. They pulled me aside and asked me if I wanted some time alone with Brent before they closed the casket. So after his family left, I had some time. After the family wake, some friends had a wake later in the evening, and Brent's sister came to that, too." Brent's family cleaned out all Brent's stuff from his apartment, "but every now and then his sister raids the boxes and brings me some of Brent's clothes."

For David, the most difficult aspect of Brent's death was "when Brent's father locked me out of Brent's apartment two days after he died. That was hard for me, because I was there the day after he died—I took a nap there. It bothered me because that's where we spent most of our time, next to my place. It was weird not to be able to go in there—that was my home too." David was also upset because the police found a suicide note after Brent's father arrived. "It was a three-page note, but I didn't get to see it. The coroner gave it to Mr. Bloom. I asked about it, and he wouldn't let me see it. He told me he didn't know where it was, and at one point he told me that he destroyed it. I asked my counselor if he could get it for me—it was a closure thing, and I thought it would help. My counselor wrote a letter to Brent's parents. Mrs. Bloom called my counselor and told him that she had received the note and didn't show it to her husband because it would make him mad. Brent was afraid of his father, who had abused him when he was younger. Brent's mother broke down when she was talking to my counselor and said she wanted to get together with me. That's the last thing I wanted, but my counselor thought it would do me some good. When we got together for lunch, she didn't have the note with her. I have a lesbian friend whose mother works in the police department, and she called the coroner's office and told them that she needed a copy for the police files. I finally got to read the note. It made me feel good that he thanked me in the note for being such a good friend, and if it weren't for me, he wouldn't have what he had. He said that I was entitled to everything he had and I assumed that was the reason Mr. Bloom locked me out of the apartment." Reading the note was helpful to David because "it brought that part of things to a close. It made me feel good that he thanked me for what he had and that I was entitled to his things."

Since David and Brent were together for eighteen years, David still receives support from the gay community. "I still hear that Brent and I were like a symbol to them of gay relationships because we were together for so long. It's not real common for a gay couple to be together for so long. They said we were like an inspiration to them—that's nice to hear." David's biggest regret is that he and Brent did not live together. "To hell with our families—we should have been together. If I'm lucky enough to be in another relationship, that's something we're going to do." Another regret is that "we should have been more open around his family. That caused some of these problems—maybe Brent would still be here if we had been more open. But that was also the time—twenty years ago—when you came out, you thought you were the only ones in the world. 'What's wrong with me?' Now, it's on TV all the time."

David believes that Brent's death has changed him in many ways. "I know I've definitely become more of a hermit. I don't get out as much." Before Brent's death, David was very social and was in charge of setting up their social activities. David has also decided to take better care of himself and has been going to a local gym to exercise. "I decided I'd better look better if I'm going to attract anyone else. I'm also not as close to my family as I was two years ago. I feel a little badly that I don't see my parents as much as I did. Sundays were always the day that he would go to his parents and I would go to mine. Now, without that routine, I'm doing things more with friends. I made up my mind after Brent died that I wouldn't turn down an invitation." One of the first social events that David attended was a small Christian group for gays, lesbians, and transsexuals. David has continued attending this group on a biweekly basis and finds it has replaced going to church—something he and Brent did together. "I became gay-radical, whereas prior to Brent's death I always underplayed it. I put a gay bumper sticker on my car, and one of my sisters told me I was 'in your face being gay.' I'm calming down a bit now and have taken the bumper sticker off my car." David has also begun to read the newspaper regularly and has found it interesting to "follow politics." Brent was the partner interested in politics, and would report various events to David. David has also become very interested in music, which was "his [Brent's] job in our relationship." David now buys CDs that he likes as a way of having music in his life.

David has found that reading books on grief has been helpful to him, especially books about men and grief. He has been helpful to a neighbor who recently lost her spouse. She asked David, "When can I go back to the cemetery?" David's response was, "Right now. For the rest of your life, you can do whatever you want." David is happy to help anyone who is grieving, because he has discovered for himself how helpful it is to talk to others, "just to know how normal I was."

In a written postscript to our interview, David said, "I was up part of the evening thinking about the parts of Brent that are still with me, such as his enjoyment of music, his smile, and his love of politics. Although I lost some sleep, it was good to think of the things that he left with me. I forgot to mention how couples with children are lucky following the loss of their partner because the remaining partner has the children as a living part of the deceased parent. Not only would they have been a distraction, to help keep

me busy in the days and months after, but they would also be another av-
enue through which memories of Brent would have been saved and revis-
ited. To hear children use phrases and see them use gestures that he used
would have been nice. Just like it is good to hear our friends reminisce
about things Brent did."

Analysis

David's story, like that of Tom, clearly illustrates how painful the experience of disenfranchised grief can be for a bereaved partner (Doka 1989,
2002b). David's most difficult experience occurred when Brent's father was
unwilling to allow David to enter Brent's apartment following his death.
Since David and Brent had spent so much time together in the apartment,
David felt cut off from the support and comfort he might have derived from
being in this space. David readily admits that Brent's refusal to tell his parents about their relationship was a problem from the beginning. Brent's father was not told until the weekend before his son's death, so that he did
not have a chance to absorb this much powerful information in such a short
time. Doka (1989, 2002b) reports that when a relationship is accepted, there
is a greater possibility for social support from family and friends. In David's
case, although their friends knew that he and Brent shared an intimate relationship and provided support for David, Brent's family (except for his sister) provided no support and, in fact, were rude to David. As was true in
the case of Tom, the dead partner's family refused to recognize or value the
importance of the relationship between their son and his bereaved partner.
David's name was also excluded from the obituary, even after he had asked
that he be listed as the surviving partner. David also had to fight to see the
contents of Brent's suicide letter, because Brent's family refused to share it
with him. Furthermore, Brent's family took all the responsibility for making the funeral arrangements, which prevented David from beginning to
work on his grief through participation in an important ritual at the time of
a severe loss.

Brent's death from suicide may have complicated an already difficult situation for parents who learned their son was gay just before his death.
Death by suicide is still stigmatized by our society, so that the social support
survivors receive is limited. This support can also be limited by the reluc-
tance of the survivor to seek support due to his or her experience of shame,
embarrassment, isolation, and guilt (Doka 2002b). Brent's father's extremely
hostile reaction to David, Brent's partner, may have stemmed, in part, from

his own pain, shame, and embarrassment about the suicide. Although David did not mention discomfort about Brent's suicidal death, he may also have experienced some of these reactions.

David has stayed connected to his memory of Brent by assuming some of the tasks that Brent had taken on in their relationship. David enjoys music but allowed Brent to provide that for them. David now initiates this soothing activity for himself. David has also become interested in world news and politics, an area that he had completely relied on Brent to provide when he was alive. In accordance with what postmodern theorists (Neimeyer 1998, 2001; Klass et al. 1996; Rubin 1999) have written about making new meaning from an experience of loss, David has joined a Christian group for homosexuals and transsexuals, which he has found helpful as he begins to build a new life. David and Brent had gone to church together, but David has found a new way to express his spirituality that is more satisfying to him than attending church.

Like Jim and Tom, Don lived with his partner, Eric, for a long time before Eric's death. Unlike David and his partner, Don and Eric shared the same house for twenty-three years.

Don

Don was fifty when his life partner, Eric, died of liver cancer at age forty-nine. Don and Eric met in their late twenties and had just celebrated their twenty-three-year-long partnership before Eric died. Don works in management for a public relations firm, and Eric worked in construction. Eric was involved in another relationship when he met Don.

Eric had been a heavy drinker, "a maintenance alcoholic," but had stopped drinking several years before he was diagnosed, only four months before his death, with primary liver cancer. "He went in to have an operation where they were going to put a pump in . . . he came home and had to go right back in because things weren't working right. That was probably the first reality check, because the woman at the hospital said, 'Do you want me to put the paddles on him if I have to?' I didn't know what to say. I had medical power of attorney, but I didn't have to show it to them. They ended up transferring him to another hospital, and we were on our way there when he collapsed. I called 911 to transport him. After he came out of the hospital, it all moved very fast. He got into hospice care right away and had a temporary nurse for half a day. . . . At some point, he just stopped talking, or was not as agitated, and it turned out it was blood poisoning. I think I decided to go back to work just a half a day. It was really . . . not to go to work . . . it was just a break. I had someone to help who was living with us. . . . They called me at the office to tell me had died. Sometimes I feel a little guilt about that, but I was there all the other times. I think one of the last things he said to me was, 'Nobody else would've done this for me.'"

Don did not feel prepared for the suddenness of Eric's death. "He stopped working in August, and by early September we had gone through two operations, hospice, and death. Things were moving so fast—I slept every night down in the lounge where Eric slept and gave him his medicine." During Eric's last month friends and relatives came to visit, which was very supportive to Don. Eric's family was supportive of Don and his relationship with Eric. "They never even asked to see the will, which I think is remarkable." Don put the obituary and the announcement of Eric's death in the paper and made most of the funeral arrangements, which he and Eric had discussed before his death. Eric was also a musician. When Don planned his funeral service, he "wanted the service to become what Eric was about and not anything else." During the service three musicians played and sang different types of music. Don felt a great deal of support during Eric's illness, his death, and afterward. "I got so much support from everybody. My parents came from the West Coast, and my one brother and three sisters were there." Don and Eric's relationship as gay partners was known to family as well as the community.

Don knew of other gay friends who had horror stories to tell about people "getting thrown out of their homes when the family comes in." Don knew that Eric had already told his youngest brother that "once I die everything is Don's." However, Don learned through Eric's death that you need to be prepared for the death of a loved one, so that the estate is protected from exorbitant taxes. Following Eric's death, Don had to use all of the insurance money to pay the estate taxes. Don's words to his friends are, "You should each have your own account some place, where at any time of crisis, you just move financial assets to that account and leave them there. If you have a home equity loan, you write a large check and put it into your account." Gay life partners do not receive the marital deduction given, upon the death of a spouse, to those partners who have been in traditional, legally approved relationships.

Following Eric's death, Don went in and out of depression. "Now I go back over the three years and see that I've come a long way. I know myself better now. I'm not happy for having gone through the experience, but

I understand myself a little better. I understand Eric better. I appreciate him more." Don better understands his own needs—"What do I want out of life? You learn what your needs are because there's such a void and a loss. You say to yourself, 'What's going to make me happy—what's going to make me feel better?' I finally admitted that I was clinically depressed and started taking medication." Don began dating someone several months after Eric died, but "it was wonderful and magical and we parted company." Later Don became involved with another partner, a relationship that also ended within a year. Don finally was able to purchase a summer home at a resort and has enjoyed spending leisure time there with friends.

Don believes that he is "no longer the same person he was when Eric was alive. You're just defined by that other person. I don't do the same things. I used to like to garden and keep house. I've become more of a homebody. I think I know my emotions better. I understand them more. I understand what I need in a relationship. I need more communication with someone. I need more touching and feeling than I had with Eric. To be honest, I was unhappy in the relationship toward the end. I wanted to be in love with somebody else, but it was not a bad life, and 'Where was I going to go?' In retrospect, I'm glad that I didn't leave, because I was glad to be there when I was needed and felt good about that. I couldn't make decisions whether to leave or to stay, and Eric made that for me. It was always Don and Eric and 'Who was Don without Eric?' That I didn't know. I had grown up, I had become an adult." Don was quite young when he met Eric and believes, "You grow up, and you build a life together, and you do certain things. Eric always took care of the air conditioning and the heater and the repairs around the house, and I made the critical decisions and decided how things were going to be done. I've had to run a big house by myself and on one salary. That's a critical thing. How do you go from a two-income lifestyle down to one? It's really what you can and can't do." Don has redecorated and rearranged things in the house he once shared with Eric. "It's just having to lead a whole life and doing those things that the other person did."

Don believes that he has changed in terms of what he wants from a relationship. "I understood my needs, and I understood more about who I was, and I came to value true intimacy. That only comes from open communication both on a physical and an emotional level—and just talking. It also comes from not being afraid to tell somebody who you are, or what you want, or what's good about you and what's bad about you." Don has found himself sharing more of himself in new relationships than he did with Eric.

However, he also believes that "at the beginning, when we were seeing each other on the side, we'd lay in bed and talk for hours and at the kitchen table." Don wonders, "Where did that sort of relationship end? You lose it along the way . . . it happens to everybody. So I've learned that you have to work at this sort of thing and I've tried to carry that in whatever relationship I've been in since Eric died." Don has also been more open at his workplace regarding his sexual orientation and has received "support from a wide variety of people. It was sort of a big outing at work, which is kind of nice, because now I can talk about boyfriends and that sort of thing. Not that I do, but I can. Everybody knows and there's no big deal about it, so in a sense, it's made an easier environment for me to work in."

Don knows that deep down "I need to be in a relationship, but I'm tired of looking for it, and I'm just sort of sitting back and letting it find me and not passing up any opportunity. If somebody says, 'Do you want to do this,' if I've never done it, I go. I need to get out and break wide wherever I can. I'm spending more money now. I don't need to save money anymore. I'm going to go out and enjoy it. I took a cruise with some friends this year. Life's meant to be lived and enjoyed. You have to get out and participate in it—it's hard, sometimes, because I'm so addicted to the Internet now, but I force myself. So it's about what your needs are and what your emotions are. It's time to connect with somebody to get that emotional bond. It's very important to me now. Sharing your life with someone is much more interesting and much more enjoyable than doing it alone. I think this (the death of Eric) has been a learning experience in redefining myself about who Don is without Eric. It comes in little bits and pieces, and it comes at funny times. I'll think, 'I never did this before' or I look at life a little differently now, and I realize that it's more precious. You are literally here today and gone tomorrow."

Don keeps Eric's memory in his thoughts. "I think about him a lot more in different ways, and I started talking to him." Don finally turned to a minister who had psychic abilities and found that "it was the most phenomenal experience of my life. I sought him out because I was at a loss as to what to do with my life—whether to move out West or not. I said to myself, 'I believe in spirituality.' The psychic tuned in to Don's relationships with Eric and others with whom he had been involved. When the psychic identified specific characteristics about these men, Don left and "cried the rest of the way home. I left there with this huge weight off of my shoulders." Don has been very comforted by remembering Eric this way. "I felt so good. I'm not afraid of death anymore. There were times when I would have willingly gone, you know, take this road and die tomorrow. Loneliness and the loss—death is more peaceful." Don no longer believes that death is the end of life. He returns to see the psychic every year and finds it's a way to stay in touch with Eric and others he has lost in his life.

Don believes that he connects with Eric in different ways. "Something will happen around the house and I think, 'Oh, is that you?' . . . or 'Did I smell cigarette smoke?' . . . or the light went off. These things happen, and the psychic told me, 'They don't know how to communicate, so they'll try different things.' He told me, 'If you have that feeling, you say 'If that's you Eric, I heard you.' So I've found myself doing that lately, and it's kind of fun. I feel better about his death, if you can. There's times that I feel sorry for what he missed. But knowing that there is this other place, I don't feel sorry for him as much in that sort of way." Don finds it comforting to know that Eric is in a different place where he is out of pain. "It gave me a sense of death not being that bad."

Analysis

Unlike Tom and David, Don did not experience disenfranchised grief. He and Eric were partnered for twenty-three years and had been open about their sexual orientation to both of their families and their friends. In fact, Eric had made it clear to his brother that Don would be receiving Eric's inheritance and had made provisions in his will to cover this matter. Following the loss of Eric, Don became very open about his gay relationship with everyone at his workplace and received a lot of support from "a wide variety of people." As Shernoff has reported (1998), the more open a gay, lesbian, or cohabiting couple have been with their families and friends, the more likely it is for them to be recognized as lifelong partners and treated with the respect and support that spouses receive when their partners die. Don was also able to have more closure because he made the funeral arrangements based on what he and Eric had discussed. Richmond and Ross (1995) report on the lack of closure for partners who were excluded from funeral preparations. Don's negative feelings about our societal laws concerning death were related to his not being given the spousal deduction at Eric's death, which forced him to use much of the inheritance to pay estate taxes.

Don's story illustrates the changes that a bereaved partner undergoes following the loss of a partner. Don believes that in some ways you are defined by your partner when he is alive. Looking back over the three years since Eric's death, Don can see how he has gained a better understanding of himself and his needs. He also realizes that he wants to become involved in a relationship different from the one he had with Eric. He would like this new partner to be more communicative and sensual than he and Eric were with each other.

Like the other men in this chapter, Don realizes how precious life is as the result of his loss of his partner. Don is enjoying his leisure time by traveling and is willing to spend more of his assets to meet his needs for fun and pleasure. "Life is meant to be lived and enjoyed." Don keeps Eric's memory alive by talking to him and by seeing a psychic who has helped Don realize that death is more peaceful than he had previously imagined. Don's spirituality has grown since Eric's death, and he believes that some type of life exists following death. He has found himself very comforted when he experiences Eric's presence in his life and communicates with Eric verbally the moment he feels his presence around the house. These experiences of connecting with Eric provide Don with a sense of comfort and peace. Just as the postmodern thinkers (Klass, Silverman, and Nickman 1996; Neimeyer 1998, 2001; Rubin 1999) have indicated, bereaved partners tend to remain connected to their deceased partners. In some ways, this connection may provide them with the assistance they need to move forward with their lives.

CHAPTER SUMMARY

Just as the literature suggests (Shernoff 1998; Doka 1989), the degree to which the gay couple has come out to their family prior to the death of a partner determines how the couple's relationship will be respected and how much support will be provided by the family. As the narratives of Jim and Don suggest, when a gay partner has not hidden his sexual orientation, he is more likely to have a network of supportive friends and family who will help him in the mourning process. Jim found that Matt's sister and Matt's parents were very supportive to him following Matt's death. Although Jim's parents had been aware of their gay relationship for some time, Matt's parents had known for only one year before his death. Don and his partner, Eric, had been very open about their sexual orientation with both of their families and their friends. Eric had informed his brother that Don would be receiving his inheritance and made provisions in his will to cover this matter. Don planned the entire funeral service for Eric, based on requests that Eric had made.

In contrast, Tom was rejected by Rob's family following Rob's death. Although Tom was designated as the executor of Rob's estate, he did not have legal rights to Rob's body. At the funeral service, which was planned by Rob's family, Tom "was treated as if I wasn't there." He was deeply hurt when Rob's business partner was chosen by Rob's family to stand in the receiving line at the funeral. In another narrative, David found the funeral to be a very difficult experience because Brent's family made all the arrangements. Brent's father completely rejected David following Brent's death, to the point of locking David out of Brent's apartment, where David had spent so much time. It is significant that David and Brent had not shared one living space but had lived in separate quarters, although they spent many hours together in each other's apartments. David's biggest regret is that he and Brent did not live together. David revealed the lack of knowledge their families had of their sexual orientation when he said, "To hell with our families, we should have been together."

The issue of the way in which AIDS complicates the bereavement of a gay partner is illustrated in the narratives of Jim and Tom. Just as the literature suggests (Richmond and Ross 1995), Jim found that watching his partner, Matt, die of AIDS was a rehearsal of his own death. Jim lost many friends to AIDS and said, "in some strange ways, it felt like a legacy—this is what happened to everyone and this is what's in store for me. Living with the knowledge that I had the same infection that I had watched devastate healthy young men of my own age was awful." Tom, whose partner, Rob, died of AIDS said that he had questions about his own health as he cared for his partner.

For Jim, the issue of "survivor's guilt" was paramount. Boykin (1991), Sanders (1989), and Murphy and Perry (1988) reported that the conception of "Why him? and Why not me?" was present in their studies of bereaved gay partners. However, according to Boykin (1991), there was a trend toward a higher degree of survivor-guilt scores in the HIV and/or AIDS subgroups. Jim was HIV positive at the time of Matt's death and may have wondered if his HIV status was responsible for Matt's infection. As the literature suggests (Boykin 1991; Sanders 1989; Murphy and Perry 1988), survivor guilt may be one of the coping mechanisms for denial of the kind of intense pain experienced by Jim. Jim suffered multiple losses of friends from AIDS, which put him in a constant state of mourning. Jim's guilt was intensified by the fact that he was not present at the time of Matt's death. Jim states, "I've had some issues in terms of 'Why me of all the people to survive?', after I lost the last friend in that group of twelve."

The narratives of Jim, Tom, and Don seem to corroborate the findings of Ferrell's 1992 study, which suggests that "the managing care process" of the gay caregiver led to positive psychosocial growth following the death of their gay partner. Two of the critical factors in making this managing of care more positive were the caregiving partner's ability to take care of himself and his ability to share the care with family and friends.. Jim speaks directly about being glad to have been able to care for his friend George during the last four months of his life. This caregiving experience occurred directly after he had cared for his partner, Matt. Jim did continue to work outside the home while managing the care of his friends. Tom was pleased to have been able to care for his dying partner, Rob, but did so with the help of his friends and continued with his work. Don took care of Eric near the end of his life, but did so by returning to work outside the home, with the help of a nurse for half of each day. Don was pleased that one of the last things Eric said to him was, "Nobody else would have done this for me."

Chapter Six

Loss of a Lesbian Partner

ISSUES FACED BY A BEREAVED LESBIAN PARTNER

Although there is much research about widows, and a growing literature on both homosexual and heterosexual widowers, there is a severe lack of research on lesbians who have lost their partners through death. Except for the dissertation research presented in chapter 2, little has emerged that is useful in understanding bereavement among lesbian women. The narratives and analyses of the five lesbian women who are presented in this chapter will add to the much-needed literature on this subject.

Lesbian women lead double lives as they work among the heterosexual majority, but they develop hidden networks of support, activity, and resources within lesbian communities (Deevey 1997). Lesbian women create families from the networks they develop, and although these families often substitute for "blood family," the kinship networks in lesbian communities differ from traditional heterosexual nuclear families (Deevey 1997). The review of literature on lesbian kinship suggests that heterosexual models of family relationships cannot be assumed to be universal.

Although mutually supportive partnerships among lesbian women are satisfying, "relationships in the larger community can be problematic for lesbians" (Mirkin 1994). Life-cycle issues such as bereavement can be difficult in the face of homophobia, sexism, and ageism. "For example, lesbians are frequently denied the recognized status of widows when their partners die. Families can prevent lesbian partners from participating in hospital visits, caregiving responsibilities, and funeral services by leaving them out of the arrangements" (1994:100).

In Deevey's (1997) study of lesbian women who have lost a partner, she found that the theme of "disenfranchised grief" identified by Doka (1987, 1989, 2002b) and presented in chapter 4 emerged from some of the narratives. Deevey (1997) and Jones (1985) conclude that the unpredictability of community and family responses remains a source of stress and fear in the lives of lesbian women who have lost their partners. Most of the women Deevey (1997) interviewed who found their families to be unhelpful or hurtful at the time of their bereavement had concealed their sexual orientation from their families or were aware that the families disapproved of their lifestyle. In contrast, women who found their families most helpful had never formally told their parents they were lesbians, but assumed their parents knew.

Pauline

Pauline was thirty-two when her partner, Jean, age twenty-six, was tragically killed in an automobile accident. Pauline and Jean met by telephone through a friend and maintained a long-distance relationship for sixteen months. During this time they flew back and forth to see each other because Jean was in nursing school on the West Coast. Following Jean's graduation, she moved east to live with Pauline. Shortly thereafter they had a union ceremony—"which was very, very nice. It was really neat." Pauline's brother attended the ceremony, along with friends of both Pauline and Jean. One of those friends is now sharing a life with Pauline. Pauline works as a counselor with teens and enjoys her work. Her current partner, Linda, is a physician.

At the time of the accident, "we were officially in a committed relationship for two years, but we considered ourselves as partners for almost five years. At the time I had taken some time off to work at a barn—I love horses—to pursue a particular type of riding that I really wanted to do. Linda was using our apartment to study for her medical boards. It was a beautiful day, and I had gone out to the barn in the morning. Jean had started working on her Master's degree upstate, and I was always worried about her traveling, but that morning she said, 'What do you want for dinner?' and I said, 'Be careful, I love you, goodbye.'"

"A few hours later, I was out in the field with the horses, when I saw a police car pulling up to the gate of the farm. I didn't think anything of it, but as I brought the horse closer, Linda came flying through the indoor arena—she was hysterical—saying, 'Jean was killed, Jean was killed!' About ten minutes from home she was crossing over a highway, and she had the green light, but a tractor-trailer ran both red lights and T-boned her, dragging the car into a telephone pole. She was killed instantly. Linda and I went back to the apartment, and I kept saying, 'No, no, this isn't true.' You can imagine the shock. The first thing I had to do and the most awful thing I had to do was call her parents on the West Coast." Jean's mother had visited Pauline and Jean twice and was supportive of their relationship, but her father and brother were not. "Fortunately, when I got them, her mom and dad were both there. I didn't know what to do if it was just her dad, but luckily they were both there."

Pauline and Linda went to the hospital to claim the body. Pauline immediately thought about organ donation and discovered that they could take the cornea and tissue. "Organ donation was a big thing for Jean. She worked in critical care and ICU, and it was always something she spoke to families about when it came to that point. We had to call to get a verbal okay from her parents to do that. The next thing I did was to call my folks, and I called my brother, who came up right away—he was wonderful."

Jean's parents and Pauline agreed that Jean would be cremated. Jean's ashes were split "so I could bury half here and half went out to the West Coast, where she and been born and raised." Although Pauline's mother and brother attended the memorial service, her father chose not to attend. "One hard thing about that was that my dad did not come up from his work for the service. If it had been my husband, he would have been there. He was supportive verbally, but if it had been my husband he would have been there in a heartbeat. It's nothing we've ever talked about—that's just the way it is." Although it bothered Pauline, once she was out of shock regarding Jean's death, "I finally let it go because it wasn't worth confronting him. A lot of wonderful friends came and a lot of people she worked with— a lot of support."

Pauline had come out to her parents, who are born-again Christians, "under great duress" and regrets doing so. Pauline's brother had been in recovery for an addiction and "one of the things was coming out to everybody. Well, I had come out to him, and he was great, but he felt like he was hiding this secret from my folks. He backed me into a corner and said, 'If you don't tell them, I will.' I told them, and it was not a good thing.

When Jean and I would visit them, they would not let us stay overnight—they really never talked about our relationship. We just didn't talk about it; it was like 'Don't ask, don't tell.' They felt that, by letting us stay with them overnight, they were condoning our relationship. Even to this day, we just don't talk about it, and they adore Linda. So we stay with them when we visit but always in twin beds."

Pauline had extreme anxiety about the court case that followed Jean's death because "what they found out over the course of a couple of years was that the truck had less than 50 percent of its braking capacity." Pauline didn't "pull any punches as to who I was in the relationship with Jean and demanded that I wanted to be part of things." Jean's parents did not come for the trial, and Pauline still remembers the prosecutor's opening line, "The last thing Jean McDonald saw on February 3, 1992, was the bulldog on the front of a Mack truck." Pauline says, "To this day I have a hard time driving around trucks. I don't like to be near them. They make me so nervous." During the court proceedings, Pauline also felt some discrimination concerning her role as a lesbian partner.

"You know how the family of the defendants make statements about how they can't imagine not having their husband home . . . I remember standing up and saying, 'I'm sorry, I don't have pity for you not having your husband home, but my partner's gone and I will never see her again.' I made no bones about who I was. At this point I didn't give two hoots about what they thought. I tried to plead that these people should be punished to the highest extent." Pauline believes that her anger toward the truck drivers, who received only a six-month jail sentence, affected her healing process. Another impediment to Pauline's healing was the civil case, which Jean's parents pursued. Pauline and Jean had never prepared wills, which brought Pauline much frustration, because "I wanted to have some control in this matter." Pauline found herself quite angry with Jean's parents for what she felt was mishandling of the civil case.

According to Pauline, "the hardest thing about Jean's accident was that it was not acknowledged. At work and among the neighbors in the apartment building, Jean was seen as a good friend, my roommate. I did force myself at the time of the accident to come out to one of the neighbors and to a woman who worked at the barn—they were great—because at that point I had nothing left to lose. In the obituary I put 'life partner,' but Jean's parents sent me a copy of the obituary they placed in their local paper, and it made no mention of me at all." Pauline discovered that whenever she did reveal her lesbian relationship with Jean to others, "all the responses were extremely positive, much more than I had anticipated. Except, of course, for my parents. I was glad I'd gotten to that point, where I didn't have any energy to hide it. So now I'm feeling that it's okay to take that risk, because 99 percent of the time they're going to be supportive."

Pauline "just muddled through" the first year following Jean's death. "I couldn't do anything with clothes. It took me the whole year of living in the apartment alone before I actually cleaned out the closet. I just couldn't change anything." Pauline suffered a deep depression for six months following Jean's death and "had a hard time functioning. I went on medication, which really helped, because I simply didn't want to get out of bed." Before Jean's death Pauline had been in therapy to help her cope with family conflicts regarding her relationship with Jean. When Pauline returned to therapy following Jean's death, she found it helpful that her therapist had met Jean during several joint sessions.

Pauline has made meaning for herself and her life from the loss of Jean in several ways. Pauline decided on organ and tissue donation immediately after Jean died and began to attend monthly support meetings that helped her cope with her feelings. Pauline received letters from those who had received the cornea transplants from Jean and found this particularly supportive. "The people at the Organ and Tissue Sharing Network were just wonderful. They couldn't have been more supportive. Part of the organ and tissue donation experience is, whether you like it or not, you've become part of a special club. And it's true. I feel that I have such a different compassion and empathy for other people. Even people I see on the news and that I don't know—there's much greater compassion for that loss and what that could possibly mean to them. I feel that I've become much more aware of what to say and what not to say to people, especially pertaining to a recent loss for them. . . . I apply this extra awareness of loss, having walked that path. Of course the one thing you can't say is, 'I know how you feel.' You realize everyone's loss is different." Pauline has experienced other benefits from her association with the Organ and Tissue Sharing Network. She has been invited to speak on panels with organ donor family members and recipient family members. She has found this to be a powerful experience. "Each of us took ten minutes to tell our story, and I had no problem saying who I was, who my partner was, what it had meant to be part of an organ donor family, and the response was wonderful."

Pauline also found great comfort in attending a six-week grief support group, which was very informative, rather than a "go-around-the-room-and-tell-your-story" approach. It was helpful for Pauline to learn that it was normal to see someone who was a double for the partner you had lost and to begin reading obituaries. "Another thing that helped me make meaning out of the whole thing over time was becoming involved, wanting to do something with grief and loss issues." Pauline contacted someone at a national organization and is now doing hospice volunteer work. Finally, Pauline reached out to two lesbian woman who had lost their partners and helped them to discuss issues that they hadn't been able to share with others. Pauline felt "really good about helping them, because somebody had done that for me. Pauline reported, "You know, I had nobody to talk with because it's hard to find a support group. All the support groups I tried to seek out were for gay men with AIDS, or support groups for people with terminal illness. All of that was different from what I was going through. You can't go to widow/widowers. It's the whole disenfranchised thing." Pauline did not make much use of the Gay and Lesbian Community Forum on the Internet, which was created for women who have lost partners. "There were a lot of women in there who were gay but had lost other people in their lives. I didn't play around in there much, but I would go in periodically and read things. I knew it was out there, even though I didn't use it."

Pauline actively keeps memories of Jean alive by placing photos around the home that she and Linda established together. Since Linda was a friend of both Jean and Pauline, they frequently discuss Jean. Pauline also keeps an old photo album from Jean's childhood and a Bible that belonged to Jean. Pauline is considering returning these family mementos to Jean's parents because she believes they would enjoy having them. Pauline has also maintained contact with another very good friend of Jean's. "That was a hard thing for a while because slowly, over time, I was meeting new people who didn't know Jean. That was really weird, to get over that spot where there was a loss. It's hard for lesbian couples. There have been new people drifting in and some drifting out of my life, so there were less and less people who knew Jean. For a while I remember feeling this as another loss."

Another way in which Pauline is connecting with Jean is by "dreaming that we were trying to reconnect. A lot of times it was as if she were still here and we had split up. It's been interesting, because the dreams always have the same theme of me trying to reconnect and to say I'm sorry for those disagreements and fights. The hard part is that in the dream, we've never done that. These dreams catch me off guard. It's not as if I've been consciously thinking of something that I see could have caused the dream, such as her birthday. They just happen out of the blue, and it's always that theme of trying to reconnect and finish that unfinished business." Pauline is still concerned about unfinished business with regard to her relationship with Jean because they "had a pretty heavy fight a couple of nights before the accident that we didn't resolve." Pauline has been in therapy for several years and feels that processing her dreams with her therapist has been helpful.

Since Jean's death, Pauline has struggled to become more of a "present-moment person. "My personality is such that I've always been one to be doing one thing and thinking ten steps ahead. Even as a kid I've always been driven, sort of a type A person, very perfectionistic." Jean "was more laid back. She'd suggest doing something, and I'd think, 'No, I should be doing this and this.' I can't just kick back. We were very opposite in that respect. So that's one thing I've gotten from Jean, in a way." Linda, Pauline's new partner, "is the same way, very spontaneous. I would say that I'm really trying to learn, not just from my personality style, but just from having this whole experience happen. I'd never had a significant loss before. I'd never had any experience with death. . . . I'm trying to work on this whole business of who cares if the floor is not clean, it's probably more important to go out and sit and chat with neighbors. The priorities of what's really important are something I'm still struggling with."

Pauline is enjoying her relationship with Linda but is struggling with how you "put that relationship behind you (and you are putting it behind you but not forgetting it) and move into your current one. I struggled with that for a long time because there wasn't a huge gap of five years in between. For a long time, I had that whole thing of 'Oh, I don't want to forget her, I might be disrespectful, am I in denial?' . . . One of the best things I can say is that because Linda did know Jean and our relationship, she's been unbelievably supportive through the whole process. She didn't push me at all to go through the closet (Jean's clothes) or that kind of thing. I think it's hard—that transition of putting that relationship wherever it's supposed to be without forgetting it. It's only through talking about it to other people who've been through it that you can discuss what you do with some of these things that are special. You don't want to negate the importance of your current relationship, but you don't want to put away or deny the importance of the other relationship, since it's not something you chose to leave."

Analysis

The theme of disenfranchised grief is evident in Pauline's story when she speaks of the reactions of others toward her regarding Jean's death. Pauline says, "The hardest thing about Jean's accident was that it was not acknowledged" as a life partnership by people at work or her neighbors, who viewed her as Jean's friend or roommate. However, Pauline discovered that when she did risk telling others about her lesbian relationship with Jean, she received support she never expected. In talking with other lesbian partners in this study, this interviewer noted that because lesbian women often assume they won't get support from others, they don't say anything. Pauline agreed with the interviewer that lesbian women who have lost a partner need to hear that they should take the risk of telling, because they are often a good judge of who will be supportive.

Despite her efforts with others in her life, Pauline felt that the responses from her parents were not positive. They had been unwilling to allow the couple to sleep at their home when they visited. Although Pauline's mother and brother attended the memorial service for Jean, Pauline's father did not. Pauline expresses feelings of discrimination in her comment, "If it had been my husband, he would have been there." It was also very difficult for Pauline to call Jean's parents after Jean had been killed because Jean's father and brother were not supportive of the couple's relationship. Pauline was also distressed that Jean's parents never mentioned her or her relationship with Jean in the obituary they prepared for their community.

Instead of being certain of support from family, neighbors, and colleagues at a time of severe grief, Pauline, like many other lesbian partners, had to encounter the unpredictability of family responses, which remains a source of stress and fear in the lives of lesbian women who have lost their partners (Deevey 1997).

At the time of both the criminal and civil trials regarding the accident that took Jean's life, Pauline felt that her relationship with Jean went unrecognized. During the criminal trial, Pauline experienced discrimination from others involved in the case because of her role as a lesbian partner. During the civil proceedings, she believed that all her rights were disenfranchised, since Jean's parents took over the whole thing and mismanaged it. Unfortunately, Pauline and Jean had never prepared wills, considering themselves too young. Thus Pauline had no control over the civil case. Nor did she have access to funds from the settlement.

Despite these impediments to the grieving process, Pauline has been able to move forward both personally and professionally. She has used this experience of loss to make new meaning in her life. Pauline's efforts to help bereaved partners who come from both same-sex and opposite-sex partnerships, and her new understanding of how to give that help, come from her own loss of Jean—the first death she has ever experienced. Pauline has also found comfort in joining the Organ and Tissue Sharing Network, which provides a direct way for her to stay connected to the memory of Jean as well as to help her make new meaning in her life. Rubin's 1999 work corroborates the importance of transforming the loss of a loved one into "something beyond grief and mourning" (1999:687) in order to move forward in one's life.

In Pauline's story it is evident that she has integrated some of Jean's qualities into her personality. This is particularly evident when she describes her attempts to become more "laid back" and to live "in the moment," as these were qualities that she admired in Jean but has never attained in herself. This integration corroborates Jones's 1995 findings that "the most frequent theme (among bereaved lesbian partners) was of having incorporated some of the dead partners' positive qualities within themselves" (1995:193).

Pauline has found many ways to keep memories of Jean close to her as a source of comfort. However, she is currently struggling with how she can validate her current relationship with Linda without negating her relationship with Jean, "since it's not something you chose to leave." Pauline's struggles in choosing a life partnership with Linda are reflected in Walter's 1997 research in which she discusses how the loyalty to one's dead spouse plays a part in one's struggle over dating. The issue of loyalty to the dead partner seems similar for widows, widowers, and bereaved lesbian partners. Pauline's struggle to find a way to validate her relationship with Jean while becoming involved with a new partner also reflects the importance, in adaptation to loss, of "finding a suitable place for the spouse in the psychological life of the bereaved—a place that is important but that leaves room for others" (Schuchter 1986:116). This same struggle is observed in the stories of spouses and heterosexual life partners described in chapters 3 and 4.

The following story differs from the others because the death was a suicide, but it reveals similar issues of lack of support from family and the workplace.

Gretchen

Gretchen was forty when her life partner, Carol, committed suicide at the age of thirty-three. Gretchen and Carol had been living together as a couple for seven years and had had a commitment ceremony before Carol's death. Carol had suffered from depression for two years prior to the severe depression that preceded her suicide. Gretchen is a music teacher, and Carol was a "vibrant, bright, talented musician."

Carol had worked very hard to get good medical care for her mental health problems because her HMO had never provided adequate coverage. Carol's workplace "let her go, and she tried to get health coverage, but couldn't, because she was sick, and they didn't want to admit that. They tried to word it in other ways. Really, it was horribly illegal. . . . So she really never had the right kind of coverage. I tried to get more involved as things went on, but that was a tough balance—trying to allow a person their own autonomy and allowing them to be in control of their life, but when they're in a severe manic or depressed state, they can't make decisions. So there were times when she would allow me to help out, and then there were times when she'd be angry and belligerent, if she was in a manic state, and that was tough."

The last six months before Carol's death "she was feeling pretty good and she didn't want to be in the relationship anymore. She wanted to be out on her own. She wanted to move out." Because of Carol's manic-depressive illness, Gretchen had mixed feelings about Carol moving out on her own. A few months after moving out, Carol "was getting depressed again. She was calling me up, wanting to come and spend a lot of time at my house, and I was worried again. I said, 'Are you okay? Do you need to go someplace? I'll help. Do you need to go to the hospital? Are you going to hurt yourself?' She said, 'No, no, I'm too chicken. I'm too scared. I would never do anything like that.'" Carol spent the weekend with Gretchen, and on Monday afternoon, when Gretchen returned from work and saw Carol's car there and "the lights were off, I was really panicked. So I went in and I found her. I just started screaming. I vaguely remember calling a very good friend of mine and she said to call 911, get out of the house, don't look at it. She'd hung herself." Afterward, Gretchen questioned her own behavior, whether she should have known what would happen, but then realized she had asked all of the right questions.

Gretchen organized a memorial service at the church she and Carol had attended. Although there was an outpouring of support from friends to "say their farewells," Gretchen feels that the "whole experience was so different because it was suicide. As far as we've come as a society, there's still that stigma around suicide. . . . People aren't sure how to react. If somebody's killed in a head-on collision, it's tragic, it's awful, but it's more acceptable. That acceptance level, coupled with the whole thing about the same-sex relationship, makes it difficult to find people to talk with about it." Gretchen experienced a lot of anger and disappointment toward Carol's parents, who did not accept Carol for "who she was in a lot of ways, and one is her sexuality. Although her parents came for the funeral and the memorial service, I did the memorial service and they did the funeral. Carol and I had had a commitment ceremony, so in my mind, we were spouses. But it was funny, at that point, after being totally nonsupportive for two years during her deep depression and two hospitalizations, her parents swooped in and made decisions about the funeral arrangements. But I thought that was not the important part. The important part to me was trying to honor Carol's life. Carol was a talented musician, so I invited some of our music friends, who performed at the memorial service, and it was fine."

In contrast to Carol's parents, Gretchen's father and stepmother were extremely supportive. When Gretchen called her father to tell him that Carol had committed suicide, he said "We're coming out." Gretchen said, "Before you do, I just want to talk to you about something we've never talked openly about. We've never really said the words, and I've never talked openly about the nature of my relationship with Carol. I don't want you to make the trip and not know fully. . . . He said, 'Oh, no,' and cut me off. I think he didn't want me to say it. It was kind of cute. He didn't want to hear the words uttered, but he said, 'No, no, it's okay. I know.' He acknowledged it. He said, 'That's not what's important. What's important is you need us and we're on our way.' So I was glad they were here that whole week. They just dropped everything and came."

Gretchen's workplace was not aware of her same-sex relationship with Carol until the obituary, in which she was listed as the surviving partner, appeared in the paper. Gretchen had spoken to a few people before Carol's death, but "It wasn't everybody's business. Anyway, some people who probably had wondered, but whom I hadn't said anything to, were really nice. It was good because they came up and tried to lend some support. The whole partner thing was just weird, because you're not quite as free to talk openly about it because you never know how some people are going to deal with it." Gretchen did experience pressure to return to work. "I felt there was a little bit of an expectation there . . . that they needed me to get back, . . . and I only took five days off." Although Gretchen believes a few more days would have helped her to cope with her grief and the nature of her partner's death, she also realized that she needed to keep busy.

Gretchen discussed several ways in which same-sex couples are discriminated against in our society. When Gretchen and Carol bought their house together, they received "funny looks and had to deal with two credit checks and the mortgage and all that. . . . The frustrating part in Carol's illness was that when she was let go from where she worked, I couldn't pick her up on my plan even though she was my marital partner—that just made additional stress. I got very frustrated."

Throughout Carol's struggle with serious depression, Gretchen felt extremely isolated. Because of Carol's parents' indifference to Carol's illness and their lack of support for the same-sex relationship, "my experience was that I started feeling really, really isolated and a lot of stress, because there wasn't anybody else to pick up the pieces. There was no local or active family on her side. We had our friend network, but it's not as if you could be totally out with everybody where you work. The daily reinforcement was lacking." Finally, Gretchen asked Carol's permission to "at least get some of our friends involved and talk about this. She agreed and it helped a little bit—broadened things a little, just trying to bounce things off of people and getting a little support."

Gretchen's memories of Carol four years after her death are mixed—sadness and the good times. "I teach lessons, and I play gigs, and just doing that and going through those motions, I often think of her. We used to perform in a couple of groups together. We had that common interest, that love of the arts and music, and that's still with me, so in a sense, the positive part is still with me. But you have those other times too, like, oh God, the sadness just floods in, and you say, 'Why?' We don't know why." (Gretchen is crying hard at this point.)

Gretchen is now in a new relationship and spoke about how she is able to keep memories of Carol separate from the new relationship. Gretchen goes to Carol's grave by herself most of the time, although once her new partner went with her and "it was fine. Initially, in my new relationship, memories of Carol would come in a lot because I was still grieving, and the smallest thing would allow those tragic, sad memories to come flooding in, all that hurt and loss. As the grief slowly decreased, there were fewer times when the grief about Carol came into the relationship with Marilyn. Occasionally it still happens. But at first I thought Marilyn was going to get so tired of me always crying over somebody else. We talked about that very openly. She had a very healthy attitude, that I'd loved that person and would always love that person, and it didn't diminish her. She was very supportive, in that if I needed time to cry or be by myself, I could do it." Gretchen spoke about how things get "stirred up in the new relationship that have nothing to do with the new relationship but are related to the lost partner. It is difficult for the bereaved partner to cope with that because it is not logical, it's just an emotional connection with that past that the new partner doesn't understand and isn't a part of."

Gretchen has changed in several ways since the death of her partner, Carol. She believes that "there's a certain seriousness because of what happened, because losing her makes you appreciate the little things and be more carefree. It's a bizarre mix, because you realize the importance of taking care of things and enjoying the moment. Before Carol died, Gretchen "became a very stressed-out, worried person, wondering what was going to happen to her (Carol), was she going to be safe, would we be able to pay for the care she needed. I just became a nonspontaneous, 'not-a-lot-of-fun' person. Carol's death and the way she died created an additional kind of awareness of taking your time to do what you want to do instead of going through the motions of what you have to do to please other people." Gretchen also believes that she is now good to herself and takes care of herself more. "I still work a lot—I've always been a bit of a workaholic—but I make time for things that I enjoy doing, whether that's playing the saxophone or spending time with friends, or making the effort to see my kindergarten buddy. Just making the effort to make those connections."

Gretchen believes that the most helpful aspect of her healing came through therapy. She saw a therapist with whom she already had a good bond, so that it was easier to deal with the aftermath of Carol's death. She also believes that her increased socialization with friends helped provide her with nurturing and support. In fact, Gretchen met her current partner, Marilyn, through some friends who "were trying to get me out because they knew I was going to isolate and be depressed all the time." Gretchen keeps her memories of Carol separate from her new relationship with Marilyn, partly because Marilyn's interests are different from Carol's. "My new partner played a musical instrument when she was younger, so she can appreciate my teaching children to play an instrument, but she's a scientist by profession and is in a lot of different circles. I think that's good, because instead of always talking about the same profession, it opens up new worlds for each of us. I also think, because her job and personality are very different from Carol's, when I spend time with Marilyn, I don't think that much about Carol. Maybe that's good, because it's truly a new relationship, and the connections I have to Carol are still through things that I'm still active with—teaching and performing." Although Gretchen still has contact with some of Carol's friends, "you honor those friendships, but when the connecting reason isn't there, it makes sense that those friends would drift away a little." Gretchen is pleased that both her friends and those of her new partner, Marilyn, "have blended well together."

Analysis

Gretchen's story presents struggles similar to those of Pauline. Both experienced lack of support from family and the workplace at the time they lost their partners. Gretchen felt isolated from Carol's parents because they neither approved of Carol's sexual orientation nor supported Carol during her deepest depression. At Carol's death, although Carol's parents attended the funeral and memorial service, they and Gretchen split the responsibilities for each service. Deevey (1997) found that families were hurtful or unhelpful at the time of bereavement if the families disapproved of the couple's sexual orientation. In contrast, as the literature suggests, families tended to be helpful if they had never been formally told about the relationship, but the lesbian daughter assumed they knew. In Gretchen's case, she found her father to be very supportive, despite the fact that she had never "formally" told him that she and Carol shared a lesbian partnership. Although Gretchen "had never really said the words," her father indicated that he knew about her sexual orientation.

However, Gretchen reported suffering from societal stigma regarding death from suicide. She believed that following Carol's death, people's uncertainty about how to react to her was intensified not only by her involvement in a lesbian relationship but discomfort with a death from suicide. Doka suggests that "how one dies can radically affect the level of support that survivors receive" (2002a:323). When deaths like suicide are stigmatized it limits the "social support" or shames survivors "so that they are reluctant to seek out support" (2002a:323). The experience of disenfranchisement relates to the cause of death, whether it stems from society's difficulty in addressing suicide or from the survivor who "internalizes the stigma experienced by the death" or feels embarrassed and isolated and experiences low self-esteem or inadequacy (Doka 2002a: 323, 327). Gretchen reported that she "questioned her own behavior" and wondered whether she should have known that Carol would commit suicide, but believed that she had asked all of the right questions.

Like Pauline, Gretchen found that following Carol's death, when she did open up about her lesbian partnership to certain colleagues at work, they tried to lend her support. This felt good to her. Again, perhaps lesbian women who have lost a partner need to take the risk of telling others. In doing so, they may receive much-needed support, because they are often a good judge of who will be supportive.

Gretchen's story presents a good example of a bereaved partner who has been able to maintain and yet change her relationship with her deceased partner. She has relocated the memory of her partner in a place that allows her to engage with her new partner, Marilyn, more fully. Rubin (1999) speaks of the importance of "maintaining and changing their relationships with the deceased" as a way of providing "warmth and solidity to the experience of the bereaved" (1999:696).

Gretchen demonstrates how a lesbian partner "takes in" the memory of the deceased partner by remembering her connections with Carol when she is involved with teaching music or playing the violin. These are activities that this lesbian couple shared. Gretchen claims that it is this very "taking in" that allows her to separate the two partners in her mind and fully enjoy her relationship with her new partner.

The following story provides a contrast to those of Pauline and Gretchen, who lost their partners to sudden death.

Denise

Denise was forty-eight years old when her lesbian partner, Diane, died at age fifty-one, after a four-year battle with ovarian cancer. Denise and Diane were involved in a twenty-year partnership. The couple met at work when they were both in heterosexual relationships. "We had never had a gay or lesbian relationship with anyone when we first met—we didn't even like each other—it was kind of funny." At ages twenty-one and twenty-four, Denise and Diane "started going out and we started to be friends. Within a couple of years, we discovered that we were falling in love with each other. It was a shock to both of us." Unlike Pauline and Gretchen, Denise and Diane "were never open—we were never out—so nobody in our family and none of our friends knew about our relationship. We lived together, but we were so careful about it. We were never physical in front of anybody as far as even kissing or holding hands or anything like that." When Diane died, Denise "felt like my life was over." Denise describes their relationship as one of "soul mates, as we were together practically constantly. We had a relationship that a lot of people don't have. It was a very, very special relationship."

Diane's cancer was diagnosed four years before she died and it was the last two years that were particularly difficult, because Diane had been in remission for almost two years following her chemotherapy. "At that point, when it came back, we had read about it and we knew things were not great—that things looked pretty bad. We were both very, very open. We had a great relationship, and at that point, we really started talking about the possibility of her passing. We discussed it but we didn't dwell on it. We said 'Okay, we understand these facts, but we're going together to give it our best shot and go with the stem cell transplant program.' We decided not to dwell on the negatives, but to see the positives and fight this together. We tried to maintain a normal life style, but at that point, when she started the transplant, she had to quit her job. It was just too much. It was high-dose chemo, and it was just too unbearable for her. Our lifestyle changed drastically at that point, because I would go to work and I would also be her caregiver. Looking back, at the time it was what I wanted to do. There was nothing that I wouldn't have done. I think my adrenalin was going so much that it just kept me doing things. Now I wonder how I did it all, but at the time, it was 'Just do it.' Things went up and down for awhile, as Diane needed dialysis and did well for a few months, but following a colostomy, "things started going downhill rapidly. That was just emotionally a pretty terrible time. But we never really gave up hope. No matter what the doctors wanted to try, Diane was more than willing. She was a fighter, and she was just going to do what ever it took. We drew strength from each other. Maybe I knew this at the time, but after I lost her, then I really discovered that a lot of my strength was tied in with hers. I just fell apart.

"When Diane passed away, I pretty much couldn't believe it, for one thing. The fact that she was just such a fighter, I just had this hope that she was somehow going to pull through. It was one of those times in September when they told us there was nothing more that they could do that I think I almost started realizing then that I was losing her. That time was just unreal, because we both knew that there was nothing else that could be done. We would just sit and talk about things. Diane never even had a will. She was as certain as I was that she was going to lick this thing. We had to talk about wills—we had to talk about things that you just never think that at your age you're going to have to deal with. She was very thorough, and she wanted to make sure everything was in order to make it easier on me. During her illness she tried to make it easy on everybody, especially me. She never wanted to be a burden—she never wanted me to quit work or stay home if I didn't need to."

Because Denise and Diane were never open about their lesbian relationship to anyone, including family, friends, and work colleagues, when Diane died, Denise found it very difficult to be treated as though she had lost her life partner. "Really, what do you do when you lose your partner and nobody really knows that you're partners?" Denise had many concerns about whether or not Diane's family was "going to give me the responsibility and the respect and the authority to do the things that I wanted to do with this funeral and viewing and everything else. It was a very, very nervous time for me. Not only was I completely distraught and depressed and beside myself, but I also had to wonder how this was all going to go down. At that time, I never had any intentions of saying anything to them. I was just overwhelmed with grief. In the back of my mind I'm thinking, 'Please don't give me a hard time. I know what I want to do; Diane and I discussed it.' Right before Diane died, she went into a coma, and that day we were supposed to meet with her two sisters because she wanted to tell them that whatever I wanted, I was in charge. She wanted to clear the air about a few things—she didn't want anyone to give me a hard time. She wanted it to be known that this was her wish. That never happened. She was not going to tell them about our relationship but was just going to set the record straight and say, 'If Denise wants to do this let her.' Luckily, since we did have good family relationships, her sisters and her one brother-in-law who lives here with his wife gave me full reign of what I wanted to do. They knew that I knew what Diane wanted. Looking back, I think it was more out of respect for Diane rather than because we were partners that they gave me the freedom to choose Diane's funeral plans."

However, Denise found it very difficult that others viewed her as "the friend, the grieving friend. That wasn't my lover, my partner, you know, my soul mate, there. That was a good friend of mine in the eyes of a lot of people. So in that respect it was very difficult, because you're not treated as a heterosexual partner would be treated as a spouse. People treat you as a friend, no matter how close of a friend you were—and people knew how close Diane and I were—it's still different. It's still not the same. I didn't really think about that ahead of time. That was something that never entered my mind. And why would it? We were perfectly fine with keeping our relationship hidden. It was never really an issue. We talked about it once or twice, especially when my brother died of AIDS, and that was a rough time. Yet we said, 'This is something we're comfortable with and this is how we're going to live.' We didn't care. But when I lost Diane, it became a very big issue for me. I felt like I had no one that I could talk to and say, 'You don't understand—I lost my spouse.' She was my best friend, but she was more than that. I knew real quick that I had to change that. I knew if I didn't, that I would go insane. I didn't want to live but feared killing myself and being in Hell while she was in Heaven—Catholic teaching."

During those early days following Diane's death, Denise found one person with whom she could share her feelings because she had accepted Denise's lesbian relationship with Diane prior to Diane's death. "There was this hospice nurse, who happened to also be a nun, who was unbelievable. When she walked into our home, she knew immediately it was just Diane and I, and we talked to her, and she approached me and knew. She came in and was open to it and said right away, 'I know exactly what you're going through as far as your partner.' When she said that, I was taken aback, but only for a second, because I trusted this woman so quickly. As soon as I met her there was something there that I knew she was going to be not only a help as a nurse but somehow spiritually. It was strange, but looking back, I said there was a reason that God sent her into our home. After Diane passed away, I stayed in touch with Mary." Because Denise could confide in Mary, with Mary's support, she was slowly able to confide in her three closest friends about her relationship with Diane. "These were three of my friends that I've known since high school, and I was scared to death to tell them something like that. I did it one-on-one, and each time the reaction was more than what I could have hoped for. Each one, in their own individual way, was so understanding and so supportive and just felt so bad. They all wondered why we didn't think they could handle knowing about our relationship. We (Denise and Diane) never even thought about that—it wasn't an issue. We were all friends and we were happy. It wasn't like we were trying to hide it—it was just our lifestyle. We were happy with it, but now that I didn't have her, I had to be open about this. I had to confide in somebody and be able to say that these are my feelings—this is what I am going through. I didn't just lose a friend. I started on my grieving path. I realized that I had to be open with a few friends, and I told my sister. She told me that she kind of had an inkling."

Denise went through an extremely difficult period of mourning following the loss of Diane. Although she returned to work after some time off, "I walked into my office and I cried. I couldn't focus on anything. I just shuffled papers and kept thinking this will get better. I was so angry. It was difficult for my coworkers. A lot of people just avoided me, while some people understood. It was like everyone was afraid to say her name. I wanted to talk about her. I didn't want them to ignore the fact that she even existed. I wanted to hear their pain too. Some of these people had worked with Diane for twenty years. The hardest thing was the fact that some people wouldn't come in and say, 'I understand how hard it is without Diane.' Just say her name—that's all I wanted. It was weird, because her family was the same way. I was struggling to find someone that I could say, 'I have to talk about Diane, you have to talk to me about her.'" Finally, Denise found support from one of her friends at work who was also a friend in whom she had confided about the nature of their relationship. This friend was sympathetic to Denise's expressions of grief about Diane, although she helped Denise to understand what makes it difficult for a young person to respond to someone who has lost a friend or partner. Denise's friend told her: "We don't know what to do, we don't know what to say, we've never gone through anything like this. We never lost a friend. You lost your partner, but I never had a friend who lost a partner. I don't know what to say." However, Denise found much relief in just being able to talk with her friend daily about the loss of Diane and felt she was beginning to stabilize her emotions.

Then, in a few months she "hit rock bottom" and wanted to commit suicide. "I woke up one morning and thought, 'This is it, I can't go on, this is useless, I have no life without Diane.' I just stayed at home, and my mind was going a mile a minute, and I thought, 'How can I do this?'" Denise called the hospice nurse and said, "I just want to die and I don't know how to do it." The nurse "talked me through it at that point and said, 'You have to go to a counselor because you've gone beyond where I can help and you need to see a counselor.' I didn't want any part of that. I told her, 'I'm not going to some stranger who I'm sure is not going to be able to help me.' She told me to try to get out of the house. I spent the rest of the morning figuring out whether or not I was going to live or die. I ended up going to work, plus my friend was calling me and saying, 'What are you doing?'"

Denise finally contacted a counselor, recommended by the hospice nurse, and was urged by two of her friends to try it out. "Once I told my friend that I had the appointment and was still debating whether or not to go, she came over and said, 'I'm not leaving until you leave.' She said, 'Diane would want you to go. Diane doesn't want you to kill yourself, and she doesn't want you to go on like this.'" Once Denise began therapy, she realized that her counselor was not going to be judgmental about her relationship with Diane. "I was sitting there, pouring out my life to this person that I just met. For some reason, there was a trust as soon as I met her. I told her from the very beginning that I was in a relationship that was hidden. Nobody knew that Diane and I were partners. She said, 'Stop right there. I just want you to know that I'm fine with that. I would never ever be judgmental; I have friends in the same type of relationships, and I just want you to know that, up front, I don't have a problem with that.'" Denise credits this counselor with saving her life. Denise was still in therapy with this counselor at the time she was interviewed, and "it was pretty much on a weekly basis. Once a week I would go down and spend an hour, and she got me through some really bad times. She turned my life around and saved my life. I'm talking about months of counseling through all the rough spots. She pretty much gave me hope. She held onto hope for me. I told her everything. I told her about the dreams I had, about the physical pain, spiritual pain, and emotional pain. There is nothing I would hold back from her, whereas with your friends, you say, 'Well, I don't know if they need to know this.'"

For a long time Denise did not have any dreams about Diane, and "I was dying to have contact with Diane. Denise kept Diane's memories alive by talking with her. " 'Please just talk to me, a vision, anything.' When Diane was sick and I would tell her that I didn't want to go on without her, she would say, 'It's not your time, and I will help you get through this.' We talked so much and those words just stayed in my mind. What did she mean? 'Are you coming back? Are you going to help me through other people? Are you going to come back and sit with me in the living room? What are you going to do?'" Looking back, Denise realizes that she was in such deep grief during the first few months after Diane's death that "you're just so unaware of anything. When you're in that deep grief somebody would have to come and hit you over the head and say, 'Here I am, look at me.' I journal a lot. I put my dreams down and ask my counselor for an interpretation, but she told me she wasn't into dreams but did know a bit. We'd talk and I'd give her my interpretation, and that was helpful. Journaling played an active role in my healing. It was the best way for me to look at my feelings. When I would write, I didn't hold anything back. I would let the words flow. This was a tremendous help and still is as I look back and see all that I documented."

Denise found that she began to have flashbacks about the time when Diane was sick. "I was having some hard times with that. My whole grief process, I presume, was normal. You go along one day and you think you're doing okay, then you hit bottom and you're there for a couple of days, and then you go back up a little bit, then you go back down." Denise tried to get away by visiting her sister, but it seemed so painful "it was not really worth it. You think about it ahead of time, and you think this is going to be good—I need to get away—and then you come back and think, 'Why did I go?'"

Now that Diane has been gone for almost nine months, "I'm beginning to notice the difference as far as the easing up a little bit. I had so much anger and was so hard on myself. No matter what I did, I was wrong. I was just beating myself up about everything. I didn't want to do anything for myself. I lost about twenty-five pounds within a month, and I wasn't eating or sleeping. Now I'm easing up on myself. You have to like yourself, and you have to learn to love yourself, or you're going to be in bad shape."

After her suicidal ideation subsided, Denise "made the commitment that I'm going to live. 'Do you want to be depressed and have no life or do you want to try and make something out of your life and show Diane that you are grateful to her and to God for everything that's she given you, for the years that you spent together.' I got to the point where I thought there has to be some good that comes out of this. There has to be a lesson."

With her counselor's help, Denise came to realize that there had to be a reason why she was still alive and "realized that, spiritually, I had to get to a point where I had to regain my faith in God and make a difference in somebody's life. There was a reason why Diane left and went on to the next life, and there is a reason why I'm still here. I'm not exactly sure what it is, but I know that I'm compelled now to get into some kind of volunteer work. I want to do something that's a tribute to Diane's memory."

Although Denise is not yet certain what her contribution will be, she is currently involved in healing her physical, emotional, and spiritual self. "When I made the commitment that I'm going to turn my life around I started reading a lot of books about spirituality and that helped emotionally. I began meditation and I ran my first 'Race for the Cure,' which I did in honor of Diane—in her memory. I feel more than ever that she's with me and that she has been all along."

Denise keeps memories of Diane close to her and is now in the process of changing her relationship with Diane's memory by shifting from "remembering her at her sickest point in the sunroom" to feeling that "I had to kind of release that from my mind and really remember her as I want to remember her, before her illness." Denise has used certain rituals to make this shift, such as "changing the one chair she sat in to a different location. I'd go out to the porch and it would be like she should be sitting there, so I'd cry and couldn't stay out there. Now I'm to the point where I did these couple of things, and at least I'm able to be out there and remember her before she was really, really sick." Denise has also decided to remain in the house that she and Diane shared, but to work at making the garden look the way she'd like it to look. "Maybe not plant the exact kind of flowers but do something a little bit different."

During the summer that followed Diane's death, Denise traveled to Omega Institute in New York. "This holistic learning center was extremely helpful. I knew I had to learn to do things alone. Omega was the first place I tried to do that. I was told that it was a safe place, and I would be with like-minded people. I was scared, but I did it." Denise traveled to Omega three times during that summer and was drawn to workshops led by authors whose books she read after Diane's death. "I proved to myself that I was capable of traveling alone. My self-esteem needed all the help it could get. All of my trips played a vital role in my healing process. I was finding out who I was. I was discovering that I could do things without Diane. Not that I wanted to, but I could."

Denise believes that she has changed dramatically since Diane's death. "I think it's going to be a change for the good, because I think I'm going to find my spirituality—a deeper spirituality than what I ever had. I was always a Catholic, but it's beyond my Catholicism. I read so many different books about Buddhism—for some reason I'm drawn to that right now. I'm learning different ideas and becoming more aware of things in the spirit world. I just firmly believe that there is another dimension, that Diane is not gone per se, but that her spirit is still here with me now."

Denise believes that if she is patient she will discover how she can make a difference as a result of Diane's death. "Patience is something I really have to concentrate on, because I find myself still wanting to make Diane proud of me. I want her to know that I grieve, but the gratitude I have for our lives together is something that I'll have for the rest of my life. The relationship we had was very, very special. The years that we had together were tremendous, and I'm compelled to make sure that her memory lives on."

Denise does have some regrets about not having been more open about her relationship with Diane. However, she is aware that when she and Diane began their same-sex relationship it was 1975, and "we were working in the same company, which was not really open minded. I think that would have been a problem. . . . Looking back, I regret not telling my mom. She adored Diane and saw her as another daughter. I think she probably would have been okay with it. I guess I'm saying that now because the people that I talked to are so open. I almost think I want to tell the world, but what good will it do, because you still run into the prejudices that are out there. You still have to be careful. There are still people that say you're a friend, but when you tell them something like that, then guess what, things change."

Just before Denise went on a trip to a ranch, "I decided that another part of my healing process was to admit to others, and myself, that I was a lesbian. This was something I never thought I would do. However, it was clear that I couldn't run from this if I was going to continue to heal. I came out to family and friends. It was the turning point in my grief process, because now I was truly discovering this new person that I was becoming. It took a couple of months to tell the people most important to me. Now it is a nonissue. It is second nature, and I am very proud of who I am, and even more proud of the relationship that Diane and I shared. I have gone full circle—from hiding it all to now being totally open about everything. What a freeing feeling. This was probably one of the best decisions I made in that first year and by far the most difficult."

Several months later, in a letter to me following her interview, Denise shared other major changes that have occurred in her life since Diane's death. Denise believed that she needed more direction in her life and left a job she had had for thirty years to return to college and obtain a degree in social work. "I have set goals for myself and plan to pursue a career of helping others, and in the process, I will be helping myself reclaim new meaning in my life." Denise has been invited to volunteer at a bereavement support center in the city where she lives. She has been working with the executive director to help get this organization on its feet.

Denise believes that "the best tribute you can give someone is the life you live after they are gone. I will never forget Diane. I will never stop loving her. I want her to be proud of me, and I want to remain open to the different avenues I am being pulled towards. I still believe that Diane is helping me to find what it is I am supposed to be doing." Denise believes that the "loss of my partner has been a life-changing experience that has ripped my heart out and exposed it to the world. Though extremely painful, this has helped me see life much differently. I believe that I have become a more compassionate and loving human being. Perhaps another way of saying it is that I am a better person for having loved Diane and having gone through the pain of losing her. Yet, it seems as though there should be an easier way."

Analysis

Denise's story represents a departure from that of Pauline and Gretchen because she and Diane met at work when they were both in heterosexual relationships. Although Denise did not experience lack of support from either her family or Diane's, she did find it extremely difficult to function in a world where no one knew that her relationship with Diane went beyond friendship. Denise and Diane had been completely closeted about their lesbian relationship, and this proved to be a disadvantage to Denise following Diane's death. As the literature on disenfranchised loss (Doka 1989, 2002b) suggests, when a partner suffers a loss that "cannot be openly acknowledged, publicly mourned, or socially supported" (Doka 1989:4), the grief of this bereaved partner is disregarded because society does not recognize the relationship of lesbian partners.

As Doka (1989, 2002b) suggests, the emotions experienced by the bereaved are often intensified in a nontraditional relationship. This certainly seems to be true in the case of Denise, who became suicidal. She movingly asked, "Really, what do you do when you lose your partner and nobody really knows that you are partners?" Denise found her grief to be extremely isolating because she was viewed as a "grieving friend." As she so clearly states, "in that respect it was very difficult, because you are not treated as a heterosexual partner would be treated, as a spouse."

Following Diane's death, she had no one that she could talk to and say, "You don't understand; I lost my spouse." Denise changed that situation quickly. She was able to confide in a hospice nurse and three friends who she thought might support her in her grief. To her pleasant surprise, she found her friends to be very supportive and wondered why she hadn't thought they could handle knowing about the nature of her relationship with Diane. This theme is similar to one expressed by both Pauline and Gretchen, who had assumed they wouldn't get support from others, and so were reluctant to say anything. Yet, when they did share with others, they found the support they needed and realized that they are often capable of judging who will be supportive. If lesbian partners could take the risk and trust their judgment, perhaps they could handle the unpredictable responses from society that Deevey (1997) claims are a source of stress and fear in the lives of lesbian women who have lost partners.

Denise has developed a way to have a continuing relationship with her deceased partner, Diane, by talking with her about issues and by dreaming about Diane and recording the process. In fact, her ongoing relationship with Diane was the key her counselor used to help Denise understand that she still wanted to live. Denise's counselor told her, "Diane would not want you to kill yourself and doesn't want you to go on like this." Memories of Diane are beginning to shift, from those that remind Denise of the time when Diane was most ill to those of Diane prior to her illness. As Rubin (1999) has pointed out, if memories remain "frozen" in time they tend to draw emotional energy from the bereaved and can impair functioning. Once the memories are available in a balanced way, they can provide a measure of strength and warmth to the bereaved partner. After eleven months, this is beginning to occur for Denise.

Just as the postmodern writers (Neimeyer 1998; Klass et al. 1996; Rubin 1999) have suggested, Denise has made some profound changes in her life since Diane's death. She has learned to ease up on herself and to love herself. Denise left her job of thirty years to return to college for a degree in social work so that she can find meaning for herself in helping others. Her first step was to become involved in a Race for the Cure in Diane's memory. She has also decided to make meaning from the loss of Diane by doing some volunteer work for a new bereavement support center that is a tribute to Diane's memory. Diane has deepened her spiritual self by becoming involved in meditation and Buddhism.

Lea

Lea was forty-six when her partner, Corky, died from cancer at forty-seven. Lea is a special-education teacher who has a twenty-three-year-old son. She had been divorced for more than twenty-five years when she and Corky met. They met professionally, and within about six months formed a close friendship, which developed into a loving partnership. At the beginning of their relationship, Lea was aware of her own sexual orientation but did not share that with Corky, who had not yet come out as a lesbian. At first they would go to a movie or out to dinner. Then Lea and Corky "started hanging out in small groups and talking a lot. . . . I think from her perspective, I can think back over twelve years ago, I've never seen anyone more excited at the prospect of learning their sexual orientation. She rejoiced in it. She accepted it with open arms and felt as if she were finally home. She had been raised in a fundamentalist Christian environment that forbid her from even thinking that was the case as a youngster. So she repressed it, and it tormented her throughout most of her life." Both Lea and Corky were in their late thirties when they entered into a lesbian partnership. "We were the sisters we never really had. We became family to each other. We loved each other as any two adults certainly do."

Throughout her relationship with Lea, Corky remained married to an abusive husband with whom she had three children. Corky stayed with her husband and children most of the time for the sake of the children. "I respected that. We worked together seven days a week—from the moment we got up in the morning until about midnight. She went home to help her children with their homework, cook their meals, go to their baseball games." About six years before Corky's diagnosis of cancer, "I purchased a house at the beach which was ours. We decorated and set up the house together."

At first Lea and Corky lived together three days of the week, but during Corky's diagnosis, Corky moved in permanently. "We lived together for three days out of the week for many years, and then we moved in my home for two years toward the end. We had a live-in relationship, a commitment ceremony—we had a partnership. That was the good stuff. The bad stuff was that she came from a community that was very myopic in their thinking on this issue. Corky came to the realization that she had to be silenced. So we remained silent. Her husband was not aware. He was not told by us or anyone else that we were in a relationship. He had let go of her long before, certainly sexually and socially. We had a community of friends. We had a family unit. But we were very much old-school, in that we saw no reason to put it in the faces of our children if our children elected not to want that. Why would they want to know that when they could be raised in heterosexual family units? God bless the young guys and gals coming up through the ranks and making babies and saying 'This is daddy and daddy and this is mommy and mommy, and this is how you were conceived.' It's marvelous, but we weren't in that group. We were both born in 1950, and we both had a clear understanding that our maternal instincts dominated. There were four kids between us, and we did what we thought was in their best interest, and we sacrificed as mothers do. I'm not out to my son formally."

By the time Corky was diagnosed with cancer, it had spread to her bones, her liver, and her lung. The cancer center told her and Lea that although the usual time remaining is six months, with experimental treatments and special nutrition to maintain her weight, Corky could live one to three years. At this point, Lea and Corky were advised that Lea should get legal power of attorney because Corky's husband might give them a difficult time in allowing the type of treatments that Lea wanted. Corky told Lea, "Absolutely, I'll give power of attorney to Lea as primary and to you (to a physician friend of theirs) as secondary."

Soon Lea discovered that what was best for Corky was for Lea to obtain a medical power of attorney. "So we rewrote it, she signed it, and we then took her from the care of her husband's physician to a special cancer center and to our friend who was a physician." During most of this time Lea felt that "there was no one accepting of the relationship between me and Corky." Lea's husband was still the "legal person," because Lea did not have her own insurance card but was on her husband's medical plan. When Corky explained to Lea's husband that the specialized cancer center could offer more time, "He reluctantly said, 'Okay, here, you can have the card; you take her for the treatments.'" Lea did so and fed her and provided for her. Before receiving care for her cancer, Corky had contracted hepatitis and was never given the proper care for this serious illness. Lea even felt that the specialized cancer center had a "very formal, strained professional relationship" with her over Corky's illness.

Corky endured many treatments for her cancer, but Lea believes that the last year of Corky's life "was a good year. . . . We had parties and luncheons with friends almost daily." Things went well until "Corky's husband, sisters, and parents decided that the routine of her only going home on the weekends and them having to take care of her a little bit on the weekends was a drag. . . . I don't know how to say it. They were truly wanting it to be over. Of course, she did get sicker. Toward the end, she was more difficult to care for. I would have cared for her at that stage for the rest of my life. The fact is—she was not in intolerable pain, which hospice helped me with. Corky's sister flew in and wanted to dominate the situation. At no point was I challenged as far as being the primary caregiver. Even when she chose to spend that last two weeks at home, knowing that she was going to die and feeling that it was in her kids' best interest to die at home and not to be humiliated by dying in the home of her girlfriend. . . . When the family gathered with the family physician, they took the case away from me. Her sister said, 'Well, this cancer center isn't making any progress—I mean she's going to die anyway.' And the family doctor said, 'Yeah she's gonna die anyway.' Her sister said, 'This is going to be a load of litigation. A woman who has medical power of attorney, but there's a legal husband and two sisters, a brother, a mother and father who are opposed to the continuation of treatment.'"

The specialized cancer center terminated the treatment. Previously, the cancer center had told Lea that the treatments were working and she was maintaining her weight. "In the most horrendous bedside manner, the physician in charge said, 'There's nothing more I can do.' Well, the prior week he had said, 'The treatments are working, things are going well, you're maintaining your weight. There are no more tumors on the liver.'"

"When we got back to the house, Corky said, 'Why didn't you tell me that I was going to die?' I said, 'I don't know that you're going to die. Unlike the doctor, I don't play God, and I suggest we go over to another cancer center and pick it up again.' We went at it for about fifteen minutes, and she convinced me at the end of that time that she wanted to let it go. Without the chemotherapy, it was a death sentence. So medically, the cancer center was superb. But when push comes to shove, and partners are involved, and there's potential litigation from either a parent or a sibling, you're up the creek."

Following the episode with the cancer center, "for the first time in those twelve years, the rumors started to circulate that I was not only a dominant friend that tried to take medical control, but that Corky and I were in a relationship, because no friend would care for another friend the way that I did. At least that's what most people think, because friends do do that for friends. One day, when I was leaving the hospital and I was sobbing, a woman approached me the way that you would approach a wounded animal and screamed at me that I had some nerve taking Corky away from her beloved husband and children."

Lea soon found that Corky's sister was not supportive of Lea's involvement and help with Corky's care. "She must have been told by Corky's husband that I hurt his marriage by giving her a job and being her friend and being aggressive . . . *aggressive,* which is the code word for *lesbian, dyke.* When Corky called her mom to tell her that she had cancer, Corky was quite upset when her mom said to her, 'What are you doing at Lea's house?' I said, 'Tell her it's serious cancer and you need her love and support.' She said it into the phone and her mother said, 'Go home to your husband.' Corky said, 'Well, Mom, I don't know what this is about, because Lea's helping me with this, and if you want me, I'll be here.' Her mother said, 'I won't call you at that house.' But she did call, and the calls weren't easy for Corky.

"I had to fight the disease with Corky, and I had to fight her entire family and entire community. It was the most bizarre case of homophobia I think I've ever seen. If I had to put my finger on it, I would say that people from that community and her family did not support Corky in her time of need. Although she had been great friends to them for many years, they did not reciprocate. I believe that they feared the unknown of the political bisexual; the idea of what they consider to be a married woman moving out into the gay community was not accepted. They don't like their choice or their lifestyle. They're horribly threatened, particularly men, with the concept that another woman can come in and take someone's wife away. I didn't take Corky away—he (her husband) had lost. Corky had set up a file for divorce long before she met me. Strangely enough, she realized when she met me that she couldn't proceed with that, because if she had lived with me, she would lose custody of her kids."

The one outside source of support for Lea was the hospice organization with which Lea and Corky became involved in order to help manage Corky's pain near the end of her life. "The hospice nurses came in and said, 'What's going on here? Why do you have power of attorney?' And I said, 'I'm a partner, and there's a husband,' and they said, 'Well, forget him.' The hospice nurses had met him, evaluated the situation, and legally looked at the fact that I had the right to be requesting the meds. Every single one of them, even the ones who might not have known anything about dealing with gays and lesbians, were respectful and absolutely incredible. That was the one group that was not from our community that was marvelous."

During the last three weeks of Corky's life, the hospice chaplain came to talk with Corky, and between the two of them, they decided that Corky should spend her final weeks in the home with her children and husband. Lea "feared Corky's quality of life more than I feared my loss. As a mother, I accepted her choice and carried her back out to her home. When she entered that home, I told hospice that 'I need backup, because it's been my experience that when she's in this house, she's not getting the meds all around the clock that she needs.' You can't miss a dose and, for whatever reason, they apparently withheld it. She was in excruciating pain. She did experience some bruising where her husband said he dropped her. She was bruised on her face. I called hospice, but her husband wouldn't let hospice in the house."

Lea derived her strength during this ordeal from having cared for her mother, who had died from a chronic illness shortly before Corky was diagnosed. In addition, Lea's extended family, including aunts, uncles, and cousins, were very supportive. "We also had a lot of good friends." When Corky was still living with Lea, the hospice organization recommended that Corky write a letter to her children to be opened on graduations and weddings. In addition, Corky decided to plan her own funeral. Lea and Corky together created the service "as we thought it should go." Lea became acutely aware of Corky's lack of denial about her impending death when she sat up and said, "I want you to get your butt out there and go on with your life and live it for both of us." Corky even described the person that she thought Lea should look for following her death. This helped Lea to have "some idea of how much love this woman had for me."

After Corky's death, making the final funeral arrangements was difficult. Corky's husband did not like the idea of cremation, although Corky had clearly stated that this is what she wanted. At that point, Lea "reached over and lightly touched his shoulder to get his attention to look at me, and I said, 'You're doing as you have always done, precisely what you want and not what she wants, and I won't have it. I will pay for this funeral.' He backed off. He feared at that moment that I was going to make a laughing stock of him in the community. The funeral service went exactly as Corky had planned."

The months following Corky's death were very difficult for Lea. "I came out of it without any of that inner strength. That all got used up. I came out of it with nothing left for me. I walked away from it having lost my future, my present, the joy of the past with her. I also realized that if I ever allowed myself to love again, to that degree, that I wouldn't survive another loss. I sold the business that we owned together. I couldn't practice without Corky. My credentials went in a box with her death." The hospice organization realized Lea's struggle and sent a "brilliant counselor, who started the process of helping me to cope with the loss and the grief—the work I needed to do to get myself back on my feet. Slowly, I stopped selling things and throwing things away, making believe that they would no longer hurt. . . .After some time, I did sell the house that we bought together and agonized over that one, because the memories were there—our commitment ceremony took place there."

Lea believes that she has changed in many ways since Corky's death. "I shifted gears from academia and a service profession to going back to where I started as a retailer—something I had never done with Corky. I've changed considerably. I'm certainly a softer, kinder, more introspective person than I was. I think I was a real hard-core businesswoman, who was much more aggressive in my quest for fixing things and improving the quality of life for the people I love. What I learned from this experience is that there are things I can't fix, and I didn't know that at the tender age of forty-six. I had previously been called 'the fixer,' and that label is gone forever. I never use the word *forever* anymore. I find people will say to me, 'We're going to be friends forever,' and I can't allow myself to reciprocate. I can't allow myself because I don't know what that word means anymore."

Lea believes that she carries her relationship with Corky forward because "half of who I am is because of my relationship with her." Lea has never been affiliated with a religious group as an adult, although she was trained as a youngster in a Christian Orthodox religion. Lea does not have any faith in an afterlife and claims, "It's a whole lot easier for those people who have faith." Although Lea is now involved in a relationship with another woman "who is marvelous, it's not the same—nor could it or would it be—it's not even at the same level as it was with Corky in that first year. But it's a marvelous relationship."

In terms of memories of Corky, Lea says, "She's always with me. She will always be with me. I've tried to let my new friends, who didn't know her, know her better by telling them a little about Corky. They're very receptive to learning more about her because that's a way of getting to know me.

I have a picture of Corky that people have told me to take out of the bed-room. . . . I feel Corky's presence in terms of decision making and how I would have kicked an idea around with Corky. It's not really a conversa-tion, but relates to her thinking process when I knew her and how she would have analyzed and evaluated the situation."

Lea believes that including Corky's story in this book is one of the ways that she has chosen to honor Corky's life. Lea said, "I wouldn't be here if I didn't think she wanted me to be telling you everything I'm telling you. I knew her best. I talked to a couple of friends last night, and they told me to answer any questions you had about Corky, because this is what she would have wanted. Corky loved to write. She kept a journal and a diary. Before she died, she said, 'We've got to somehow tell the story so people will make the choice that's in their own best interest.' Corky wanted the story writ-ten, and she basically wanted it said that although she laughed at the very political gays and lesbians who were constantly talking about 'you have to come out,' she would not have come out in the political sense, but she would have made the break from her marriage to be with the one she loved. That's something she would have done differently and part of the process of coming out to yourself. The realization that you're making a choice with a different life partner puts you in a category where you will be the recipi-ent of prejudice."

Lea has also chosen to honor Corky's life by creating a pet-loss bereave-ment foundation at the local hospice where Lea and Corky received sup-port. Corky loved all animals—"the dogs, the cats, the birds, the guinea pigs, the rabbits—she probably had close to fourteen animals at one time, and she talked to the animals. I've never seen anyone with animals the way this woman was with animals." Lea has just suffered the loss of a pet she had for eighteen years, which provided "the last link to my mom and Corky—it brought up a lot of that stuff from the past." Lea is now using services for herself from the pet-loss bereavement program that she helped to create at the hospice.

Lea openly discussed the fact that, although she has dated others since Corky's death, Corky was "the one and only love of my life." Lea believes that she will live with another partner, but "I don't think I'll ever give that much of myself to another human being. I gave Corky 100 percent. She re-ciprocated with 100 percent, and that percentage that I no longer have to give died with her. Because I am who I am, and I love my life and have a zest for life, I always will give 80 percent." Lea believes that in any first, strong relationship there is a recognition that you shared a lot of yourself in that relationship. When you become involved in a new relationship there is probably "a holding back of oneself from a new relationship in some way that may not have been present in the first relationship." Lea believes that this is healthier in some ways, because you emerge as a person, "more than as just a part of the other person."

Lea also shared her impressions of what occurs when lesbian partners lose their partner. "When death occurs for those partners who have been together for seven years or more, there are no legal ties. Usually there are no children. When death occurs, it's different from a breakup. Some of them will react with blood and guts—I had my first panic attack of my life when Corky was diagnosed. I had my second panic attack when I buried her. I never had that happen to me, ever. It happened when I started to try to fall asleep. When I was out of control, I woke up screaming. I don't see that with other partners. I've buried a lot of lesbian friends and I've sat with their partners and I've seen their partners pair off within three months into another 'business' relationship. Right or wrong, that's the way it is." Lea believes that it was different for her and Corky because they both had children and came from the world where they were both "moms." "The extreme devotion, love, and lifelong commitment that we had for each other exists, but not in huge numbers within the gay population." Lea believes that, in general, whether partner loss occurs through death or separation, lesbian women partner again very quickly. When I shared the difficulty I was experiencing in locating lesbian partners for this book, Lea said that she believes that early partnering following a death contributes to the difficulty, because "the new partner really doesn't want their partner to share about the loss they've experienced."

Analysis

Lea's story demonstrates the negative effects of a homophobic community upon the bereavement process of a lesbian partner. Like the previous narratives, the theme of disenfranchised grief described by Doka (1989, 2002b) is clearly apparent. Lea found that once some of the community members discovered that she had been more than a friend to Corky, they became hostile and abusive toward her. Lea felt that she had to fight the disease with Corky, and once Corky died, Lea had to "fight her entire family and community." Lea believes that the idea of a married woman moving out into the gay community was not accepted and led to the increased difficulty she had in receiving necessary support when she was grieving. Lea discovered that Corky's mother was angry that Corky chose to live some of her last days with Lea instead of her husband. Lea also found that, although she and Corky had obtained a medical power of attorney, so that Lea could help make decisions about Corky's care, no one, including the doctors and the hospital, accepted this document. Lea's grief was again disenfranchised when she was unable to facilitate the type of medical treatment that she and Corky wanted. The one community agency that supported Corky and Lea in their lesbian relationship was the hospice organization, which was respectful of their needs.

As with the other lesbian partners whose stories are described in this chapter, although Lea found the months following Corky's death very difficult, she believes that she has changed in many ways since her partner's death. Lea changed her career, moving from academia and a service profession to retail. Lea had no experience with this type of career when she was living with Corky and now finds it more supportive of her needs. Lea also sees herself as a softer, kinder, more "introspective person." She believes that she learned, from her experience of Corky's death, not "to fix" things as aggressively as she did before Corky's death. She will also never use the word *forever* anymore.

Despite her involvement in a new relationship, Lea remains connected to Corky through active memories of her. "She's always with me. She will always be with me." Just as with some of the other lesbian partners, Lea allows her new friends to get to know her better by describing Corky to them. Lea also experiences Corky's presence when she is making a decision "in terms of how she would have analyzed and evaluated the situation."

Rubin speaks of how the bereaved "transform the relationship with the deceased into something more" (1999:687) in formal or informal memorials. Lea has chosen to honor Corky's life by including her story is this book. Corky loved to write, kept a diary, and wanted her story told. Before her death, Corky said, "We've got to somehow tell the story so people will make the choice that's in their own best interest." Lea has also memorialized Corky's life by creating a pet-loss bereavement foundation at the local hospice where she and Corky received support. Corky loved animals, so that this memorial is a way for Lea to transform her relationship with Corky into "something beyond grief and mourning" (Rubin 1999:687) and enter Corky's memory into the fabric of her own life.

The following story is similar to Lea's, in that both partners died from a serious illness. In addition, their partners remained married while in a lesbian relationship, because their spouses had serious emotional problems that they feared would have negative effects on their children.

Pat

Pat was fifty-one years old when her partner of twelve years died from serious side effects of treatment for a brain tumor. Pat is an office manager, and her partner, Francine, was a tennis instructor. Pat has been divorced for twenty years and has three adult daughters. Two of her daughters are thirty-two-year-old twins, and the other daughter is twenty-eight and newly married. Pat has two grandchildren. Francine was never divorced from her husband. She lived with Pat most of the time and spent the last year of her illness in Pat's home, where Pat cared for her. Francine did not want to divorce her husband, a Vietnam veteran, because of his serious mental and emotional problems.

As Pat told the story of Francine's illness, she began to cry and cried at several points during the interview. "Francine was in good health, but one day she was driving down the highway and had a little seizure. Following this, she lost the use of her left leg, and then her whole left side didn't move. I took her to the emergency room. Her brain tumor was diagnosed and she started radiation treatments." After three months Francine returned to work on a limited basis and was walking with a cane. Several months later, her neurosurgeon ordered an MRI and discovered that the tumor was growing again. We went to Sloan Kettering for experimental chemotherapy treatments, but the side effects were difficult for Francine. She was run down and couldn't even get out of bed." Although Francine had a few extra weeks of normal life during the experimental chemotherapy treatments, she developed pneumonia, which could not be treated. Because she had extreme difficulty breathing, she was admitted to the hospital, where she slipped into a coma for three weeks. When she regained consciousness, the doctors performed a tracheotomy to enable her to breathe. However, because of Francine's loss of weight and body functions, Pat had to locate an appropriate nursing home for the final days of Francine's life. This was a very difficult time for Pat, because Francine was so confused, and Pat had total responsibility for securing an appropriate facility.

Although Pat was providing all of the care for Francine, she was denied access to the doctors' consultations. The doctors provided Francine's husband with information, and he was willing to sign so that she could continue with the experimental treatments, which both Pat and Francine's sister opposed. Pat was surprised that she was denied access to the doctors who were caring for Francine, because she and Pat had secured medical power of attorney for each other. Furthermore, Francine's mother-in-law was very angry that Pat had secured this medical power of attorney.

Pat and Francine's sister planned a memorial service for Francine, which Francine's husband attended. The service was held at a summer camp where Francine had been employed. Francine's ashes were spread over the lake near the camp. Pat's family was very supportive during this time.

An important factor that has helped Pat to cope with her grief has been the support of her own family. Although Pat has never told her family directly about her same-sex relationship with Francine, she suspects that they know about the relationship and have always respected and loved both her and Francine. Pat's three adult children and her father have been available to her on a regular basis. Pat visits with her family on weekends, which are the toughest time for her. Pat also enjoys her relationship with Francine's sister, who lives on the West Coast. Pat and Francine's sister exchange visits on a regular basis and find it comforting to share memories of Francine. Pat also keeps a connection with Francine through Francine's former employer when Pat spends time stringing tennis racquets at his store. She finds these times very special as they exchange memories of Francine.

Pat has found therapy with a chaplain at a hospital to be very therapeutic. Soon after Francine's death, Pat attended a mixed grief group but found it difficult to continue because all of the bereaved partners were spouses. Pat felt uncomfortable discussing the real nature of her relationship with Francine within this group, and instead referred to Francine as her deceased friend. Pat has explored various resources for same-sex partner-loss groups but has found nothing available within a reasonable commute.

The most difficult aspect of the loss of Francine has been the loneliness. "Trying to fill the void of Francine's loss is so hard." Pat is learning to do some things on her own and has finally gone to a movie alone, but "I haven't yet attempted dinner out." Pat has no interest in finding someone else and thinks about her relationship with Francine every day. However, she has been crying less often and is hoping she can move forward during the next year.

Pat feels that she has become "more skeptical of people" since Francine's death and says, "I've learned to depend on no one." Friends have disappointed her by not helping her with household chores since Francine's death. In fact, one best-friend couple of both Pat and Francine, who were supportive during Francine's illness, have avoided Pat since Francine's death. She calls them, but "they never call me." Pat also believes that she has become "more withdrawn into herself" and is moodier since Francine's death.

On the positive side, Pat finds that gardening is a real source of pleasure and feels that "I'm doing gardening as a tribute to Francine." Pat never enjoyed gardening before; Francine was the one who enjoyed nature and gardening. Pat also appreciates the outdoors more as a result of her relationship with Francine and says, "I'm walking more than ever before and loving it." Pat also finds that just being out of doors is a comfort to her. It provides a link to her relationship with Francine, who was so involved in outdoor activities. "I think of Francine when I'm outside." Pat has considered moving to a new house but believes that she will wait until her retirement. Although Francine was very sick during the last year that the couple lived together, Pat continues to enjoy the happy memories of the many years they spent together in her house.

Analysis

Unlike Pauline, Gretchen, and Denise, but like Lea, Pat did receive a great deal of support from her own family following the loss of Francine. This support has been paramount in her beginning recovery. As the literature (Deevey 1997) indicates, women who found their families most helpful, although they had never formally told their parents about their lesbian relationships, were women who simply assumed their parents knew. This was clearly the case with Pat, who stated that she suspected that her family knew about her lesbian relationship with Francine and that her family respected and loved both her and her partner.

Like most of the other lesbian partners, Pat discovered that securing a medical power of attorney did not allow her access to the doctors, who were making decisions about Francine's care without her input. Just as Lea found with her ill partner, the doctors relied instead upon the input from the patient's husband. This kind of behavior only increases the grief felt by a partner who has provided all of the care during a prolonged illness, and it is an example of disenfranchisement.

Pat keeps her connection to Francine alive in several ways. She enjoys an ongoing relationship with Francine's sister and Francine's former employer, with whom she shares many memories of Francine. Pat has also "taken in" some of the qualities of Francine, such as her love of the outdoors and, in particular, gardening. Pat never enjoyed gardening before the loss of

Francine but now finds real pleasure in this activity. She finds that being out of doors provides a link to Francine, whom she thinks about when she is outside.

CHAPTER SUMMARY

The theme of disenfranchised grief is present in all but one of the narratives of the lesbian women who shared their stories in this book. After Jean's tragic death, Pauline found that her life partnership with Jean was not acknowledged by family, neighbors, or colleagues. Instead, the community viewed her as Jean's roommate or friend. Pauline also felt that the responses from her own family were not positive. Although her mother and brother attended Jean's funeral service, her father did not attend. It was very difficult for Pauline to contact Jean's parents because Jean's father and brother had never supported her relationship with Pauline. Pauline was very hurt that Jean's family never mentioned her in the obituary they prepared following Jean's death.

Following Carol's death, Gretchen felt isolated from Carol's parents because they did not approve of Carol's sexual orientation. These reactions seem to support Deevey's (1997) research, which suggests that families were hurtful or unhelpful at the time of bereavement if they disapproved of the couple's sexual orientation. Although Denise received support from her family and Diane's, she found it extremely difficult to function in a world where no one knew the nature of their relationship, assuming that it was a friendship. Denise, feeling more and more isolated without the support of a community, considered suicide. Lea's story demonstrates the negative effects of a homophobic community upon the bereavement process of a lesbian partner. During the final stages of Lea's partner's life, when some of the community members discovered the nature of Lea and Corky's relationship, they became hostile and abusive toward her. Lea believes that because the idea of a married woman moving out into the gay community was not considered acceptable, she experienced increased difficulty in receiving support.

Unlike Pauline, Lea, and Denise, Pat received a great deal of support from her own family following the loss of Francine. This support has been paramount in her healing process. Pat's experiences corroborate Deevey's (1997) suggestion that women who found their families most helpful, although they had never formally told their parents about their sexual orientation, were women who simply assumed they knew. Pat clearly stated that she suspected that her family knew about the nature of her relationship with Francine and were loving and supportive of them. This was also true of Gretchen's father, who was very supportive following the death of her partner. Although Gretchen had never officially told her father about the nature of their relationship, she realized that her father knew when, as she began to tell him, he said, "No, it's okay. I know. That's not what's important here."

It is clear from some of the narratives of bereaved lesbian partners that friends become family, as the available research suggests (Deevey 1997; Oktay and Walter 1991). This is especially critical when a lesbian woman loses her partner and is in need of support during her bereavement. Pauline speaks of the community of lesbian women who were supportive of her at the time of Jean's death. She is now sharing a life with one of those women. Gretchen believes that her increased socialization with friends helped provide her with nurturing and support. Gretchen met her new partner through the friends who encouraged her to "get out more." Although Lea and Corky chose not to tell their children about the nature of their relationship and were surrounded by an outside "homophobic" community, they "had a community of friends. We had a family unit." This "family" was extremely important to both partners while Corky was ill and to Lea after Corky died of a long-term illness.

The available literature also points to how the unpredictability of community and family responses during bereavement remains a source of stress and fear in the lives of lesbian women who have lost their partners (Deevey 1997). However, following the loss of their partners, some of the bereaved lesbian partners who took a risk and shared the nature of their relationship with friends or colleagues found that they received the support they needed. Pauline discovered that whenever she did reveal her lesbian relationship with Jean to others (neighbors and colleagues), "all the responses were extremely positive, much more than I anticipated. Except, of course for my parents. So now I'm feeling that it's okay to take that risk, because 99 percent of the time, they're going to be supportive." Following Carol's death, Gretchen found that when she revealed the nature of her relationship with Carol to her colleagues at work they did lend her support, which felt good to her. Denise and Diane had chosen to keep their lesbian relationship hidden from colleagues and friends, so that Denise was extremely isolated following the loss of Diane. However, she slowly began to tell three old high-school friends about the nature of her relationship with Diane. "I did it one-on-one, and each time the reaction was more that what I could have hoped for. Each friend, in her own way, was very understanding and so supportive. They all wondered why we didn't think they could handle knowing about our relationship." Some of the narratives of lesbian women suggest that they are able to perceive who will be supportive to them following the loss of a partner. If lesbian partners could take the risk and trust their judgment, perhaps they could handle the unpredictable responses from society, which Deevey (1997) claims remain a source of stress and fear in the lives of lesbian women.

Another example of the discrimination facing Lea, Pat, and Gretchen concerned legal and financial matters. Although Gretchen viewed Carol as her marital partner, because they had held a commitment ceremony, Gretchen was unable to include Carol on her medical insurance at work following Carol's loss of her job. This created additional stress in coping with Carol's depression, because they could not secure the help they needed. Lea found that, although she and Corky had obtained a medical power of attorney before Corky's death, no one, including the doctors and the hospital, accepted this agreement, which would have permitted Lea to help make appropriate decisions about Corky's care—decisions that Corky and Lea had agreed upon. Similarly, Pat discovered that securing a medical power of attorney did not allow her access to the doctors, who were making decisions about Francine's care without Pat's input. This discrimination only increases the grief for a partner who has provided all of the care during a prolonged illness.

On a positive note, some of the narratives in this chapter suggest that hospice organizations provided much-needed support to the bereaved lesbian partners. Lea and Corky received much support from their local hospice organization, which helped them to manage Corky's pain near the end of her life. The hospice nurses recognized the importance of their partnership and supported Lea's effort to secure the medication that Corky's husband did not want her to have. A hospice chaplain helped Corky to decide where to spend the final weeks of her life. During the earliest days following Diane's death, Denise found that the hospice nurse was the one person with whom she could share her feelings. The nurse had accepted Denise's lesbian relationship with Diane prior to Diane's death. This marked the beginning of Denise's healing, as she was extremely isolated from her community.

However, a need for support groups for bereaved lesbian women emerged in some of the narratives. When Pauline sought a group experience that would suit her needs, none was available except those for AIDS partners, terminally ill partners, and widows and widowers. Pat attended a grief group for partners, but soon discovered that all of the partners in the group had been spouses. Pat felt uncomfortable discussing the nature of her relationship with Francine within the group and referred to Francine as her friend. She explored various resources for same-sex partner-loss groups but found nothing available.

What helped some of the bereaved lesbian partners to cope with their loss was to incorporate some of the positive characteristics of their deceased partners into their own personalities or daily lives. Following Jean's death, Pauline integrated qualities into her own personality that she had admired in Jean, such as being "laid back" and living "in the moment." Lea incorporated some of Corky's qualities, like being a "softer, kinder, more introspective person." Pat has discovered that she is comforted by participating in outdoor activities, such as walking, which her deceased partner, Francine, enjoyed. Similarly, Jones found that most of the lesbian women she interviewed "incorporated some of the dead partners' positive qualities within themselves" (Jones 1985:193).

Chapter Seven

Similar and Diverse Themes Among Bereaved Partners

This chapter presents underlying themes that emerged from the narratives of widows, widowers, domestic partners, and gay and lesbian partners, with excerpts from various narratives introduced to highlight the similarities and differences among the various partner groups.

There is little literature available that discusses the similarities and differences among different types of partner loss. However, a small body of literature contrasts experiences of widows with lesbian partners and another contrasts experiences of widows and gay men whose partners died of AIDS. The available literature has been introduced into the appropriate sections of this chapter.

AMBIVALENCE REGARDING EXISTING TIES WITH THE DECEASED PARTNER

A bereaved partner, confronted by the reality that the deceased partner is gone forever, will do whatever it takes to sustain the relationship. Conversely, evidence of the partner's prior existence can easily trigger painful feelings that the surviving partner is trying to avoid. Excerpts from the narratives presented in the preceding chapters illustrate one of the major themes in the literature. This theme concerns the bereaved partner's ambivalence about his or her continuing ties with the deceased partner (Schuchter 1986; Marris 1986; Simos 1979; Bowlby 1980; Stroebe, Schut, and Stroebe 1998).

Most partners whose narratives are included in this book, regardless of legal status or sexual orientation, spoke of contradictory impulses, or tugs, that they experienced when trying to preserve the loss in some way while, at the same time, wishing to avoid the pain of their loss. For example, Frank, widowed at age forty-nine, said, "It's an interesting phenomenon . . . what do you remember, what do you hold on to and what do you let go? It's a tough question sometimes—it's an interesting question sometimes. . . . With me, now, . . . sometimes I don't want to remember because it makes me so sad. So who wants to be down like that? . . . But there's that remembrance that you do want to hold on to. There's that person that you want to know, you want to remember."

John, widowed at thirty-seven with three children, demonstrates the dynamic nature of the grieving process in which he can go for "long periods without feeling connected" to Bobbie, and yet can be driving a car and "puddle up" with tears for little or no reason. John says, "Things get better, but they never get totally better." This is the voice of a man who has been widowed for almost sixteen years.

Laura, aged forty-five, expressed her difficulty in wanting to be involved in making decisions regarding her deceased partner's material possessions yet wanting "to remove" herself because it was "just too difficult." Laura couldn't bear to be in Jake's old office—"it was too hard." Francine still hears from families of the air crash victims in the accident in which her partner, Steven, died. Yet she is unable to go to the site of the crash, despite the fact that other families go regularly and have purchased land to improve. Francine's ambivalence about continuing ties with Steven is reflected not only in this reaction but in her reaction to the upcoming "spreading of ashes" of her partner's body. She is apprehensive about the pain that certain memories will bring her.

Tom, a forty-two-year-old gay man, talks about the contradictory impulses in a slightly different way. Because his partner, Rob, was dying from AIDS, Tom found that just prior to Rob's death he had to create some distance, because he had been gearing his whole life to Rob's care. Tom says, "I still loved Rob and cared about him deeply, but I needed to feel some independence."

Pauline, a lesbian woman whose partner died in an auto accident, reports that she has dreams of trying to reconnect with her deceased partner, Jean.

Many of the dreams make her feel as though Jean is still here, yet "we are split up." More similarities than differences are observed when examining various partners' ambivalent reactions toward existing ties with the deceased. Perhaps this is because this dual process of mourning (which suggests that the bereaved individual allows himself or herself to experience the pain of the loss while attempting to move away from it to reinvest in the world) is a necessary component of the healing process.

DISCRIMINATION EXPERIENCED BY SURVIVING PARTNERS IN NONTRADITIONAL RELATIONSHIPS

Reactions of Family Members and Medical Personnel

Little research compares the experiences of bereaved partners who were married with those who cohabited prior to the loss of their partner. However, Ferrell (1992) found in his work with bereaved gay partners that they experienced the common grief reactions identified earlier in studies of bereaved adults by Lindemann (1944), Bowlby (1977), Freud (1957), and Parkes (1972). In examining the themes in all of the stories contributed to this book, it appears that grief, as an emotional experience, is similar for all of the partners, regardless of their status in society or their sexual orientation. However, some of the differences in the experiences of deceased partners can be attributed to societal reaction toward the bereaved partner. For example, Ferrell (1992) found that the common issues of grief that gay survivors face are compounded by the problems of stigma and homophobia. The grief of gay survivors is also complicated by their relative youth and by issues related to AIDS, discussed in chapter 5.

Doka (1989) states that, although the grief experiences of bereaved non-married partners are similar to those of widows and widowers, partners who cohabit do not share with married partners the societal sanctions that allow them to receive support in their grief. Doka (1987, 1989, 2002b) suggests that the emotions of a bereaved partner (such as anger, guilt, sadness, and loneliness) are often intensified in a nontraditional relationship. However, because of the narrative approach used by the author, it is impossible to compare the intensity of emotions experienced by the deceased partners whose stories are included in this text. In Deevey's (1997) study of lesbian women who have lost a partner, she found that the theme of disenfranchised grief, identified by Doka (1987, 1989, 2002b) and discussed in detail in chapter 4 of this book, emerged from many of the narratives of lesbian women who participated in her study. It is clear from the narratives of partners who shared their stories in chapters 4–6 that those partners who were unmarried, in both same-sex and opposite-sex partnerships, experienced discrimination from family, hospital personnel, and clergy. Widows and widowers who shared their stories never discussed such discrimination.

Most of the partners in nontraditional relationships, whether same-sex or opposite-sex, pointed to the pain they experienced when negotiating end-of-life decisions and issues with medical personnel. Marie was angry that the visiting nurses who came to her home while she was caring for her partner, Bert, questioned her role. They were judgmental toward the couple when they discovered that she and Bert were not married. Laura felt angry when doctors, upon discovering that she and Jake had never married, informed her that she could not make any decisions about what would happen to Jake, despite her care of him throughout his entire illness. Lea discovered that although she had obtained a medical power of attorney so that she could help make decisions about Corky's care, no one, including the doctors and the hospital, accepted this document. Similarly, Pat discovered that securing a medical power of attorney did not allow her access to the doctors, who were making decisions about Francine's care without her input. It is significant that the lesbian partners whose narratives are shared in this book are the only group of nonmarried partners who experienced difficulties executing a power of attorney. Domestic partners who shared their stories in chapter 4 did not mention this difficulty, nor did the gay partners whose narratives are presented in chapter 5, although they were similarly excluded by hospital personnel.

The medical staff at the hospital where Rob died prevented his partner, Tom, from being at his bedside when he was dying of AIDS. Although before Jake's death Laura had provided all of the care for her partner, when she took him to the hospital as he was dying, the doctors told her that she could make none of the decisions, since she wasn't married to Jake. Laura is angry that although she knew Jake's wishes better than anyone else, "I had no rights." Furthermore, when the doctors came to talk to Jake's family at the hospital, they addressed all of their remarks to Jake's brother. Laura felt negated and ignored at the very time she was experiencing deep sadness. Barry was deeply hurt during the funeral service for his partner, Julie, who died from cancer. The priest mentioned Julie's love for the entire extended family by name, but never mentioned Barry. These varying types of discrimination only increase and complicate the grief for a partner who has provided all of the care during a prolonged illness.

The degree to which gay and lesbian bereaved partners experienced disenfranchisement of their grief seems related to the degree to which the relationship was known or accepted by each partner's family prior to the loss. Furthermore, this degree of disenfranchisement is related to how open the couple decided to be regarding their relationship with their family and the community. The experiences of bereaved gay and lesbian partners presented in chapters 5 and 6 of this book parallel the work of Doka (1989, 2002b), who states that when the relationship is accepted, there is greater possibility for social support from family and friends, which facilitates the resolution of grief.

Following her partner's death, Pauline discovered that no one understood the nature of her relationship with Jean, and instead, viewed her as a roommate or friend. This was extremely painful for Pauline. Jean's family had never supported her lesbian relationship and excluded Pauline from the obituary they wrote following their daughter's death. Gretchen was isolated from Carol's parents following Carol's death because they did not approve of the couple's sexual orientation. Contrary to the experiences of Gretchen, Pauline, Lea, and Denise, Pat received a great deal of support from her family following the loss of Francine. Pat and Francine had been open with their parents about their relationship prior to Francine's death. These experiences corroborate Deevey's 1997 findings that women who found their families most helpful and supportive had either told their families about their sexual orientation and had been accepted or assumed they knew.

Similarly, the literature (Shernoff 1998; Doka 1989) suggests that the degree to which the gay couple has come out to their family prior to the death of a partner determines how the couple's relationship will be respected and how much support will be provided by the family. In chapter 5, the narratives of Jim and Don suggest that when a gay partner has been open regarding his sexual orientation, he is more likely to have a network of supportive friends and family who will help him with the mourning process. Don and his partner had been very open about their sexual orientation with both of their families and friends. Prior to Eric's death, Eric informed his brother that Don would be receiving his inheritance and made provisions in his will to cover this matter. Unlike other gay and lesbian partners, Don planned the entire funeral service based on requests that Eric had made before his death. Eric's family did not interfere with this planning, unlike many of the other families in the narratives.

In contrast, Tom was rejected by Rob's family following Rob's death. Although Tom was designated as the executor of Rob's estate, he did not have legal rights to Rob's body. At the funeral service, which was planned by Rob's family, Tom was treated as if he weren't there. David and Brent had never told either of their families about their relationship and maintained two apartments, although they always stayed in one of them together. Following Brent's death, Brent's father completely rejected David, locking him out of the apartment in which David and Brent had spent time together. Had it not been for a supportive gay community, David would have been completely isolated in his grief following Brent's death.

The experiences of domestic partners seem somewhat different compared to those of the lesbian and gay bereaved partners. All of the families of the cohabiting partners were informed about the nature of the partner's relationship prior to the death. In some cases, families or family members accepted this relationship, supporting the bereaved partner, but in others they did not. For example, Laura was surprised and hurt that, following Jake's death, both of his children rejected every attempt that she made to remain involved in their lives. Following Steven's death, Francine felt rejected by his mother, who told her that she did not deserve any of the proceeds from the lawsuit regarding Steven's death or any of the inheritance.

All of these rejections make it more difficult for the bereaved partners to receive the support they need to grieve and go forward with their lives. For example, Barry and Julie's relationship was not accepted by Julie's adult daughter, which made it very difficult for Barry to negotiate end-of-life issues or to be as involved as he wished in planning Julie's funeral. However, Julie's adult son, who was not particularly accepting of their domestic partnership while his mother was living, was very supportive of Barry following his mother's death. Julie's son often calls Barry for advice and told him that it would have been great to have had him as a stepfather if his mother had lived. Peter found both of Marilyn's adult children to be supportive following their mother's death. Furthermore, his own adult daughter wrote him a letter in which she stated that Marilyn was "more than my Dad's girlfriend, she was my stepmom." The pattern with domestic partners seems less clear than with gay/lesbian partners as to whether the degree of acceptance or recognition of the relationship determines the degree of support provided by the family following the loss of a partner.

Community Reactions

Domestic partners, as well as gay and lesbian partners, expressed concern about community reactions to their loss of a partner. Differences and similarities are revealed when the experiences of various partners are examined.

In chapter 4, Laura, who was forty-two when her male partner died at forty-six, states, "partners live in a very small segment of society that sanctions a lot of things but this isn't the rest of the world. We have a tendency to forget that. What I was doing was crossing a boundary. As long as I was within that little circle it was fine, but every time I had to cross that boundary it was one of the great difficulties. Losing a partner is an experience that brings home in a very fundamental way how different our lives are. I have friends who are gay and have lost partners. They have a community that supports them and gives them sustenance. It's funny, but I think they have more in the sense of an understanding community than I did. People who were around me—my friends and colleagues—were really great. But the difficulty is that when you negotiate death and all of its ramifications, you end up making that leap out of that immediate community. It makes it much harder. I couldn't have anticipated some of what occurred because it wouldn't have dawned on me that those things would happen." Other opposite-sex partners who had not married their loved ones prior to their death never mentioned any community support system that helped to sustain them during the illness or following the death of their partner.

All of the narratives of the gay men presented in this book seem to corroborate what Laura has stated: the gay community supports bereaved partners following the death of a partner. Although Jim lost twelve of his friends to AIDS during or shortly after the time that his partner was dying, he believed that he had a community of support for his grief while it was the most painful. Tom, whose partner, Rob, died of AIDS, spoke very clearly of the support he received from his involvement in a support group and from an organization, Action AIDS, for coping with his grief. Tom says, "Knowing that my pain was not just my pain, but respecting the fact that it is my pain, yet there are others that join me in the universe with that challenge, helped me to cope." Don and his deceased partner, Eric, were part of a large gay community in a large urban area. Don believed that this involvement has helped him to move forward in his life. Finally, David, whose partner of eighteen years, Brent, committed suicide, continues to receive support from the gay community several years after Brent's death. David said, "I still hear that Brent and I were like a symbol to them of gay relationships because we were together so long. They said we were like an inspiration to them— that's nice to hear." However, David's pain and grief about his loss were exacerbated by the negative reactions of Brent's parents.

Several of the narratives of the lesbian women who shared their experiences illustrate the difficulty they had in locating a support group that might have been helpful to them. Denise was forty-eight when her lesbian partner, Diane, died of cancer. Denise's isolation following Diane's death was intensified by reactions of community members who did not understand the importance of her relationship with Diane and perceived them as just friends. "Diane was a good friend of mine in the eyes of a lot of people. So in that respect it was very difficult, because you're not treated as a heterosexual partner would be treated, as a spouse. . . .When I lost Diane it became a very big issue for me. I felt like I had no one that I could talk to and say, 'You don't understand, I lost my spouse.' I didn't lose my spouse—she was my best friend, but she was more than that." The pain over her loss of Diane was increased by the difficulty of finding support from a community that understood her needs. Denise considered suicide until she became involved in a therapeutic relationship that helped her to begin to heal. Denise found her therapist through a hospice nurse, who had been the one person to accept the lesbian relationship shared by Denise and Diane. Denise's difficulty may also have been related to the lack of a role for the bereaved lesbian partner, a role that parallels that of a widow, who undergoes a transition into this status following the loss of her spouse. Doka (1987, 2002b) suggests that, although partners in nontraditional relationships lose significant roles when their mates die, "there is no transitional role for them to assume" (1987). Lea also lost her lesbian partner, Corky, to cancer when both women were in their late forties. Lea found the outside community to be extremely homophobic, although she and Corky did have a circle of friends who were supportive. Like Denise, the only group from which Lea experienced support was a local hospice organization.

Pat was fifty-one when her partner of twelve years died of a brain tumor. Like Denise, Pat felt extremely isolated in her grief following Francine's death. Although Pat received support from her own family, when she attended a mixed grief group, she found it difficult to continue attending, because all of the bereaved partners were spouses. Uncomfortable discussing the real nature of her relationship with Francine within this group, Pat referred to Francine as a friend. Pat explored various resources for same-sex partner-loss groups, but found nothing available to her within a reasonable commute.

Jones (1985) found that the experience of bereavement for the lesbian women she interviewed paralleled the experiences of heterosexual widows in many ways. The process and length of grief experienced by the lesbian women in her study (Jones 1985) confirm the findings of previous research.

However, the major differences were found in the establishment and involvement in social networks. In contrast to heterosexual widows, who found family members to be more helpful than friends during their bereavement, lesbian women found friends to be the most helpful group (Glick, Weiss, and Parkes 1974). Just as Oktay and Walter (1991) found in their study of breast cancer patients, lesbian women referred to their friends as family. In *Breast Cancer Through the Life Course: Women's Experiences* (Oktay and Walter 1991), Diane, a forty-six-year-old lesbian woman diagnosed with breast cancer, derived support throughout her cancer experience "from her close network of women friends who became like family to her." Diane said, " I have a lot of friends . . . every weekend and on all the holidays someone would come to visit . . . So at some incredibly deep level I realized that I had family" (1991:137).

Jones (1985) found that although friendship groups of the lesbian partners were composed primarily of other lesbian women, they also included gay men and heterosexual men and women. The friendship network served a function similar to that served by the family for heterosexual widows. Friends provided practical and emotional support during the final illness and the first few weeks of bereavement (Jones 1985). However, like heterosexual widows, almost all of the lesbian women interviewed (Jones 1985) found that the amount of support they received dropped away shortly after the first month.

In most cases, the lesbian women who shared their stories in this book created a community of friends but were unable to locate a support group that might help them navigate their grief. In contrast, the gay men found available support groups, largely because of the AIDS epidemic. The surviving opposite-sex partners who were living with their partners when they died found few friends and no community to help to support them during this difficult time. The implications seem to be clear. Hospice organizations and others who offer support groups for bereaved partners need to be sensitive to the special needs of lesbian women and bereaved opposite-sex partners, who feel uncomfortable attending groups for spouses.

USING MEMORIES AND CONTINUING BONDS WITH THE BEREAVED TO COPE WITH GRIEVING

Rubin (1999) is concerned with "how people are involved in maintaining and changing their relationships with the deceased." This includes the memories, both positive and negative, associated with the deceased and how the bereaved partner has transformed the relationship with the deceased into something more—with how he or she has "entered the memory into the fabric of the life" of the bereaved partner. Klass, Silverman, and Nickman (1996) emphasize the importance of using continuing bonds with the deceased loved one to enrich functioning in present relationships. For example, Marion, who lost her spouse when she was forty-four, demonstrates various ways in which she has used continuing bonds with her husband, Sam, to help her cope with her grief. Marion feared that she would forget Sam after he died. For the first year following his death, she found herself talking to Sam all the time. At times Marion has felt as if she were going crazy, and it helps her to remember that Sam told her, "You think you're crazy. I'm crazy too. I just have it under control." Even two years later, Marion 'talks' to Sam "when I'm trying to figure something out—'Sam, what should I do?'" Marion is deeply religious and finds that praying to Sam is more helpful than praying to God, "because God doesn't have a face, but Sam does." Marion also keeps her connection with Sam by wearing his T-shirts, and "now my son can wear some of his clothes." As a way of helping her family keep bonds with Sam, Marion has asked her brother to type some of the stories that Sam wrote about his youth in the South, to help her children understand how their father grew up in a community that was basically self-supporting. Memories and thoughts of Sam seem to provide a measure of strength and warmth for Marion and her children, which Rubin (1999) suggests is a significant sign that the memories have found an "appropriate resting point in the life of the bereaved" (Rubin 1999:697).

In Richards's 1999 study of gay men who have lost a partner, he reviews the following themes from the interviews in which a link to the deceased partner was maintained: (1) stating that the deceased is in some way a part of the self, (2) maintaining an active relationship with memory, (3) feeling guided by the deceased partner, and (4) experiencing the presence of the deceased partner. All of these themes were present in Marion's story about the loss of her spouse. Similarly, some of the narratives of gay men in this book demonstrate some of these themes. For example, Don (who was fifty when his life partner, Eric, died) keeps Eric's memory in his thoughts by talking to him and by seeing a psychic who has helped Don to realize that death is more peaceful than he had previously imagined. Don is comforted and communicates with Eric verbally whenever he feels Eric's presence around the house. Don says, "Something will happen around the house and I think, 'Oh, is that you?' . . . or 'Did I smell cigarette smoke?' Then I say, 'If that's you, Eric, I heard you.'" These experiences provide Don with a sense of peace.

David was forty-five when his life partner of eighteen years committed suicide. David believes that one sign that Brent has become a part of him is that he now reads the newspaper and is finding it interesting to follow politics. Before Brent's death David was not interested in politics and relied on Brent to report on various current events. David has also become interested in music, which was "Brent's job in our relationship." David now takes the initiative in purchasing CD's that he enjoys as way of having music in his life.

Some of the narratives of lesbian women who lost their partners illustrate how they are using memories of their partners to help them cope with their loss. Pauline was thirty-two when her partner, Jean, died at age twenty-six in an automobile accident. She actively keeps memories of Jean alive by placing photos of Jean around the home that she and her new partner, Linda, have established together. Pauline keeps an old photo album of Jean's from her childhood, as well as a Bible that belonged to Jean. Pauline has also maintained contact with a very close friend of Jean's. Another way in which Pauline connects with Jean is by "dreaming that we were trying to connect. A lot of times it's as if she were still here and we had split up." Pauline is concerned about unfinished business with Jean because they had some pretty heavy arguments just before the accident. Pauline believes the dreams are a way of helping her to resolve some of her feelings.

Pat was fifty-one when her partner of twelve years died of a brain tumor. Pat, like David, has taken on some of the interests and characteristics of her deceased partner, Francine. Gardening has become a real source of pleasure for her, and she believes that "I'm doing gardening as a tribute to Francine." Pat never enjoyed gardening or the outdoors prior to Francine's death, but because Francine enjoyed nature and gardening, Pat "walks more than ever before" and feels linked to her relationship with Francine when she is outside. Pat also enjoys an ongoing relationship with Francine's former employer and her sister, with whom she shares many memories about Francine.

Barry lost his partner at seventy-six. He keeps Julie's memory close to him by talking to her and by staying in touch with her son and her brother, with whom he can share memories. Like Marion and Don, Barry also talks to Julie. "If I have a problem, if something's bothering me, I talk to her. I just have feelings in my heart that she's listening and that I'm communicating with her." With behavior similar to John's, who lost his spouse, Barry is trying to carry on some of the tasks that Julie performed in their relationship—for example, by taking a sewing class. Barry also finds (like Marie and Peter) that Julie's dog provides comfort to him and a way for him to remember Julie. Barry has reached a point where his memories and thoughts of Julie are available in a balanced way, so that he finds what Rubin (1999) suggests is a measure of strength and warmth from his reconstructed relationship with Julie. It is interesting that Barry, Marie, and Peter were all unmarried and living with their partners at the time of their loss.

After more than sixteen years of widowhood, John stays connected to memories of his wife, Bobbie, who died when John was thirty-seven. He stays in touch with Bobbie's aunt and cousins through phone calls and Christmas cards. He also honors the memory of his wife on the anniversary of her death by lighting a candle in the Jewish tradition. In his wife's memory, John started a memorial fund for Girl Scout troop travel and is now a life member of the Girl Scouts. John's use of his memories to honor and memorialize his wife demonstrate Rubin's 1999 suggestion that the memorialization process is a way for the bereaved person to transform the memory of the deceased into something beyond grief and mourning. This transformation can lead to new meaning for the bereaved partner. The narratives of all of the partners, whether married or cohabiting in same-sex or opposite-sex relationships, seem to reflect more similarities than differences in the way they use continuing memories and bonds with the deceased in order to cope with their grieving.

DEVELOPING NEW RELATIONSHIPS
WHILE CONTINUING BONDS WITH
THE DECEASED PARTNER

Another theme common to all the partners who were considering or were involved in a new relationship was concern about how they could make a place for the deceased partner in their minds and hearts as they struggle with a new relationship. Walter (1997) suggests that loyalty to the deceased spouse, for both men and women, plays a critical part in the bereaved partner's struggle with dating. Frank, widowed at forty-nine, openly discussed his ambivalence about dating other women, which seemed to be related to his memories of Sarah. Frank says, "I'm a little bit too involved with one person right now, and somehow I let that happen. I'm not totally involved. I still have a relationship with Sarah." Yet Frank remembers when "there was no room for anybody else" during the first year after Sarah's death.

Kristen, the twenty-nine-year-old widow who lost her spouse in a car accident, spoke of how she has "emotionally relocated her memory of Carl" as she enters her new relationship with Brian. Kristen says, "It's not that you've forgotten him. It's not that you've moved on without him, because you can't. It's just that you are in a place where you can have somebody else and you can have him too, and they're not all mixed up." Kristen's comments corroborate the work of Klass et al. (1996), who speak of how the continuing relationship with the deceased is transformed in such a way as to allow for new growth. In Kristen's case, this involves a new relationship. Kristen speaks of how her relationship with Brian cannot replace her relationship with Carl. Her experience corroborates Rubin's (1999) insistence that "involvement with the past relationship cannot serve as a replacement for relationships of the present, but only as an adjunct to them" (Rubin 1999:696). One year following her interview for this book, Kristen wrote that when she remarried, two years following the death of her husband, the father of her late husband and her own father shared in giving her away at her wedding. This experience seems to validate some of the postmodern thinkers who speak of how maintaining continuous bonds with the deceased partner can enrich the functioning of the surviving partner (Rubin 1999; Klass et al. 1996).

Like the widows and widowers in chapter 3, Pauline, a young lesbian woman, said, "I think it's hard—that transition of putting that relationship wherever it's supposed to be without forgetting it. It's only through talking about it to other people who've been through it that you can discuss what you do with some of these things that are special. You don't want to negate the importance of your current relationship, but you don't want to put away or deny the importance of the other relationship, since it's not something you chose to leave."

Gretchen, whose lesbian partner committed suicide, presents a good example of a bereaved partner who has been able to maintain and yet change her relationship with her deceased partner. In this way she can relocate the memory of her partner in a place that allows her to become more fully involved with her new partner, Marilyn. Gretchen believes that she has learned how to keep the memories of Carol separate from her thoughts about Marilyn. Initially, in her new relationship, "memories of Carol would come in a lot because I would allow those tragic, sad memories to come flooding in— all that hurt and loss. As the grief slowly decreased, there were fewer times when the grief about Carol came into my relationship with Marilyn. Occasionally it still happens." Gretchen's new partner remains comfortable when Gretchen cries with her about the loss of Carol. Rubin suggests that the importance of "maintaining and changing their relationships with the deceased" is a way of providing "warmth and solidity to the experience of the bereaved" (Rubin 1999:696).

The bereaved partners from lesbian relationships seemed more insistent that the new partner and their new friends know about their deceased partner. For example, Pauline's new partner, Linda, was a friend of both Pauline and Jean, her deceased partner. During my interview with Pauline, Linda was in the house and would comment on details of her memory of Jean. Gretchen and her new partner, Marilyn, would often discuss Gretchen's relationship with her deceased partner, Carol. Gretchen's new friends mixed with her old friends and were interested in hearing about her life with Carol. By contrast, in examining themes from the narratives of widows, widowers, cohabiting partners, and bereaved gay partners, this involvement of the new partner with the deceased partner was never mentioned.

Peter was involved in a partnership with Marilyn for several years prior to her death. He keeps memories of Marilyn close to him and believes that his relationship with Marilyn has greatly influenced his new relationship with Nancy. Peter believes that the tremendous respect and sense of dedication that he had for Marilyn has been brought to his relationship with Nancy. "If you want to have a special relationship, you cannot take someone for granted. That relationship needs to be fed and cared for. That's something I did naturally with Marilyn and that I am doing with Nancy." Here is an example of how the new relationship has grown from and is an adjunct to the prior relationship. Peter's use of his continuing bonds with Marilyn to enrich his new relationship with Nancy illustrates the postmodern belief that the continuing attachment with the deceased can be used as a resource for enriching the functioning of the bereaved in the present (Klass et al. 1996).

On the other hand, the experiences of Don and Jim, two gay men whose partners died from illness, are somewhat different from those of the partners described above. Although Don was glad "to be there for Eric" when he needed him, he was unhappy with the relationship. Don believes that since Eric's death, he has changed in terms of what he wants from a relationship. He better understands what he needs from a relationship and wants more open communication on a physical and emotional level. From his relationship with Eric, Don has learned how to "share more of himself in new relationships" and realizes that he needs to be more open at his workplace regarding his sexual orientation so that he can receive support from more of his colleagues. Although Don was dissatisfied with the relationship with his deceased partner, he is still able to use his continuing bonds with Eric to enhance his conception of what he wants from a new relationship.

Jim's story is distinct because he lost twelve friends to AIDS during the time that his partner, Matt, was dying of AIDS. Jim believes that "one of the damages that the amount of losses from AIDS has created is a decreased ability to invest in being a partner in the future." Jim thinks that he is "much better with friendships than trying to make a go of a partnership." Because Jim has had so many losses within a few years, he may have more difficulty allowing his continuing relationship with Matt to be transformed in a way that can provide him with the balance and strength that Rubin (1999) believes enable the bereaved to move forward with new relationships. From Rubin's work, it seems that Jim may be having difficulty in reducing the "intensity of focus on the reworked attachment to the deceased" (1999:698).

MAKING MEANING FROM THE EXPERIENCE OF THE DEATH OF A PARTNER

Another theme that emerged from the grief reactions of all of the partners was the way in which bereaved partners' lives were transformed by their response to the death of their partners. Robert Neimeyer (1998, 2001), in his postmodern works, has postulated that "meaning reconstruction in response to a loss is the central process in grieving" (Neimeyer 2001:4). The death of a partner is a life-shattering and worldview-shattering experience. Neimeyer (1998) urges us to appreciate more deeply the extent to which losses of those we love can create profound shifts in our sense of who we are. Grieving requires the bereaved partner, whether married or cohabiting when their partner dies, to reconstruct a personal world that makes sense and restores a sense of meaning and direction to a life that is forever transformed. The following excerpts from narratives from each chapter illustrate the ways in which different types of bereaved partners have been transformed by their experience with death. These examples come from partners who represent a wide age range, from twenty-nine to eighty-nine.

Kristen was twenty-nine when her young husband was killed in an automobile accident. The literature (Schaffer 1993; DeGiullo 1992) indicates that spousal loss at an earlier time in development allows younger widows to remake their lives and start over in a way that might seem unrealistic to an older widow who loses a spouse later in life. Kristen firmly believes that the death of her husband deeply affected her personal and professional goals. She believes that she is a "much healthier person now. I have much more insight into who I am." As a result of personal changes, she has fewer friends because she doesn't have "a lot of superficial relationships any more." Kristen believes that some of her professional growth emerged from her new status as a single woman as well as the experiences surrounding the death of her husband and her own "near death" experience. As a married woman, Kristen felt "like I was just a wife. I just really never had to exercise my strength." Kristen left her job in animal research to pursue a master's degree in counseling. Her professional dreams now include creating a grief center that will provide animal therapy, because she knows that her own animals gave her much comfort following the loss of her husband.

Frank was forty-nine when his wife died from a serious illness. He believes that his personality has changed significantly since Sarah's death. He often thanks Sarah "for making me grow up. I think at times I would let Sarah deal with the hard stuff and now I have to do it. I think I'm maturing. . . . I don't think I'm quite as goofy as I was before. I'm more vocal. There's a weightiness that I feel." Sarah's death has provided Frank with "an opportunity to find my own adultness. I'm the captain of my own ship. I think it keeps me in the here and now. I think I try to be true to myself more than I did before."

These two excerpts clearly point to the theme of "becoming stronger as a result of surviving the pain of death and stepping forward to handle things that previously were done by the deceased person" (Frantz, Farrell, and Trolley 2001:204).

John, who lost his wife when he was thirty-seven, provides another example of a bereaved partner who has assumed a role once held by the deceased spouse, which helps him to construct meaning out of his experience. When Bobbie died, John was left to parent three young children, ages nine, eleven, and thirteen. John believes that he has changed since his wife's death. "I wasn't much of a dad because I didn't have to be, because she was so much of a mother. She did so much for them and with them. I thought it was important, but I didn't have to do it. . . . I learned from her that it was important to show certain attention to the children . . . getting my daughter to music lessons became a reason for being." John's story corroborates Carverhill's 1997 findings that widowers are forced to examine and change their values and priorities and to reevaluate the meaning of their work outside the home.

It is truly remarkable to note that an eighty-nine-year-old widow believes that she has changed as a result of the loss of her spouse. Flora and Jim were married for almost sixty years at the time of his death. Flora reports that "you're never the way you were. You're a different person." Flora has realized that although she finds relating to new people in a professional role quite easy, she has difficulty in more personal situations. However, "I've realized that I'm much more comfortable with myself than I thought I'd be." Being alone has certain advantages for Flora, who can do what she wants at any time of day without disturbing anyone. She also enjoys dining at fancy restaurants, which is something her husband did not enjoy.

Francine's life partner, Steven, died in a plane crash. Like Kristen and Frank, Francine believes that she has become more independent and no longer "needs to feel protected by a man." Francine reports that "My friends who have lost partners all talk about who we've become—we've become independent and have grown tremendously. We'll never be who we were with our mates—you decide who you want to be on your own. I'm a strong force and a lot more proud of who I am now. When I was with Steven, there was a part of me that didn't want to be as successful as my partner. I held back." Francine's art work is flourishing since the loss of Steven. She believes that she has "grown more from this relationship and the loss of it than people could grow in a lifetime."

Jim's partner, Matt, died in his thirties from an HIV-related illness. During the years surrounding the death of his partner, Jim lost twelve friends to AIDS. Despite all of the depression and isolation that followed these multiple losses, Jim has been strengthened by his recognition that he has a real reason to be alive. Jim says, "I do feel amazingly strong and capable of doing anything. I lost my lover and my best friend in the same week. . . . If it doesn't kill you, it makes you stronger. I've learned to live with the demons and have a newfound ability to channel my emotions." Like other bereaved partners, Jim's experience has made him "value the human experience—the ability of the mind and body to cope and to survive." Jim wants to make each day count!

Tom, who lost his life partner, Rob, noted similarly how Rob's death has made him "dramatically more aware of the scarcity of time and the precious nature of life." Tom also tries to stay "in the present moment," yet believes that he has learned "to live with a certain amount of uncertainty."

Lea and her partner, Corky, had both been married, and each had children. Following Corky's death, Lea felt that she had "nothing left" and sold the business they had owned together. Now Lea believes that Corky's death has changed her own identity in many ways. Lea says, "I'm certainly a softer, kinder, more introspective person than I was. I think I was a real hardcore businesswoman who was much more aggressive in my quest for fixing things. . . . What I learned from this experience is that there are things I can't fix." Lea believes that she carries her relationship with Corky forward, because "half of who I am is because of my relationship with her."

As a part of her healing process following the death of her partner, Francine, Pat has incorporated some of her partner's interests into her life. Pat never enjoyed gardening or nature prior to Francine's death. Since her death Pat finds that gardening and the outdoors provide her with a real source of pleasure.

Lea and Pat provide two examples of how a bereaved lesbian partner can incorporate some of the deceased partner's characteristics into her own personality as a way of making meaning from the experience. Lea and Pat corroborate Jones's 1985 study of bereaved lesbian women, in which she found that several women described a "conscious sense of having taken in valued parts of their partners' personalities" (Jones 1985:193) as a way of coping with their grief. Similarly, some of the gay men who shared their stories expressed this sense of taking on some of the characteristics of the deceased partner or performing tasks he had done and pursuing some of his leisure-time interests. This seems to have occurred more frequently for the gay and lesbian partners than for the widowed and nonmarried partners.

CHAPTER SUMMARY

Most of the partners whose narratives are shared in this text experienced what may be a universal component of grief process—the contradictory pulls toward giving in to the pain of grief and avoiding the pain, so as to reinvest in their world. Additionally, all of the partners, in one way or another, expressed their newfound appreciation for making each day count—for enjoying the moment. This corroborates the conclusions of other researchers that "many bereaved people say that they have learned to appreciate the value of life more than they ever did before. They have learned that life is special and precious and that it has to be lived in the moment as much as possible" (Frantz, Farrell, and Trolley 2001:204).

Partners from varying types of relationships constructed meaning from their experience of loss in different ways. Most of the gay and lesbian partners seem to have taken on characteristics of their deceased partners by performing tasks and pursuing leisure-time interests previously associated with their partners. This behavior was less common among the widows, widowers, and opposite-sex partners, who more often described changes in their personalities that reflected a newfound sense of independence or professional and personal growth, separate from their partners' personalities.

Because of the small number of participants, it is difficult to speculate on these differences. The dissimilarity may be related to differences in the degree of emotional bonding that same-sex and opposite-sex partners experience with one another prior to the death of a partner. The literature suggests that one of the coping mechanisms adopted by lesbian couples to handle the stresses of growing up and living in a heterosexist society is to create "a bond between the partners . . . strong enough to compensate for both the denial and the danger that the (lesbian) family faces from the society at large" (Slater and Mencher 1991:378). These authors suggest that this is a burden rarely shared by heterosexual families, who are inherently validated by a society that assigns them various norms and rituals. Furthermore, emotional fusion in lesbian couples may be ego-syntonic, because women of all sexual identities tend to prefer a high degree of intimacy through connection with others (Chodorow 1978; Gilligan 1982; Miller 1986; Slater and Mencher 1991). "Two women sharing a partnership may be expected to have a high degree of relatedness" (Slater and Mencher 1991:345). This high degree of relatedness between lesbian partners may also explain why the lesbian partners who shared their narratives in this text were more insistent that their new partners and new friends know about their deceased partners. In Pauline's case, her new partner, Linda, had been a close friend of both Pauline and Jean, her deceased partner. Gretchen and her new partner often discussed Gretchen's relationship with Carol, her deceased partner. Gretchen's old and new friends often met together and were interested in talking about Carol. No other group of deceased partners communicated this type of response to the deceased partner.

Chapter Eight

Interventions

A CLASSICAL MODEL OF INTERVENTIONS
WITH BEREAVED PARTNERS

Many grief researchers (Raphael, Middleton, Martinek, and Misso
1993; Rando 1984; Worden 1991, 2002; Silverman 1986) have identified the
establishment of a relationship with the bereaved spouse as a key issue in the
counseling process. Worden (1991, 2002) and Raphael et al. (1993) urge the
counselor to develop a relationship that offers human comfort and care and
that encourages and accepts appropriate grief. Rando (1984), in her classic
work on clinical interventions with caregivers, suggests that an accepting and
nonjudgmental listener helps to facilitate the expression of emotions and "the
necessary review of the relationship with the lost loved one" (1984:79).
Rando urges counselors to be fully present in order to provide the griever
with security and support. Another common intervention, providing general support, can include work with family members, work with relevant others from the bereaved person's social network, and suggestions from the
counselor to become involved in support groups for bereaved spouses.

Raphael et al. (1993) urge grief counselors to explore the loss, which includes "the circumstances of the death, its reality to the bereaved, the psychological trauma associated with it, and personal and social responses to it"

(1993:431). Raphael et al. have outlined a clinical model for an intervention process with bereaved spouses. They suggest asking several key questions during the initial phase of therapy that help to identify crucial issues to explore with a bereaved spouse. The first question, "Can you tell me about him/her?" enables the client to discuss the history of the relationship, "including its positive and negative aspects, its elements of ambivalence and dependence" (1993:427). The second question, asking about how the death occurred, facilitates an exploration of the circumstances surrounding the death. The third question asks bereaved partners how others have responded to them, allowing for "an exploration of various aspects of social support and their perceived significance" (1993:430). The final question asks the client to discuss how the loss has affected his or her family and assesses how families are facing the grief and how each member is grieving. These questions help to decide whether or not intervention is needed and to set goals during the therapeutic intervention as well as to facilitate natural grieving processes.

For those who had been married for many years and had been socialized into the acceptance of very narrow gender roles, the bereavement experience revealed a lack of specific skills. Lund, Casserta, and Dimond (1993) suggest that one of the best ways to enhance self-esteem is to learn new skills. "Fifty-eight percent of our respondents reported feeling better about themselves as a result of learning new skills" (1993:253). These researchers recommend that the grief counselor acknowledge and integrate "the reciprocal relationship between self-esteem and personal competencies" into intervention plans (1999:254). Positive self-esteem, combined with the ability to use one's personal resources and skills, helps to provide successful adjustments to the demands of a new environment.

Just as the classical theories of grief presented in chapter 1 were stage-oriented, the interventions of the classical grief researchers emphasize the importance of helping the bereaved partner work through the various stages. Worden (1991, 2002) and Kubler-Ross (1969) believe that grief counseling involves helping the survivor work toward a healthy completion of the tasks of grieving that are outlined in chapter 1. Bowlby (1980) also includes a stage approach in his work with the bereaved (outlined in chapter 1), but does highlight the importance of the counselor or therapist in understanding that the "persistence of the relationship" in the world of the bereaved is a natural part of the grief process.

Rando (1984) and Worden (1991, 2002) encourage the counselor to help the griever release emotional ties with the deceased and to accept the pain of looking realistically at the loss. Worden (1991, 2002) believes that the focus of treatment should be to help the bereaved work on any tasks they seem unable to meet. The clinician must give the person permission to grieve while conducting an assessment of the bereaved partner's grief in order to determine which tasks of grief are incomplete. "Treatment needs to be aimed at making it safe to feel positive and negative emotions so grievers can work through them" (Rando 1984:85). Because the bereaved have so much difficulty facing anger, this emotion may have to be relabeled before the griever can deal with it. Worden (2002) suggests asking questions like "What do you miss about him?" which may bring out positive feelings, while a question such as "What don't you miss about him?" (2002:59) may elicit more negative feelings. This process allows the bereaved to see the deceased more realistically and to realize that both types of emotion can exist together.

Rando (1984), Lopata (1996), and Silverman (1996) urge the counselor to help the bereaved discover his or her new identity and the psychological and social roles that he or she must assume. The counselor must be aware of how painful this transition may be and ask the bereaved what roles, expectations, and opportunities she has had to relinquish and what new ones have to be assumed. It is also important for the bereaved to consider how her identification with the deceased has added to or changed her previous identity. Rando (1984) emphasizes the importance of helping the bereaved to recognize what has remained consistent, despite the trauma and loss. This work can provide a much-needed sense of continuity and security.

Rando (1984), Bowlby (1980), and Raphael et al. (1993) encourage the bereaved to review and talk about the deceased and their mutual relationship. Rando stresses the importance of helping the bereaved to consider how he will keep his partner's memory alive and continue to relate to her. It is important to discover what parts of the previous life will be retained (routines, special times, mementos) and "how reminiscences can be kept life-promoting rather than death-defying" (1984:102).

Rando and Doka (2002) highlight the importance of the use of ritual in therapy with the bereaved. Rando believes that participation in ritual behaviors may provide the bereaved partner with an opportunity to "interact intensely with the memory of the deceased for a limited time without crossing over into pathological dimensions" (1984). It is significant that Rando clearly states that these rituals allow the "bereaved to hang on to the deceased without doing so inappropriately or interfering with grief work" (1984:106). According to Bowlby (1980), work on the recollection of the deceased is aimed at helping the bereaved "identify feelings that must be processed," with the goal of "slowly beginning to decathect from the deceased" (1980:94). However, Rando is one of the earliest researchers to suggest that counselors help the bereaved to understand that a "healthy new relationship with the deceased must be formed" (1984:101). Rando believes that "although death has separated the mourner from the deceased, it has not ended the relationship" (1984:101). For Rando it means that the relationship with the deceased has changed from one based on the presence of the deceased to one based on relating to memories of the past. This transition occurs during the grief process as the bereaved restructures her life to gain a perspective on this new relationship. By focusing on the importance of how the bereaved partner changes her relationship with the deceased, in order to create a new perspective of the deceased, Rando's work (1984), is similar to that of the postmodern thinkers (Klass et al. 1996 and Rubin 1999), whose ideas are discussed in the next section of this chapter.

However, the classical and postmodern thinkers differ regarding the goal implied in this process. Rando (1984), Worden (1991, 2002), Raphael et al. 1993) all suggest that the goal is to relinquish ties with the deceased, while the postmodern thinkers urge counselors to help the bereaved find ways in which their memories of the deceased can improve their current functioning.

A POSTMODERN MODEL OF INTERVENTIONS WITH BEREAVED PARTNERS

The classical theorists (Raphael et al. 1993; Rando 1984, and Bowlby 1980) as well as the postmodern grief researchers (Rubin 1999; Klass et al. 1996; Neimeyer 1998, 2001) urge therapists and other helping professionals to review the lost relationship with the surviving spouse. Although Raphael et al. (1993) and Rando (1984) suggest that the therapist explore the relationship and its meaning to the bereaved spouse, they see the purpose of doing so as "the gradual undoing of the bonds of the lost spouse" (Raphael et al. 1993:432). The postmodern thinkers (Rubin 1999; Neimeyer 1998, 2001; Klass et al. 1996), whose ideas are outlined in chapter 1, see an exploration of the bereaved partners' relationship with the deceased as a way of enhancing their current functioning and helping the bereaved with the healing process.

Within this postmodern model, "the therapist is interested in the meaning of the relationship to the deceased person," not for the purpose of relinquishment of these ties, as suggested in the classical models (Freud 1957;

Kubler-Ross 1969, 1989; Worden 1991, 2002; Rando 1984; Raphael et al. 1993), but instead to examine the "positive function served by the continuing relationship" (Neimeyer 2001:26). Neimeyer believes that the emphasis on relinquishment, as conceptualized by the classical model, inevitably leads to a lack of interest on the part of the therapist in exploring the ongoing meaning of the relationship to the deceased person. He further suggests that the effects of this standard model have been to create a fear on the part of the therapist that "the exploration of the positive meaning of the relationship will get in the way of relinquishment" (2001:28). In fact, Rando (1984) does emphasize the importance of allowing the bereaved to "hang on" to the memory of the deceased, without allowing this memory to interfere with grief work. Neimeyer (2001) urges therapists working with bereaved partners to allow the client to explore the positive aspects of his or her relationship with the deceased partner without concern that this will detract from the client's ability to invest in her life and move forward.

For Rubin (1999), an exploration of the continuing relationship to the deceased is as critical to assessment and intervention with the bereaved as is examining the current functioning of the bereaved. When examining the bereaved partner's response to loss, it is important to consider the function and relationship of the bereaved partner to the deceased partner. Clinicians need to ask questions about the meaning of the deceased, both in the past and present life of the bereaved. Clinicians also need to focus on the development and continuing changes in the relationship to the deceased.

Rubin (1999) claims it is insufficient to examine coping, function, or the ability to form new relationships as the only factors in a positive adaptive response to the bereavement process. Rubin cites the importance of examining the ability of the bereaved partner to "reorganize and access thoughts and memories of the internal relationship" with the deceased partner (1999:698). Gretchen believed that she learned how to keep the memories of Carol, her deceased partner, separate from her thoughts about her new partner, Marilyn. This process of changing her relationship with Carol enabled Gretchen to become more comfortable in her new relationship and fostered her own personal development. The preoccupation and experience that the bereaved partner has with thoughts, memories, and emotions are often not perceived by others.

Both Rubin (1999) and Silverman et al. (1992) speak to the importance of looking for a balance in the current functioning of the bereaved partner, as well as a balance in the bereaved partner's perception of the relationship with the deceased partner. The degrees of anxiety and depression experienced by the bereaved, the ability to invest in life, and the use of social supports provide markers of levels of general functioning. However, the feelings evoked by thinking about the lost partner can become markers of the nature of the ongoing relationship with and attachment to the deceased partner. The postmodern thinkers believe that meaning and dialogue are at the heart of the mourning process. Because "The human experience of loss is about our ongoing and everlasting dialogue with the dead" (Neimeyer 2001:22), the postmodern view of bereavement intervention requires that therapists help to create an atmosphere within the treatment relationship where the bereaved can discuss the relationship with the lost partner.

Klass, Silverman, and Nickman (1996) found that memories of the deceased spouse helped widows to consolidate new identities that included valuable aspects of their marriages and that helped them to ground themselves in reality. In Chapter 3, although Marion felt that she "lost herself" after Sam died, she has been able to reconstruct a new identity as a single woman by incorporating some of the strengths of her relationship with Sam. By talking with Sam and attempting to understand what he might bring to a situation, she has been able to move forward in her decision-making processes. Klass et al. (1996) suggest that this "sense of presence" seems to mitigate the loss of trust in the "continuity of life," as well as the emotional and social isolation that widows experience. Therapists and other helping professionals can encourage bereaved partners to discuss memories of their deceased partners, both within the treatment and on their own, while living their ongoing daily lives.

Postmodern thinkers (Neimeyer 1998, 2001; Attig 2001; Walter 1996) argue that the mourning process is most importantly a "crisis in meaning" and suggest that the classical view of mourning is unable to "capture the positive function of the attempt to preserve meaning in the face of disruption" (Attig 2001:22). Attig believes that "Bereavement shatters our taken-for-granted life patterns and undermines many of our life assumptions." After the death of a partner, the bereaved has to learn again "how to be and act in the world" without his or her partner (2001:41).

Many grief researchers (Lopata 1996; Campbell and Silverman 1996; Silverman 1986; Carverhill 1997; Neimeyer 2001) suggest that when a partner dies, the bereaved partner must "relearn" his or her very self. The partner may ask questions of himself such as "Who am I now?" or "How were those aspects of myself affected, shaped by, and perhaps dependent on my partner who died?" (Attig 2001:40).

For example, in chapter 3, Frank shares his belief that his relationship with Sarah and his loss of her have made him "grow up," because while they were married, Sarah made more of the difficult decisions. In chapter 4, although Francine cherishes the relationship that she had with Steven, she recognizes that their partnership limited her personal growth and independence. Attig (2001) asks, "How am I different for knowing and loving him or her?" (2001:40). Francine says, "I'll never be who I was when I was with my mate—you decide who you want to be on your own." How can we now understand these aspects of ourselves? How are we going to change our personalities and give new shape to the "next chapters of our own life stories in the absence of those we love?" (Attig 2001:40). In chapter 6, Lea believes that her personality has changed since the loss of her lesbian partner, Corky. She has changed her career from academician to retailer. Lea now sees herself as a kinder, gentler, "more introspective person," who is much less aggressive in trying to "fix" things than she was before Corky's death. Following the death of his partner, Matt, Jim found that as a counselor he was more compassionate and more "willing to listen to the mood shift of people's pain."

Therapists must move toward appreciating the grieving process as an effort on the part of the bereaved to "reconstruct a world of meaning and restore coherence to the narratives of our lives" (Neimeyer 2001:69). Furthermore, in grieving, the bereaved partner relearns his or her relationship with the partner who has died. Therapists need to explore with their clients how their relationship with their deceased partners has shifted, how the loss of their partners has changed their lives, and what new meanings have been discovered.

Further aspects of the postmodern model of grief and mourning that have implications for changes in clinical practice include several responses on the part of the therapist. First, the therapist must view each partner's response to bereavement as unique, in that what is normal as against pathological "must be considered in the context of the patient's specific personality, relationship to the deceased person, and his or her familial background" (Hagman 2001:25). It is crucial for the therapist to be open to individuality and to explore the unique bereavement response of the bereaved partner.

Second, what have often been termed "pathological responses" may, in fact, be successful attempts to preserve and maintain an attachment to the deceased partner (Attig 2001). For example, in chapter 3, Marion's narrative illustrates ways in which a spouse can cope with her grief by using connections with her deceased husband. Marion did this by visiting places where she and Sam had gone together, by writing a history of Sam's life, and by wearing some of his clothing. In chapter 5, Don connects with his deceased partner, Eric, by "talking" to him when certain things that remind him of

Eric happen around the house. Don finds comfort in knowing that there "is this other place where Eric has gone," and by saying, "If that's you, Eric, I heard you." The intervention process requires the therapist to explore the ongoing value of the attachment to the deceased by helping to reconstruct "the meaning of that person in the context of the survivor's ongoing life" (Attig 2001:35).

Classical theory and postmodern theory are similar in their understanding that, as the bereaved partner moves forward, he or she moves in two directions at once, "oscillating between the past and the present" (Simos 1979:35). Bowlby (1980) speaks of "two incompatible urges"—an urge to cling and an urge to separate. Stroebe and Stroebe (1987) describe the bereaved as experiencing the full range of feeling associated with the loss and then, at other times, "tuning out the waves of grief." Neimeyer (2001), in his postmodern approach, suggests that the bereaved returns to aspects of her life that are still viable by discovering what still nourishes her in her daily life patterns. "We revive what still works in ourselves, families, and communities" and continue to sustain ourselves from "roots already in place" (Attig 2001:43).

However, Neimeyer (1998, 2001) takes this process one step further. At the same time that the bereaved partner is coping with conflicting urges to return to the past and to avoid the pain of the past, he or she transforms the self while reshaping his or her individual, family, and community life. Because life cannot be what it was, the bereaved searches for new life while still grieving. The postmodern paradigm of grief allows for beginning a new life while continuing a relationship with the deceased. By contrast, the classical theorists (Freud 1957; Kubler-Ross 1969, 1989; Worden 1991, 2002) view the grieving process as more or less completed prior to beginning new relationships and taking on new challenges.

The bereaved partner learns to find new ways to be in daily life. In chapter 3, Kristen, Frank, John, Marion, Flora, and George described ways in which they were making new lives while still holding on to some old patterns. Some of the nonmarried partners—Peter, Barry, Laura, and Alisa—also discussed ways in which they were charting new, exciting territory that they believe would not have been available to them had they not suffered the loss of their partners. In chapter 5, Jim, Tom, Don, and David spoke about how their life patterns had changed following the loss of a gay partner. In chapter 6, all of the bereaved lesbian partners found themselves living their lives in very different ways after struggling with grief over the loss of their partners. Although these bereaved partners had no choice about what happened, they all grew positively, though at times very painfully, through their experience of loss. Some grew stronger in their sense of character, while others grew in self-understanding and self-esteem. Clinicians need to be able to encourage clients to discuss, in specific ways, how their lives have changed since the loss of their partners.

The classical and postmodern views of bereavement and interventions can be applied to all the types of bereaved partners discussed in this book. The following discussions make more specific suggestions based on research findings for particular types of partners—young widows, widowers, opposite-sex partners, and same-sex partners.

INTERVENTIONS WITH BEREAVED SPOUSES

Individual Interventions

Rando (1984) makes specific recommendations for working with bereaved spouses. The first is to help the bereaved spouse identify those functions or roles previously assumed by the deceased that will now have to adopted by the bereaved spouse or taken on by someone else. The second, especially with elderly widows and widowers, is to be aware of any loss of social connection that was provided by the deceased spouse. With the elderly, the therapist must also determine whether the living spouse can manage independently. Ida, a bereaved partner (chapter 4), shares the importance of her regular connection with her adult daughter, which has helped to mitigate her loneliness. In chapter 3, Flora, widowed at eighty-nine, and George, widowed at eighty-one, were both functioning independently at the time of the interview for this book. However, both bereaved spouses lived close to at least one adult child who was involved with helping them to cope with daily tasks. A therapist would have to reevaluate such living arrangements regularly to determine whether they continued to be feasible.

The therapist also needs to help the surviving spouse to maintain appropriate relationships with and role expectations for children. In the cases of Frank and John, they were clearly taking on many of the child-rearing tasks that their wives had performed. Frank and John reported that these new tasks were both stressful and rewarding to them as single parents. In John's case, he had three young children to care for and found it difficult to create leisure time for himself.

The bereaved spouse usually needs help in working toward an appropriate redefinition of his or her identity. The therapist needs to aid the bereaved spouse in moving from "we" to "I" and provide support for the grief that results from these changes. Bereaved spouses sometimes need help to develop new relationships with people who can validate and support their new identities. It is also important to recognize differences in the "periods of vulnerability" for widows and widowers. "Widowers appear more vulnerable shortly after the bereavement, in contrast to widows, who seem this way two or three years later" (Rando 1984:149). Finally, as needed, it is important to refer the surviving spouse to one of the many self-help widow/widower support groups. Many churches, synagogues, community agencies, funeral homes, family service agencies, and other organizations sponsor such groups.

Group Interventions

It is often difficult for a widow or widower to express genuine and, at times, intense grief, because of our society's tendency to view death as an unnatural occurrence rather than as a universal phase of the life cycle (Walter 1997). Society also tends to put the widow or widower on a time schedule for the grieving process and usually prefers that the bereaved partner "get on with living." A support group can combat this insensitive societal schedule by encouraging bereaved spouses to establish their own timetable for grieving (Walter 1997). Bereavement support groups represent an excellent approach to this highly vulnerable population, because the small-group format can specifically address and lessen the "intense social isolation experienced by most bereaved spouses" (Yalom and Vinogradov 1988:420). In general, the literature advocates support groups for bereaved spouses (Barret 1978; Folken 1991; Kay, DeZappien, Wilson, and Yoder 1993; Kinderknecht and Hodges 1990; Lieberman 1989; Lieberman and Videka-Sherman 1986). The social linkages within the spousal bereavement group are seen as critical factors in positive change; neither time alone nor mere contact with a self-help group is sufficient to enhance the mental health of the widowed (Lieberman 1989; Lieberman and Videka-Sherman 1986). In chapter 3, Frank discusses his positive experiences with a support group for both widows and widowers. "By going to the group, it puts me in touch with feelings I had a while ago and they're not active feelings now." Frank was able to process some of his work on the memories of Sarah with the group members. Frank's work with his memories of Sarah would be a process especially encouraged by the postmodern approach to grief work.

Support groups for bereaved spouses have several goals. One is to assist members to cope with the pain of grief and mourning by creating a community in which they are deeply understood by peers. Other goals are "to combat the social isolation that is so pervasive and to support members as they begin to understand the changes facing them as they begin to fashion a new future for themselves" (Walter 1997:70). For example, Frank talked about how the support group has helped him to move forward by being there with him. "These six other people, they know that darkness that I'm talking about, and it's good to be in a group of people that know that darkness, and they're not immobilized by it—that's good to see." Both postmodern and classical approaches to intervention with bereaved spouses agree that support from others who have shared a similar loss is helpful to a bereaved spouse.

INTERVENTIONS WITH YOUNG WIDOWS

Individual Interventions

Shaffer (1993) reports that the findings from her research on young widows lend support to the approaches described in the bereavement literature. However, implications from her study could broaden clinical implications and contribute significantly to meeting the needs of the widowed population under the age of forty-five. Since spousal loss at a young age can result in the rebuilding of a new, strengthened, and enhanced personal identity, the clinician can support and encourage an individual beyond adaptation to the death of a spouse, guiding the bereaved spouse in the process of personal redefinition. In chapter 3, it is clear that Kristen is working on defining both a new personal and a new professional identity as she moves through her grief following the loss of her young husband. Postmodern thinkers would conceptualize this behavior as recreating meaning in her life. The clinician needs to support the client in acknowledging her loss and pain and readjusting to new roles and responsibilities as a single woman. "Over a period of time it is important to acknowledge the succeeding stages beyond widowhood . . . the affirmation of the possibility of eventually moving beyond the self-perception as 'widow' and into a time where life is characterized by expanding horizons . . . and the formulation of a new sense of self" (Shaffer 1993:134).

Group Interventions

Shaffer (1993) reports that the young widows who participated in a support group where the members were all experiencing the "same nonnormative circumstances" derived a sense of comfort and relief from not feeling alone and unique in their experience of widowhood at such a young age. In chapter 3, Kristen, widowed at twenty-nine, spoke of how important the support group she attended was for her. Kristen was able to locate a support group for widows at a local hospice center. Although "the closest woman in age to me was fifty, . . . I don't know what I would have done without that group. It was just the universality. There were just four of us and we just talked about what we were going through. Nobody else understood." This support group ran for twelve weeks, and Kristen attended every session. The group was led by a therapist, "but she was just there to facilitate stuff. We were the ones doing the work. Just hearing the stories . . . I can't even describe how meaningful it was." As a result of her positive experience with this group, Kristen would like to cofacilitate grief support for adults and children once she receives her graduate degree in counseling.

Local hospice organizations have begun to develop and run support groups for young widows and widowers. One hospice has titled their group "Early Endings, Healing Together: A Support Group for Young Widows and Young Widowers" (Samaritan Hospice 2000). This is a time-limited group of six sessions, with topics such as "I'm Grieving as Fast as I Can," "From We to Me," "Time Heals all Wounds," "Six Kinds of Guilt and How Many Other Emotions?" "Alone but Not Lonely," and "Who Do I Hope to Be Next Year?" The coleaders have found this group approach to be helpful to this population of bereaved widows and widowers.

INTERVENTIONS WITH BEREAVED MEN

Individual Interventions

As Chetnik points out, over the past forty years, most grief research has focused on widows—because they are more numerous than widowers and because they have been more willing to participate in grief studies. Thus this research has concentrated upon how women handle loss. "Affective expressiveness, especially crying and talking about the loss with others, has come to be seen as the accepted norm for grieving" (Chetnik 2000:4). Bereaved individuals who cope with loss in other ways are often viewed as "doing it wrong." In a study of men who had lost their fathers, Moss and Moss (1997) found that men tended to control their emotions after the death by emphasizing thinking and action as alternative reactions. Some of the sons focused upon taking care of the estate, funeral planning, and supporting relatives, while others turned inward and rationalized that their father's death was better for everyone involved. To their surprise, the researchers discovered that these mourning patterns seemed to be effective for these bereaved sons. Just as Martin and Doka (2000) have found, action-oriented coping may enhance immediate mastery and bolster self-esteem.

Martin and Doka (2000), after decades of clinical experience, have found that men tend toward a style of grieving that focuses on action, mastering feelings, and thinking. In his interviews with men about the death of their fathers, Chetnik (2000) found that these men coped by "walking, running, gardening, building with their fathers' tools, and taking over the fathers' businesses" (2000:4). Through these activities these bereaved sons were able to "gradually release the energy that built up inside them after the loss" (2000:4).

Although most of the men whose narratives on partner loss are reported in this book cried during the interview with the author, several indicated that they had been unable to cry with anyone prior to the interview, except their children. In their narratives shared in this book, John (chapter 3) and Barry (chapter 4) grieved in an action-oriented way, by creating memorials to their deceased partners and by taking on activities once assumed by their wives. John took on all of the care of his three children and became involved in the Girl Scouts, while Barry began taking sewing lessons so that he could fix his own clothes and find comfort in an activity formerly assumed by his partner. Jim (chapter 5) became a caregiver to his other gay friends with AIDS.

However, Chetnik (2000) stresses that gender does not definitively determine styles of grieving. In his study, about twenty percent of the men interviewed said "crying and talking were their primary ways of coping with the loss of their dads" (2000:4). In chapter 3, Frank provides an example of a widower who copes with his grief by sharing his feelings and thoughts with others as well as with members of his grief support group, which he has attended for three years.

As Chetnik (2000) suggests, in working with male bereaved partners "it is important to be open to nontraditional styles of grieving" (2000:5). In the initial session with a bereaved male partner, it is important to focus on understanding the client's past adaptive strategies in coping with grief (Chetnik 2000). Rather than asking, "How do you feel?" Martin and Doka (2000) suggest asking, "How did you react?" or "How did you respond?" However, it is very important to remember that some men may prefer to begin counseling from an affective rather than a cognitive approach.

Golden and Miller (1998) provide some important guidelines for therapists and other helping professionals who work with bereaved men. First, it is important to help a bereaved male partner understand how our culture may have influenced the way he lives his life and how he has been encouraged to deal with his grief. Men who are grieving often value their aloneness. Therapists who are inclined to talk about whatever is hurting them may find it difficult to understand that someone else would prefer not to talk. If it is more natural for a therapist to turn to others for support, it may be difficult to understand why others would choose to go off by themselves. Because many men value their independence, when a serious loss occurs, a man may tend to believe that the resulting grief is a burden that he must bear alone. Men may try to create a "private healing space" in which they can process what is happening around them and within them. These times can be healing, as long as they connect a man with his pain. George (chapter 3) found that playing golf helped him cope with his grief, while Barry (chapter 4) found much comfort in spending time alone with his deceased partner's dog.

However, Golden and Miller (1998) also suggest that if the bereaved man is emotionally expressive, the therapist should encourage him to cry, or laugh, or rant and rave. Generally, it is important for a therapist or helping professional to support a man in doing what comes naturally to him—to listen to his thoughts and his explanations. A therapist may be able to suggest various alternatives, and his client may choose to respond in other ways.

Campbell and Silverman (1996) believe that a man must relearn his sense of himself as a separate entity—he must renegotiate his relationship with his wife. He must come to a new understanding of who he is in relation to his deceased wife. This change involves a man's relationship with himself. This renegotiation involves recognizing one's needs and finding ways to fulfill them. In chapter 3, Frank, whose wife died when he was in his forties, found that he had to redefine himself by "becoming more mature" and becoming more responsible for both himself and his young daughter. John found himself doing some soul searching as he began his new life as a single parent with three young children.

Although none of the men whose stories are shared in this book reported that they kept a journal, this can be one way of facilitating this process of renegotiation with oneself. "You set yourself down on paper one moment, then come back at another moment and look at yourself as another, as if somebody else had written that, and you interact with yourself" (Campbell and Silverman 1996:231). This may be one way for a man who is grieving to discover a different conception of himself and what he needs. Widowers will also have to change the way they relate to the rest of the world. Social support has often been cited as an aid for depression in the process of mourning. In contrast to widows, men seem to lack extensive community contacts and may need special help in learning how to create a network of support for themselves.

Group Interventions

Chetnik (2000) urges helping professionals to be innovative in setting up grief groups that are attractive to men. He believes that men tend to avoid bereavement groups because they "expect to sit in a circle and talk about their feelings" (2000:4). Carverhill (1997) suggests reframing grief groups as "mutual story-telling sessions" in which men have an opportunity to retell their loss stories. Widowers may feel more comfortable in attending a support group if they have had at least one individual session with the group facilitator before joining the group (Carverhill 1997).

Carverhill also found that a widower may need to retell his loss story well beyond the time frame of one year. This raises questions regarding inclusion criteria used by some bereavement programs.

Golden and Miller (1998) suggest that grief groups for men be conducted outside of a standard office setting. One suggestion offered to therapists was that they invite widowers for a one-day fishing trip in honor of their deceased wives. Golden and Miller (1998) found that men were more likely to come to such an excursion than to come to a group session in an office. Although Frank (chapter 3) and Tom (chapter 5) reported great benefits from attending standard group sessions held in an office, other men might be attracted to a group held outside a traditional setting.

INTERVENTIONS WITH BEREAVED DOMESTIC PARTNERS

Individual Interventions

Very little literature addresses interventions with same-sex bereaved partners. They are truly a "hidden population" (Sklar and Hartley 1990). However, Meagher (1989) speaks of the importance of the counselor in helping the bereaved partner validate the importance of the relationship. Since the disenfranchised griever is coping with loss that is not socially recognized, the central theme in counseling those who are coping with disenfranchised loss is to validate that loss. The counselor also needs to help the

survivor validate the nature of the relationship itself, because there may be a
tendency to distort the quality of the relationship because of the lack of validation from others in the bereaved partner's world. Meagher believes that
because of possible distortions, the survivor may tend to "assign blame where
no blame existed" or to construct "a picture of the self as a manipulated and
abused victim" (Meagher 1989:320). Marie, who tells her story in chapter 4,
may have done this by discussing blame and manipulation throughout her
narrative.

Guilt may be a universal response to the loss of a partner, but Meagher
suggests that "there is a strong probability that the intensity of guilt increases in disenfranchised grief" (Meager 1989:320). It is important for counselors to help the bereaved partner to examine unresolved guilt, which may
provoke "an attempt at self-punishment" on the part of the survivor. Resolution of guilt in grief requires "an internal process of self-forgiveness . . .
and a letting go of the hold on the guilt" (1989:321).

The literature (Rando 1984; Doka 2002c) has identified participation in
some type of ritual as helpful to the bereaved partner in coping with grief.
Rituals are "powerful vehicles" for providing an opportunity for the bereaved to structure their experience, to express emotions, and to "allow one
to cross a threshold from one identity status to another" (Doka 2002c:135).
Rituals also "give meaning to an event or experience" (2002c:135). This
kind of help was denied to some of the opposite-sex bereaved partners, who
were excluded from active involvement in death-related rituals and ceremonies. Francine, whose partner died suddenly in a plane crash, felt that she
was ignored by Steven's mother following his death. Francine has never allowed herself to visit the scene of the crash as most of the other survivors
have done. Perhaps Francine could benefit from an experience or ritual focused on Steven's death. Although Barry attended the funeral of his deceased partner, Julie, her daughter took control of the plans. Barry was very
hurt that his name was never mentioned during the service. He "felt like I
didn't exist."

Alternative rituals, cocreated by the therapist and the bereaved partner,
can help to "enfranchise those who have been excluded" (Doka 2002c:41).
These rituals can help a bereaved domestic partner legitimize "emotional
and physical ventilation of grief," facilitate "a sense of experiencing or
doing," . . . and encourage the partner to "reframe events or experiences"
by offering support (Doka 2002c:143). A grief counselor can assist the survivor in finding ways to say good-bye and to express feelings that go with
this experience. Meagher (1989) suggests that a counselor talk through an

imagined funeral. The bereaved partner might also be encouraged to write a eulogy to the deceased partner and express feelings that he or she could not express because of exclusion from the official ritual. Both classical and postmodern thinkers would agree about the importance of encouraging the survivor to review memories and talk about the deceased and their mutual relationship. The therapeutic relationship could provide an opportunity for the bereaved partner to review the entire relationship and to include a description of the hopes and fantasies that helped to form it.

It seems that the uniqueness of disenfranchised grief may lead to a situation in which the grief counselor becomes a social and familial surrogate for the bereaved partner. All of the bereaved partners in opposite-sex relationships felt that their relationships with their partners was misunderstood by someone in their immediate environment. For some partners, like Laura, Barry, and Francine, this was especially painful because the meaning of the relationship was denied by others. For these partners in particular, the counselor might need to represent herself as a surrogate social and familial tie. However, the most important goal may be to help design intervention strategies that will help the bereaved partner to compensate for the absence of the necessary supports. The counselor can pay special attention to the absence of others with whom the bereaved partner can share feelings and to the lack of an active participation by the survivor in any ritual observed around the death of his or her partner.

In one of the few instances of therapeutic work done with opposite-sex partners, White (1997) reports on his work nine months following Sophie's loss of Bill, her male partner. In his narrative approach with Sophie, White tells of the "turning point" in the therapy. He urged Sophie to get more in touch with Bill by inviting her to sense his presence and to share "his being" rather than "his loss," as others in her life were encouraging her to do. White (1997) invited Sophie to share with him some of the ways in which she believed that Bill had understood her. When Sophie was able to experience Bill's understanding during the session, she felt Bill's acceptance of her. Perhaps some of the domestic partners who shared their narratives in this text might have benefited from such a treatment approach.

Group Interventions

Although none of the bereaved domestic partners who shared their stories in this book used a group as a method of support to help them cope with their grief, it would seem that this population, in particular, could benefit from a support group for bereaved partners. Pesek affirms this point by asserting that because support groups "normalize the grief process," they allow "grief in a population that is often neglected" (Pesek 2002:130). Both Laura and Francine mentioned how helpful a group might have been if one had been available. Because this is a special population, which lacks societal recognition and lacks validation of the nature of the relationship and what the loss means for the bereaved partner, a small group could have provided some of this support and validation. Local hospices and other organizations, which sponsor groups for bereaved spouses, need to consider the importance of designing a group for those who have never married but have lost their significant others. Alisa, who was engaged to her partner when he died, did attend one group session for bereaved spouses but did not return because she felt too uncomfortable. Pesek agrees that groups "may have a difficult time integrating disenfranchised grievers, especially for relationships or losses that defy conventional standards" (2002:130). Specialized support groups are needed to provide the support and validation that are needed by this population of grievers.

Sklar and Hartley (1990) report on a mutual support group with thirteen participants who had lost a close friend. The group participants, as well as the other participants in their study, felt that they had not been acknowledged by others "as truly grieving to the same degree that a family member might" (1990:10). Some of the narratives of domestic partners in chapter 4 illustrate the findings of Sklar and Hartley (1990), which suggest that when bereaved partners consciously attempted to grieve in ways that might be expected of family members, they were not permitted to do so by the family. Sklar and Hartley found that within the support group they facilitated, "the mutuality of mourning was a surprise to the participants, none of whom had realized that best friends as a 'category' could mourn, although each had mourned independently" (1990:110). This report, in addition to other thoughts expressed in this section, provide evidence of how important it is to create support groups for this disenfranchised population.

INTERVENTIONS WITH BEREAVED
LESBIAN PARTNERS

Deevey found that the large majority of her population who selected psychotherapy to cope with issues related to bereavement indicated that "therapists need to be prepared to assist such clients" (1997:260).

Psychotherapists working with bereaved lesbian partners need to be educated on issues of lesbian relationships, including bereavement. The psychotherapist who can facilitate a discussion of ambivalence, guilt, and anger will be especially helpful to those clients for whom the death of a partner has left them at risk for a complicated grief reaction. In addition, most of the women in Deevey's study (1997) had contact with nurses, funeral directors, doctors, and clergy. "Training programs for these service providers, on lesbian and gay relationships and bereavement, would potentially provide even more help to bereaved lesbian women" (Deevey 1997:261) because these groups are more likely to serve all lesbian women who need such services during their grief.

Individual Interventions

Modrein and Wyers found that lesbians who seek professional help believe that the "gender of the helping professional rather than their sexual orientation is an important consideration when they choose a professional (1990:102)." Lesbian clients believed that they were more comfortable in talking with another woman, and that a woman would be more understanding (1990).

Martin (1991) found that in her bereavement therapy with a lesbian widow it was important to encourage the bereaved partner, Eva, in her wish to talk with Joanne, the deceased partner, because "for a long time after someone dies, she or he is still present in one's life" (1991:180). Martin suggests, as do many of the postmodern theorists, that if the continued relationship with the deceased is supported, it provides an opportunity "for the gradual loosening of bonds over time."

The issue of disenfranchised grief was important to address, because "Eva's parents, her brother, and her sister-in-law had not even acknowledged Joanne's death" (Martin 1991:178). Eva was encouraged to draw parallels between her marriage to Joanne and her brother's marriage, since there was little question that if her brother's wife had died, the family would have participated actively in the long illness, the funeral, and the mourning. It was also difficult, yet important, for Eva to express her anger at Joanne's family for minimizing and denying the death experience (Martin 1991).

Martin (1991) also encouraged Eva to consider coming out to her own family, who did not know the nature of her relationship with Joanne. Eva's mother responded with a "loving and emotional message on her answering machine but avoided the central issue." Martin indicated that at the time of termination of her therapy with Eva, Eva was pleased with the changes she had made as well as with her increased openness. These positive feelings that resulted from sharing the nature of the lesbian relationship following the death of a partner seem to corroborate the experiences of several lesbian partners who shared their stories in chapter 6. Pauline discovered that whenever she did reveal her lesbian relationship with Jean to neighbors and colleagues, "all the responses were extremely positive, much more than I anticipated, except for my parents." In addition to Pauline, Denise and Gretchen discovered that when they revealed the nature of their relationships to others, they were gratifyingly supportive. These narratives suggest that bereaved lesbian partners can be perceptive enough about who will support them following the loss of a partner to make it worth taking the risk of sharing. This much-needed support mitigates the stress and fear of bereaved lesbian partners that are caused by the unpredictability of responses from society (Deevey 1997).

Since bereaved lesbian partners who shared their narratives in this book reached out to local hospice organizations and received support from them, it is imperative that hospice workers be trained in some of the important issues that face lesbian partners following the loss of a partner. Neither urban nor rural centers for gay and lesbian adults seemed to be places where bereaved lesbian partners were able to turn for help.

Group Interventions

Neither the women in Deevey's study (1997) nor any of the lesbian partners whose narratives are shared in this book participated in any type of group for bereaved persons. Since this type of support has been shown to be effective in helping widows adjust to bereavement (Silverman 1970), and since a need for such support is apparent from comments made by these lesbian partners, it is imperative that groups for bereaved lesbians be developed. Significantly, when this author attempted to find a lesbian population to interview for this book, staff from both a rural and a large urban gay and lesbian center recognized that they had not considered establishing support groups for bereaved partners. Yet they agreed that the need is present. At a state conference for hospice workers (Walter 2000), professionals indicated that they needed to consider developing bereavement services for this underserved population. As early as 1997, Deevey noted the current near invisibility of the majority of the lesbian population. It is striking that little movement to create special services for this population has been made in more than four years.

INTERVENTIONS WITH BEREAVED GAY PARTNERS

Individual Interventions

Gay men all struggle with stigmatization, disapproval of same-sex relationships, lack of societal recognition, and the possibility that many of the individuals who provide caregiving and support in the gay community are likely to develop AIDS themselves (Dworkin and Kaufer 1995). Five major areas of concern for this population, and possible areas for therapeutic intervention with a bereaved gay partner, are (1) social isolation, (2) fear of contagion, (3) disenfranchisement, (4) psychological and spiritual issues, and (5) bereavement overload (Rando 1993).

Bereavement overload emanates from the persistence of death and dying in the gay community. The narrative of Jim in chapter 5 exemplifies bereavement overload. Two levels of grief—aggregate losses and individual losses—must be addressed in counseling bereaved partners who have experienced multiple AIDS-related losses. Nord (1996) suggests that the failure to recognize both levels of grief will handicap treatment and lead to frustration on the part of both the helping professional and the client. In Nord's (1996) experience with survivors, he has observed "a back-and-forth shift" in the client's focus from the individual to the aggregate losses. Jim's narrative reflects this shift, as he speaks of his grief for the loss of his partner, for his closest friend, and then for all twelve of his friends who died within a short period of time.

Although gay men who are HIV positive are the group in a seven-year long-term study (Martin and Dean 1993) reporting the highest level of distress, uninfected men are also at risk for distress. Those uninfected men, such as Tom, as well as long-term survivors, like Jim, whose narratives are presented in chapter 5, need to acknowledge that they too may become ill. Dworkin and Kaufer (1995) suggest that it is "critical that the group of HIV-negative men not be shunted aside with the assumption that they are safe. In particular, those who are caregivers need social support and bereavement counseling" (1995:47). Jim felt that watching his partner, Matt, die of AIDS was a rehearsal of his own death. Jim says, "In some strange ways it felt like a legacy—this is what happened to everyone else and this is what's in store for me." Tom, whose partner, Rob, died of AIDS, said that there were con-stant questions for him about his own health as he cared for Rob.

Nord (1996) believes that "shame and guilt are likely to be underlying is-sues in the therapeutic process with gay and lesbian clients as a result of in-ternalized homophobia" (1996:408). The AIDS virus can intensify this feel-ing of shame if disease and death become an important part of one's identity. Guilt can take many forms, and when it is excessive, the therapist or helping professional needs to encourage the bereaved partner to discuss the guilty feelings and the thoughts, behaviors, and fantasies that underlie them (Rando 1993). In Jim's narrative we hear the voice of the survivor's guilt, corroborated in various studies (Boykin 1991; Sanders 1989; Murphy and Perry 1988), when he asks, "Why me of all the people to survive?" Within one year after his partner, Matt, died, Jim lost the "last friend in that group of twelve."

A further concern for both infected and noninfected gay men is the need to make sense of the loss and fit it into one's assumptive world (Parkes 1993). The effect of AIDS can be to destroy the belief system of survivors. Much of the therapeutic work will involve working with assumptions and questions of meaning. Nord believes that clients have been helped by a "frank discussion and realization that they are grappling with the significant, existential issues of life" (Nord 1996:407). Creating new assumptions about how the world functions is a necessary part of healing and growth. In his narrative in chapter 5, Jim says, "having to make sense of the person's life more than the illness is one of the hardest things for me." Jim did not want to "let AIDS be the defining factor" in his partner's life. An important part of an intervention strategy with a young AIDS survivor may be to help him find ways to define himself beyond the illness.

Emotions related to the meaning of life, sickness, and suffering are nor-mally issues that are gradually confronted by people as they age. Because AIDS most often strikes individuals at the prime of life, these issues are par-ticularly hard to endure. In order to incorporate the meaning of multiple losses and suffering at such a young age, one's value system must be re-worked (Dworkin and Kaufer 1995). Jim is reevaluating his life and recog-nizes some new strengths derived from his experience with multiple loss-es. Jim knows that there is a reason for him to be alive and believes that "I do have the sense of needing to do something important and worthwhile. My experience has made me value the human experience more—the abil-ity of the mind and body to cope and survive. I need to get something out of my days and do something that makes sense to me." Tom believes that his experience in losing his gay partner has made him more aware of the scarcity of time and the precious nature of life. "I really try to stay in the present. I value time—I am more gentle."

Dworkin and Kaufer suggest that grief can reactivate emotions that are related to the experiences involved in "establishing one's gay or lesbian identity." In experiencing partner loss, one's identity, self-esteem, and body image are challenged" (1995:47). Gay men will mourn the possible loss of their own health, and the ways in which their lives have been diminished, in addition to mourning the loss of their partner. Jim felt that watching Matt die was a rehearsal of his own death and has felt so damaged by the experience that he now has a "decreased ability to invest in being a partner in the future." Therapists and other helping professionals need to assist gay men in modifying their assumptions about the world and help them to incorporate the losses into those new assumptions (1995).

Group Interventions

Therapists and helping professionals have used group interventions to support both HIV patients and their partners. Gazarik and Fischman (1995) report their successful experience with a time-limited group for HIV-infected patients and their partners. The general goal of this group was to create a safe environment in which members could freely explore issues about loss and express feelings as they arose. The main issues that were addressed included the following: (1) debilitation and lack of effectiveness, (2) shame and guilt, (3) difficulty in informing others about the diagnosis, and (4) redefinition of roles. In chapter 5, Tom shares how important joining a support group was for him. "It was important for me to involve myself with others through a support group and ACTION AIDS . . . knowing that my pain was not just my pain, but respecting the fact that it is just my pain, yet knowing that there are others that join me in the universe with that challenge."

WORKING WITH GAY AND LESBIAN
BEREAVED PARTNERS

Dworkin and Kaufer (1995) suggest that staff who work with this population of bereaved partners require specialized training and education in a number of areas. Although traditional theories about the grief process offer a foundation for understanding the effects of loss because of HIV infection, they tend to focus on an individual's response to a single episode of loss and do not capture the experience of "multiple loss by an entire community" (1995). Also, these theories do not provide an understanding of the implications for one bereaved adult "where the onset of mourning for one loss overlaps with the end stage of mourning for another loss" (1995:42). Therese Rando (1993) discusses the implications for complicated mourning when gays and lesbians face overlapping losses, which result in a "chronic state of mourning." Posttraumatic stress, loss saturation, unresolved grief, survivor guilt, and fear of HIV infection complicate this chronic state of mourning (Rando 1993). In a study by Biller and Rice (1990), multiple losses hindered the grieving process because the bereaved adult tended to grieve over the loss he or she identified as most significant while minimizing the grief for other recent losses. In chapter 5, Jim's narrative illustrates the need for such understanding on the part of the clinician.

Mental health professionals "can enhance their understanding of the grief experience by gaining knowledge of its normative and social ramifications, and its profoundly existential nature" (Dworkin and Kaufer 1995:54). Although gay therapists may already have an awareness of pertinent issues from their own personal and social experience, they may not have analyzed or conceptualized their observations. Nongay therapists need a basic foundation in knowledge of gay and lesbian issues; they need to know about developmental and existential issues as well as "the effects of stigma on bereavement. Special attention must be given to recognition of the grief of hidden grievers and the need to take this seriously" (Dworkin and Kaufer 1995:54).

Hidden grievers are described as gay or lesbian adults "who have no real connection to the gay community. . . . They are isolated because of secretive behavior that often is shared with no other individual" (Dworkin and Kaufer 1995:48). Practitioners must try to provide support services for the "hidden griever" that are both accessible and nonjudgmental.

In chapter 6 of this book, Denise represents a hidden griever who found it very difficult to function in a world where no one knew that the nature of her relationship with Diane went beyond friendship. Denise and Diane were completely closeted about their lesbian relationship, which Denise found disadvantageous following Diane's death. Denise, with no one to confide in, considered suicide. However, once she contacted a hospice nurse who suggested counseling, and Denise began to reveal the nature of her relationship with Diane, her healing began.

Interventions with bereaved gay and lesbian partners need to respond to developmental issues, existential themes, multiple and chronic primary and secondary losses, and the collective nature of grieving. Interventions must address "lowered self-esteem, personal identity, questions about body image, and the reestablishment of meaning in one's life" (Dworkin and Kaufer 1995:50). Interventions need to be designed that help clients to do the following things: (1) create meaningful rituals, (2) gain support when their emotions become overwhelming, (3) encourage self mastery, (4) develop structures that support predictability and control, (5) cope with survivor guilt, and (6) refocus on the emotions of joy and hope (Dworkin and Kaufer 1995).

Importance of Social Support and Community Linkage

Social support has been identified by many authors (Dworkin and Kaufer 1995; Grothe and McKusick 1992; Osterweis, Solomon, and Green 1992; Sowell et al. 1991) as the key to coping with loss, especially multiple loss. Social support provides self-esteem, a feeling of being loved, networking, and provision of resources for establishing relationships and problem-solving (Dworkin and Kaufer 1995). It is important for therapists and other helping professionals to help bereaved partners to "maintain a sense of purpose while they are coping with unremitting loss" (1995:51). For gay and lesbian partners, the community rituals and social supports can provide structures for legitimizing grief, and this can help to substitute for the traditional kinship framework for mourning often available to bereaved spouses.

As we see in David's narrative in chapter 5, although his own family did not support him, the community of gay men with whom David and Brent interacted was very supportive. Because David and Brent had been partners for many years, David felt that the community recognized them as a symbol of the possibility of developing long-term relationships. Jim, Tom, and Don also spoke of the importance of their friends and/or the gay community in lending support during the difficult time following the loss of their partners. Tom specifically identified ACTION AIDS, a community self-help organization, as an important support to him in his grief.

Hicks points out the importance of developing specialized programs for lesbian women and gay men. "Although there are not enough controlled studies to demonstrate effectiveness, it is clear to many who work in these programs that they seem to be more powerful in helping patients achieve recovery and healing" (2000:93). The nurturing environment provided by such groups allows clients to share secrets and pain they have often hidden. Because of the special issues that are faced by the lesbian and gay community, it is important to advocate for specialized programs and affirmative treatments.

CHAPTER SUMMARY

In this chapter, we discussed both the classical and postmodern approaches to interventions, with an emphasis on examining both similar and different approaches that clinicians might use in working with bereaved partners. The basic similarity is the belief that all bereaved partners struggle with two incompatible urges—to cling to the pain of the loss and to move away from the loss, so as to focus on reinvesting in the present. The postmodern approach takes this concept one step further. Therapists are encouraged to allow clients to begin a new life while continuing a relationship with the deceased, rather than viewing the grieving process as something that should be more or less completed before beginning new relationships and taking on new challenges—the approach suggested by the classical theorists. Visually, the classical approach is more linear in its conception of the grief process, while the postmodern approach seems more spirallike in its direction.

The postmodern approach encourages therapists to help the bereaved to construct meaning from their experience of loss and to find new ways to "be" in their daily world, given their loss. This approach moves away from the phase-oriented classical approach to one in which the grief process is individualized for each person, with no time limits for the process to unfold. Both approaches suggest the importance of helping the bereaved partner to review his or her past relationship with the deceased. However, the classical approach conceives of the purpose of doing so as helping the bereaved to relinquish their ties with the deceased, while the postmodern approach views this exploration of the past relationship as an opportunity to transform the relationship, so that memories and thoughts of the deceased can enhance the bereaved's ability to function. Drawing from both the classical and postmodern models of grief, this chapter has explored interventions with various types of partners.

Both individual and group interventions are discussed, with suggestions made as to how these approaches might be applied with various types of partners, including widows, widowers, domestic partners, and gay and lesbian partners. When applicable, this chapter discusses appropriate literature and uses excerpts from the narratives in earlier chapters of the book to provide insights into applying individual and group interventions.

It is clear that all types of partners could benefit from both individual and group interventions. However, hospice organizations, as well as other types of community agencies, need to create specialized programs for domestic partners and for gay and lesbian partners who have lost their partners through death and separation. Several lesbian partners who shared their narratives in this text reached out to hospice organizations for help following the loss of their partner. Although they received individual therapy, a support group might have provided additional help. Bereaved lesbian partners and domestic partners emerged as the most underserved groups of bereaved partners. It is clear that specialized services and support groups need to be created for these two populations.

In designing both individual and group interventions with opposite-sex, gay, and lesbian partners, therapists should address issues of disenfranchised grief. The therapist needs to pay special attention to helping bereaved partners from these populations validate the nature of their relationship with the deceased partner. In addition, the therapist needs to be aware of the possible absence of others with whom the bereaved partner can share feelings about their lost relationships, This may require designing interventions that will help the bereaved to compensate for the absence of necessary supports. One of the suggestions from both classical and postmodern approaches is the use of ritual. This may be particularly helpful to those partners who were denied access to the rituals that families created following the death of the partner.

Chapter Nine

Clinical Implications

CLINICAL IMPLICATIONS FOR INTERVENTIONS
WITH BEREAVED PARTNERS

Clinicians from all disciplines who become involved with bereaved partners, regardless of their clients' legal status or sexual orientation, need to recognize and appreciate the importance of the bereaved partner's ambivalence about maintaining continuing ties to the deceased. Most partners whose narratives are included in this book spoke of contradictory impulses, or tugs, that they experienced when trying to preserve the loss of their partners while avoiding the pain of that loss. Clinicians need to design interventions that will allow their bereaved clients to experience this ambivalence, which is such an important part of the grieving process. Clinicians themselves need to be comfortable in looking for and listening to such ambivalent impulses. Chapter 1 of this text begins with a quote from Peter Marris that emphasizes a view of grieving that examines the tension between contradictory impulses. This view attempts to consolidate all that is valuable in the past and preserve it from loss, while reestablishing "a meaningful pattern of relationships, in which the loss is accepted" (Marris 1986:31, 32). Although this quote was taken from a text written more than twenty years ago, some of the postmodern thinkers (Neimeyer 2001; Rubin 1999) embrace this concept.

Applying a postmodern approach to clinical work with bereaved partners means that the therapist or helping professional must go beyond examining the current level at which the bereaved partner is functioning. The therapist must listen for and be open to all of the client's thoughts, memories, and experiences with the deceased partner (Rubin 1999; Klass et al. 1996). It is important for the therapist to help the bereaved partner to examine both positive and negative memories associated with the deceased partner. The therapist can also try to discover if and how the bereaved partner is maintaining or changing his or her relationship with the deceased. Furthermore, if the client does not mention memories of his or her relationship with the deceased partner, the therapist can inquire about the relationship and its meaning for the bereaved partner. The client may then be able to develop a new narrative that allows the relationship with the deceased to continue while the bereaved partner moves forward in his or her own life.

Nearly all of the bereaved partners who shared their narratives spoke about how they were using memories, thoughts, and "talking" with their deceased partners to help them cope with their grief. In several cases—for example, John (a widower), Barry (a domestic partner), Francine (a domestic partner), David (a gay partner), and Pat (a lesbian partner)—the bereaved partners took on characteristics of the deceased partners, or roles that they had performed, to help soothe them during the grieving process. However, it is important for the clinician to remember that, although the postmodern paradigm suggests encouraging clients to examine and process memories of their deceased partners, the therapist must always remember to individualize treatment and allow clients to chart their own course in grief work.

In addition to considering the cognitive aspects of memories that are held by the bereaved partner, a helping professional must also consider the affective components of grief, such as anger, sadness, guilt, and loneliness. As noted in the first section of this chapter, Rando's 1984 contributions are extremely helpful in working with both the positive and negative feelings that the bereaved holds toward the deceased. Rando suggests that because the bereaved often have so much difficulty facing anger, this emotion may have to be reframed before the bereaved partner can deal with it. It is easier for the bereaved partner to perceive the deceased partner more realistically if he or she realizes that both types of emotions toward the partner can exist together.

Perceiving the deceased partner more realistically seems related to the postmodern emphasis on changing or transforming the bereaved partner's relationship with the deceased partner. Klass, Silverman, and Nickman

(1996) and Rubin (1999) encourage bereaved partners and clinicians who work with this population to consider how the bereaved can change connections with the deceased partner so as to hold the relationship with the deceased in a new perspective, both cognitively and emotionally. Klass et al. (1996) also urge clinicians to examine with their clients how the bereaved partner has negotiated and renegotiated the loss over time. This process of renegotiation is clarified by Rubin in further detail; he believes that clinicians need to help the bereaved to examine (1) the extent of the imagery and memories that they experience, (2) the positive and negative affects associated with the memories of the deceased, (3) the indications of idealization of and conflict with the deceased, and (4) the ways in which all of these indicators provide a view of the bereaved partner's "cognitive and emotional view of the deceased" (Rubin 1999:22).

Several of the narratives in this text discussed how the bereaved partners were changing their relationships with their deceased partners and point out how that has enabled them to become involved in new relationships. Although the young widow, Kristen, has not forgotten her late husband, Carl, she has "emotionally relocated her memory of Carl" so that it is available to her and actually nourishes her current functioning with her new spouse. Her continuing bonds with Carl allowed her to "walk down the aisle" with her late husband's father and her new father-in-law. Pauline was enjoying her new relationship with Linda while continuing to dream about connecting with her deceased partner, Jean. In chapter 4, Peter had been divorced twice before becoming involved in a domestic partnership with Marilyn, several years before her death. Through his relationship with Marilyn, Peter learned the importance of respect and dedication in a committed relationship, knowledge that enhances his current relationship with Nancy. In chapter 5, as Don began to perceive his relationship with his deceased partner more realistically, he changed his expectations of what he wants from a future relationship. As a result, Don wants more open communication on both a physical and emotional level.

The classical approach to grief seems to suggest that a bereaved partner must complete certain tasks of grieving before they can move forward into a new relationship. The postmodern perspective on grief rejects that notion of phase-oriented mourning. Neimeyer reports that "scientific studies have failed to report any discernible sequence of emotional phases of adaptation to loss or to identify any clear end point to grieving that would designate a state of recovery" (2001:3). Critics of the more traditional models of grief have suggested that the concept of the bereaved as "passively negotiating" phases or transitions is limited and places the bereaved person in a passive and disempowered position (Neimeyer 2001; Attig 1991). Clinicians who work from a more postmodern perspective do not conceptualize the grief process as one in which the bereaved moves from one stage to another toward recovery. They encourage a more active, creative approach to working with the griever, who constructs and reconstructs his or her own narrative about the loss experience. Attig (1991) believes that the grieving process is "rich in choice" and perceives the bereaved as having the "choice" of discovering ways to build new relationships with the deceased that can give new shape to their own lives.

In addition, clinicians must be able to support partners who want to move forward with their lives while they are still working on their relationships with their deceased partners. The postmodern approach allows the bereaved partner to do both simultaneously. This latter approach can be very freeing for bereaved partners who begin a new life while grieving about the past and working on feelings and thoughts about the deceased partner.

Romanoff reports that "even in a research setting, narrative can and does have a therapeutic impact" (2001:254). The narrative process offers an opportunity for both continuity and change. In the process of gathering the twenty-two narratives for this text, my general questions changed the way the bereaved partners would have told their story prior to their interviews with me. Thus, during the interviews, each partner constructed a new story in my presence. Concurrently, this process also changed some of the questions that I asked of that partner and other partners. The bereaved partners frequently commented to me, at the end of an interview, that they perceived their loss differently as a result of the interview. Following my interview with David, he sent me a message stating that he had stayed awake the night of the interview reviewing "parts of Brent that are still with me" and concluded that, although he and Brent never had children together, he realized how good it was for him to hear friends reminisce about things that Brent had done. Several months following my interview with Denise, she sent me a letter sharing other major changes that had occurred in her life since Diane's death. She left a job that she had held for thirty years to return to college and obtain a degree in social work. As a part of "reclaiming new meaning in my life," Denise wants to pursue a career in a helping profession. Later, when I sent the partners copies of the narratives that I had constructed from the interviews, they would respond with changes they wanted to make, either to improve the accuracy or to reconstruct a story told one year before. For example, in her reconstruction of her first interview, Kristen announced her remarriage by reporting that her late husband's "father walked me down the aisle with my own father on the other side." Kristen was particularly pleased that Carl's father, who died shortly after her wedding, told her that the happiest memory he had of the last months of his life was "your getting married and seeing you happy again." These experiences clearly speak to the ways in which Kristen has used her relationship with her deceased spouse and his family to help her move forward in her new life.

In the postmodern approach to grief, there is skepticism about the concept of closure, since there are serious questions about whether people ever "recover" from a loss. This gives the clinician permission to allow the bereaved partner to work on his or her grief, regardless of the amount of time that has elapsed since the death of the partner. This approach to grief encourages "circularity" rather than "closure" and frees the bereaved partner to experience feelings and thoughts about the deceased partner at any point in his or her life. A circular approach can normalize, for bereaved partners, the ongoing or intermittent painful feelings about their loss, which friends, relatives, and society tend to believe should be worked through to a point of closure. Perhaps this need for closure is related to our society's tendency to deny the process of death and to discourage people from discussing death and all of its ramifications.

The postmodern approach encourages the clinician to help the bereaved partner to "reconstruct a world of meaning" and to explore with their clients how their lives have been changed or altered by the death of their partners. All the partners who shared their narratives offered ways in which their lives had been changed by the loss of their partners. In many cases these bereaved partners believed that their lives had been enriched by their experience with a profound loss. All of them expressed, in one way or another, how they now perceived life as precious and experienced the need to make each day count. While eliciting details about the loss and its pain, it is also important for clinicians to be able, if possible, to elicit this more hopeful recognition. At the same time, it is important to remember that clients often do not appreciate being told that something positive or "good" will emanate from their experience with loss. If therapists, somewhat insensitively, approach bereaved partners in this way, it is not only "not helpful" but may also bring on anger and wonder that the therapist could have so misunderstood them. Because the postmodern approach urges therapists to ask questions and cocreate meanings with the client during the therapeutic exchange, there is less likelihood that a therapist would "tell" a client what to feel. Instead, therapy becomes a process of discovering what the client is experiencing at that moment.

Both the classical and postmodern approaches to grief emphasize the importance of social support and involvement in support groups to facilitate the bereaved partner's moving forward in his or her life. The postmodern approach supports the idea that "we find and make meanings alongside others who are themselves struggling to find and make meaning" (Attig 2001:44). Both the classical approach to grief (discussed in chapter 1 and earlier in this chapter) and the postmodern perspective emphasize the importance of how "grieving with fellow survivors" provides support and comfort for the bereaved.

Although the postmodern perspective on interventions with the bereaved does not focus on the importance of the clinician's attitudes toward death or the clinician's awareness of his or her own concerns and feelings about death and bereavement, Rando (1984) brings this issue into sharp focus in the first and final chapters of her classic text. Rando believes that this focus is particularly important, given the death-denying culture in which we live. She provides an important exercise in her text (1984:9–13), which asks the clinician to consider such factors as the following: (1) how early experiences with loss and death leave one with reactions one needs to understand, (2) how important it is to be aware of one's own current feelings and attitudes toward death, and (3) how these feelings and attitudes can affect the way in which a clinician works with the bereaved, both positively and negatively. In her final chapter, Rando (1984) explores how the clinician and/or caregiver can cope with the stress of caring for the bereaved and the dying. She ends the book with a set of exercises that help clinicians to understand personal and professional expectations and to find ways to replenish themselves (1984:443, 444).

Other authors (Kauffman 1989; Worden 1991, 2002; Bruner 1997) have suggested that the issue of death and the loss experience of the bereaved can arouse significant anxiety in the therapist and heighten his or her own sense of vulnerability. Therapists may be reminded of their own losses when engaged in work with the bereaved and need to understand that personal reactions and feelings may emerge from this work. Clinicians need to "monitor and examine their reactions to the mourner to further the therapeutic process" (Bruner 1997). Peer support and clinical supervision can provide opportunities for clinicians to work on their reactions.

CLINICAL IMPLICATIONS FOR INTERVENTIONS
WITH BEREAVED PARTNERS FROM SAME-SEX
AND OPPOSITE-SEX RELATIONSHIPS

As was cited in the previous section of this chapter, clinicians who work with bereaved domestic partners, gay partners, and lesbian partners should have specialized training and education in issues of disenfranchisement and the impact of multiple loss. Dworkin and Kaufer (1995) argue that practitioners must attempt to provide "accessible and non-judgmental support services for the hidden griever" (1995:48). It is this author's belief that a coconstruction of grief issues can be created by the bereaved partner and the clinician. Although nongay clinicians need a basic foundation and knowledge of gay and lesbian issues, the gay bereaved partner may feel more empowered if the clinician invites the client to share his or her story with special attention to educating the clinician about issues with which she is unfamiliar. This may be important even when the clinician is gay, because although he or she may have an awareness of pertinent issues from personal experience, these issues may or may not be prominent for the bereaved gay partner.

It seems clear from the narratives of both same-sex and opposite-sex partners, as well as from the sparse literature on this topic, that our society must find a way to provide support for bereaved partners who do not have the support of another group or community. The fewer supports available to bereaved partners, the less likely they are to receive validation for their feelings and thoughts about their experience with grief. In chapter 4, Laura was most vocal about the need for such support for a group of bereaved domestic partners because, unlike the gay men and lesbian women who had lost partners, domestic partners do not have a community that "supports them and gives them sustenance." Some of the more isolated bereaved lesbian partners shared the difficulty they had in locating a support group that might have been helpful to them. Clinicians, community mental health centers, hospice organizations, gay and lesbian centers, and other community groups need to advocate for and create such support groups.

Hospital personnel need to become more sensitive to the needs of bereaved domestic partners, lesbian partners, and gay partners. These partners felt that medical personnel, in particular, were insensitive to the nature of their relationship with the deceased, and in some cases refused to honor a durable medical power of attorney, which had been set in place by the deceased partner prior to her death. Relatives, friends, clergy, funeral home owners, and all who touch the lives of a bereaved partner need to validate the relationship between the bereaved and deceased partner, as well as the pain experienced by the bereaved partner.

It may be important for the clinician working with these partners to encourage them to consider sharing more about the nature of their relationship with those close to them, so that they can receive the support they need following a separation or other loss of the relationship. Several of the lesbian partners interviewed for this book discovered that whenever they did reveal the nature of their relationship, the responses from others were positive and supportive. David wished that he and his gay partner had shared more about their relationship, so that their families would not have been so angry following Brent's death. In an earlier section of this chapter, in the excerpt from a treatment session with a lesbian woman named Eva, she was encouraged by her therapist to come out to her family, who did not know the nature of her relationship with her partner. Although Eva's mother did not discuss the relationship, she responded with warmth and love toward Eva. By the end of her treatment, Eva was pleased with her increased openness with others and with the responses she received. Despite these findings, clinicians need to allow bereaved partners to use their own judgment when considering this issue and deciding to whom they wish to reveal the nature of their relationship with the deceased.

The material presented in this book on disenfranchised grief has implications for the loss of a partner in a nontraditional relationship (same-sex or opposite-sex) even when the loss occurs for reasons other than death. The chapters that include this content can be useful both for partners experiencing losses and to professionals working with clients who have suffered a separation or loss. The ending of a partnership, whether by mutual consent or because one partner leaves the relationship, would present issues similar to those discussed in this book concerning bereaved partners whose relationships were severed by death. For example, the differences in bereavement experiences and the supports available to the bereaved partner seemed related to the degree to which a gay or lesbian partner is open about his or her relationship to friends and family. These same differences may also apply when a partnership ends for reasons other than death. The implications for the clinician would be to help the client become aware of these differences and to develop a strategy for helping the client to feel more supported and validated in his or her response to the separation.

CLINICAL IMPLICATIONS FOR A RESPONSE
TO THE EVENTS OF SEPTEMBER 11, 2001

The material presented in this text on the experiences of bereaved widows, widowers, domestic partners, gay partners, and lesbian partners has direct implications for those partners who have suffered and will continue to suffer various types of losses since the tragedy that struck our nation on September 11, 2001. The obvious implications apply to the many women and men who lost partners at "Ground Zero" in New York City, at the Pentagon in Washington, D.C., and in Pennsylvania, as a result of the four plane crashes at those sites in our nation. However, there are many couples who will be separated for undetermined lengths of time while the United States wages its "War on Terrorism." These partners will also be coping with separation, loss, and grief. There have been and will continue to be civilian casualties from the war, resulting in more deaths of partners in various types of relationships.

The events of September 11 have brought into focus the consideration of deaths that affect large numbers of people. The content presented in chapter 5 of this text on the disenfranchised grief experienced by gay men and others as a result of the AIDS epidemic may provide some important lessons for this new awareness. Traditional theories of grief tend to focus on an individual's response to a single episode of loss and fail to embrace the experience of "multiple loss by an entire community" (Dworkin and Kaufer 1995). Multiple losses can hinder the grieving process because the bereaved adult tends to focus on the loss identified as most significant, while minimizing his grief for other losses. Rando (1993) discusses implications for complicated mourning when gays and lesbians experience overlapping losses that result in a "chronic state of mourning." Posttraumatic stress, survivor guilt, unresolved grief, and loss saturation may be reactions to consider, given the mass numbers of deaths resulting from the tragedy of September 11. It is noteworthy that the widowed spouses of police officers and firefighters have now formed a new group called "The 9-11 Widows and Victims' Families Association." The emergence of this group represents more than an expression of grief; it represents a political group of people who "want a dignified almost reverent approach to the clearing of the sixteen-acre site (at Ground Zero)" as well as a "voice in how the property is developed" ("As Sept. 11 widows unite: Grief finds political voice," *New York Times* 2001). This reveals a desire to memorialize the partners who died and to construct meaning from this experience of death. Perhaps this horrific tragedy can help all of us recognize how important it is to reframe a tragic loss in a way that is hopeful. It is clear from the narratives shared in this text that partners from varying types of relationships all found ways to reframe their loss and to find new meaning in their lives. This tenet is one of the basic assumptions of the postmodern thinkers (Rubin 1999; Neimeyer 1998, 2001; Klass et al. 1996; Attig 1991) and one that can be helpful to all who suffer a loss.

September 11, 2001, and its aftermath remind us of our own vulnerability and mortality and thereby contradict "our unconscious beliefs that we are immortal." As Leviton points out, "the good news is that once the topic of horrendous death is acknowledged and discussed, nearly all respondents are willing to do something—they just want to know what to do" (2001:4).

The events of September 11 have changed all of our lives in many ways. Living with trauma and death, whether vicariously or directly, has become a way of life for most Americans. This fact may encourage us to embrace the importance of recognizing and understanding the meaning of the loss, while "capturing the positive function of the attempt to preserve meaning in the face of disruption" (Neimeyer 2001:41). These events, as well as the narratives of the twenty-two partners who shared their experiences in this text, can provide us with an increased appreciation for how new meaning can be made and life-enhancing experiences can emanate from a tragic loss.

CONCLUSIONS

This text has been devoted to integrating the literature about bereaved partners from a variety of relationships with bereaved partners' life experiences. Despite the growing number of books devoted to grief and loss, there is no other publication that juxtaposes losses from both traditional and nontraditional relationships in one text. From the literature and the narratives included in this book, it is clear that there are both similarities and differences in the grief experiences of bereaved widows, widowers, opposite-sex partners, gay, and lesbian partners. Most of the differences seem to arise from societal reactions to relationships in which the couple was not married.

Narratives presented in this text help us to understand that because there is a broad range of what can be considered normal reactions to the loss of a partner, it is essential to address each loss on an individual basis. Through the diverse reactions provided by the narratives, it is clear that each person's loss is uniquely experienced, even though certain aspects of the experience are shared by others.

As discussed in the introduction, with an increasing number of adults choosing to cohabit, it is extremely important to address some of the clinical issues and needs of this population. Some of these issues include disenfranchised loss and the lack of specialized support or clinical services to meet the needs of these underserved populations, particularly those of bereaved domestic and lesbian partners. The hidden population of grievers who have shared an opposite-sex partnership needs much attention. Unlike many gay and lesbian bereaved partners, these domestic partners do not share a common community. Designing support groups for this population is critical. Enabling bereaved partners to validate the true nature of the relationship through therapeutic conversations with the deceased partner, or through journaling about their experiences, can be helpful. In addition, clinicians can design interventions that encourage bereaved partners to experience rituals like those to which they were denied access, or to which they had limited access, following the death of their partner.

Since very little professional literature describes the experiences of bereaved lesbian partners, it is important to stress as well that there appears to be a relationship between the degree to which gay and lesbian partners have shared the nature of their relationship with others, prior to the death of the deceased partner, and the amount of support they receive following their loss. Several of the lesbian partners who were interviewed for this text discovered that whenever they did reveal the nature of their relationships, the responses they received from others were positive and supportive. Two of the gay partners interviewed for this book wished that they had shared more with others about their relationships prior to the death of their partners. They thought it might possibly have mitigated some of the anger they felt from family members. Clinicians working with this population can consider encouraging gay and lesbian partners who are coping with life-threatening illnesses to share more about the nature of their relationship both before and following the death of a partner. However, the judgment of the partners themselves always needs to be considered in any intervention.

The postmodern perspective encourages bereaved partners to begin a new life while continuing to work on their relationship with the deceased partner. This concept differs from that suggested by the classical grief theorists, who tend to recommend completing work on past relationships before beginning new ones and taking on new challenges. The narratives of the bereaved partners whose stories appear in this text support this postmodern concept; most of them were able to begin moving forward in their lives while maintaining and/or changing their bonds with their deceased partners.

In light of the new postmodern research on grief, as well as interviews with the partners who were pleased to construct and reconstruct their narratives with the author of this text, it may be important for the clinician to be active and creative in helping the bereaved partner to construct and reconstruct his or her story of loss. This method can be especially helpful with populations of bereaved partners, such as same-sex and opposite-sex partners, whose lifestyle the clinician may have little knowledge of. This co-construction of work, in which the bereaved partner is invited to educate the clinician about important issues, can be therapeutic for the partner.

Many classical and postmodern authors and researchers have documented the importance of social support and the use of support groups as critical in coping with loss and death. Social support is key to decreasing the isolation experienced by widows, widowers, domestic partners, gay partners, and lesbian partners following the loss of their loved ones. It is critical that society in general—family, friends, the medical profession, and those clinicians who serve the disenfranchised population of bereaved partners—recognize the need to validate the feelings of bereaved partners concerning their loss, as well as recognizing the importance of their participation in end-of-life activities to which they have been denied access. It is also important for those who touch the lives of all bereaved partners (whether married or unmarried) to view each partner's grief as unique, without imposing a time table for completing certain designated tasks of grieving.

Both postmodern and classical models of bereavement encourage emotional approaches to intervention with bereaved partners. Practicing clinicians and educators of future clinicians should consider the affective components of grief, including both positive emotions and negative ones, such as anger. It is often difficult for bereaved widows, widowers, and same-sex and opposite-sex partners to examine their negative feelings about the deceased partner. However, until the bereaved partner can integrate these feelings, it is often difficult to begin the work of transforming and changing the relationship with their deceased partner.

Both classical and postmodern approaches to grief have been discussed and compared in terms of how they might be applied to interventions with bereaved partners who have been married, as well as those who are living together in either opposite-sex or same-sex relationships. Narratives from the twenty-two partners who shared their stories in this book seem to corroborate some of the suggestions and findings of the postmodern thinkers.

It is clear that the partners who were involved in new relationships following the death of their partners were transforming the nature of their relationships with their deceased partners in order to make room for these new relationships. In many cases, thinking about the memories and even "talking" to the deceased partner enhanced the current functioning of the bereaved partner. All of the partners discussed the ways in which their memories of their deceased partners helped them to cope with their grief.

Finally, all of the partners discussed how their lives had been transformed by their response to the death of their partner. As Neimeyer (1998, 2001) suggests in his postmodern works, the world of the bereaved is shattered when they lose a partner. This tragic loss can promote profound shifts in one's sense of meaning and the direction of one's life. The narratives of the bereaved partners who contributed to this book vividly reveal some of these transformations.

References

"As Sept. 11 widows unite: Grief finds political voice." *New York Times*, Nov. 25, 2001, pp. A-1, B-7.

Attig, T. 1991. The importance of conceiving of grief as an active process. *Death Studies*, 15:385–393.

Attig, T. 2001. Relearning the world: Making and finding meanings. In R. Neimeyer, ed. *Meaning Reconstruction and the Experience of Loss,* pp. 33–54. Washington, D.C.: American Psychological Association.

Balswick, J. and C. Peek. 1971. The inexpressive male: A tragedy of American society. *Family Coordinator,* 20:363–368.

Barret, C. 1978. Effectiveness of widows' groups in facilitating change. *Journal of Consulting Clinical Psychology,* 46:20–31.

Biller, R. and S. Rice. 1990. Experiencing multiple loss of persons with AIDS: Grief and bereavement issues. *Health and Social Work,* 15 (4):283–289.

Bowlby, J. 1977. The making and breaking of affectional bonds, I and II. *British Journal of Psychiatry,* 130:201–210.

Bowlby, J. 1980. *Loss: Sadness and Depression. Attachment and Loss,* vol. 3. New York: Basic Books.

Boykin, F. 1991. The AIDS crisis and gay male survivor guilt. *Smith College Studies in Social Work,* 61 (3):247–259.

Brabant, S., C. Forsyth, and C. Melancon 1992. Grieving men: Thoughts, feelings, and behaviors following deaths of wives. *Hospice Journal,* 8 (4):33–47.

Bruner, J. 1997. Mourning and loss: a life cycle perspective. In J. Brandell, ed. *Theory and Practice in Clinical Social Work,* pp. 662–688. New York: The Free Press.

Campbell, S. and P. Silverman 1996. *Widower: When Men Are Left Alone.* Amityville, N.Y.: Baywood Publishing.

Carverhill, P. 1997. Bereaved men: How therapists can help. *Psychotherapy in Private Practice,* 16 (4), 1–20.

Chetnik, N. 2000. Reaching bereaved men requires innovation. *The Forum,* 6 (5):1–16. Newsletter of the Association for Death Education and Counseling.

Chodorow, N. 1978. *The Reproduction of Mothering.* Berkeley: University of California Press.

Corr, C. 1993. Coping with dying: Lessons that we should and should not learn from the work of Elisabeth Kubler-Ross. *Death Studies,* 17:69–83.

Dean, L., W. Hall, and J. Martin. 1988. Chronic and intermittent AIDS: Related bereavement in a panel of homosexual men in New York City. *Journal of Palliative Care,* 4 (4):54–57.

Deevey, S. 1997. Bereavement experiences in lesbian kinship networks in Ohio (Doctoral Dissertation, Ohio State University, 1997). Abstract in *Dissertation Abstracts International,* 58/02:630.

DiAngi, P. 1982. Grieving and the acceptance of the homosexual identity. *Issues in Mental Health Nursing,* 4:101–113.

DiGiulio, J. 1992. Early widowhood: An atypical transition. *Journal of Mental Health Counseling,* 14 (1):97–109.

Doka, K. 1987. Silent sorrow: Grief and the loss of significant others. *Death Studies,* 11:455–469.

Doka, K. 1989. *Disenfranchised Grief: Recognizing Hidden Sorrow.* New York: Lexington Books.

Doka, K. 2002a. How we die: Stigmatized death. In K. Doka, ed. *Disenfranchised Grief: New Directions, Challenges, and Strategies for Practice,* pp. 323–336. Champaign, Ill.: Research Press.

Doka, K. 2002b. Introduction to *Disenfranchised Grief: New Directions, Challenges, and Strategies for Practice.* Champaign, Ill.: Research Press.

Doka, K. 2002c. The role of ritual in the treatment of disenfranchised grief. In K. Doka, ed. *Disenfranchised Grief: New Directions, Challenges, and Strategies for Practice,* pp. 135–147. Champaign, Ill.: Research Press.

Dworkin, J. and D. Kaufer. 1995. Social services and bereavement in the lesbian and gay community. In G. Lloyd and M. Kuszelevicz, eds. *HIV Disease: Lesbians, Gays and the Social Services,* pp. 41–60. New York: Harrington Park Press.

Erikson, E. 1963. *Childhood and Society,* 2d ed.. New York: Norton.

Faberow, N., D. Gallagher-Thompson, M. Gilewski, and L. Thompson. 1992. The role of social supports in the bereavement process of surviving spouses of suicide and the older adult. *Suicide and Life Threatening Behavior,* 22 (1):107–124.

Feinson, M. 1986. Aging widows and widowers: Are there mental health differences? *International Journal of Aging and Human Development,* 23 (4):241–255.

Fenichel, O. 1945. *The Psychoanalytic Theory of Neurosis.* New York: Norton Publishing.

Ferrell, J. 1992. Managing care in the context of bereavement: A grounded theory study of male survivors of partners who died from AIDS (Doctoral Dissertation, Medical College of Georgia, 1992). Abstract in *Dissertation Abstracts International,* 53/04:132.

Fields, J. and L. Casper. 2001. *America's Families and Living Arrangements: March 2000.* Current population reports, pp. 1–16. Washington, D.C.: United States Census Bureau.

Folken, M. 1991. The importance of group support for widowed persons. *Journal for Specialists in Group Work,* 16 (3):172–177.

Frantz, T., M. Farrell, and B. Trolley. 2001. Positive outcomes of losing a loved one. In R. Neimeyer, ed. *Meaning Construction and the Experience of Loss,* pp. 191–209. Washington, D.C.: American Psychological Association.

Freud, S. 1957. Mourning and melancholia. In J. Strachey, ed. and trans. *Standard Edition of the Complete Psychological Works of Sigmund Freud.* London: Hogarth Press.

Gazarik, R. and Fischman, D. 2000. A time-limited group for patients with HIV infection and their partners. *Group,* 19 (3):173–182.

Gergen, K. 1991. *The Saturated Self: Dilemmas of Identity in Contemporary Life.* New York: Basic Books.

Gilligan, C. 1982. *In a Different Voice.* Cambridge, Mass.: Harvard University Press.

Glick, I., R. Weiss, and C. Parkes. 1974. *The First Year of Bereavement.* New York: Wiley Interscience.

Golden, T. 1996. *Swallowed by a Snake: The Gift of the Masculine Side of Healing.* Kensington, Md.: Golden Healing Publishing.

Golden, T. and J. Miller. 1998. *When a Man Faces Grief: A Man You Know Is Grieving.* Fort Wayne, Ind.: Willowgreen Press.

Grothe, T. and T. McKusick. 1992. Coping with multiple loss. *Focus: A Guide to AIDS Research and Counseling,* 7 (7):5–8.

Hagman, G. 2001. Beyond decathexis: Toward a new psychoanalytic understanding of the treatment of mourning. In R. Neimeyer, ed. *Meaning Reconstruction and the Experience of Loss,* pp. 13–31. Washington, D.C.: The American Psychological Association.

Hamilton, N. 1989. A critical review of object relations theory. *American Journal of Psychiatry,* 146 (12):1552–1560.

Hamovitch, M. 1964. *The Parent and the Fatally Ill Child.* Duarte, Cal.: City of Hope Medical Center.

Hicks, D. 2000. The importance of specialized treatment programs for lesbian and gay patients. *Journal of Gay/Lesbian Psychotherapy,* 3 (4):81–94.

Holmes, T. and R. Rahe. 1967. The social adjustment scale. *Journal of Psychosomatic Research,* 11:213–218.

Jones, L. 1985. The psychological experience of bereavement: Lesbian women's perceptions of the response of the social network to the death of a partner.

(Doctoral Dissertation, Boston University, 1985.) Abstract in *Dissertation Abstracts International*, 46/09:2566.

Kauffman, J. 1989. In J. Doka, ed.. *Disenfranchised Grief: Recognizing Hidden Sorrow*, pp. 24–29. New York: Lexington Books.

Kauffman, J. 1994. Group thanatopsis. In V. Schermer and M. Pines, eds. *Ring of Fire*, pp. 149–173. London: Routledge.

Kauffman, J. 2002. The psychology of disenfranchised grief: Liberation, shame, and self-disenfranchisement. In J. Doka, ed. *Disenfranchised Grief: New Directions, Challenges, and Strategies for Practice*, pp. 61–77. Champaign, Ill.: Research Press.

Kay, M., J. DeZappien, C. Wilson, and M. Yoder 1993. Evaluating treatment efficacy by triangulation. *Social Science Medicine*, 36 (12):1545–1552.

Kelly, J. 1977. The aging male homosexual: Myth and reality. *The Gerontologist*, 17:328–332.

Kessler, B. 1984. Personal meanings of bereavement. (Doctoral Dissertation, Saybrook Institute, 1984.) Abstract in *Dissertation Abstracts International*, 45/09:3074.

Kimmel, D. 1978. Adult development and aging: A gay perspective. *Journal of Social Issues*, 34:113–131.

Kinderknecht, C. and L. Hodges. 1990. Facilitating productive bereavement of widows: An overview of the efficacy of widows. *Journal of Women and Aging*, 2 (4):39–54.

Klass, D., P. Silverman, and S. Nickman. 1996. *Continuing Bonds: New Understandings of Grief.* Washington, D.C.: Taylor and Francis.

Kubler-Ross, E. 1969. *On Death and Dying.* New York: Macmillan.

Kubler-Ross, E. 1989. *Death Studies*, 17:69–83.

Levinson, D. 1997. Young widowhood: A life change journey. *Journal of Personal and Interpersonal Loss*, 2:277–291.

Leviton, D. 2001. Terrorism: Implications for ADEC and its members. *The Forum*, Nov./Dec., p. 4. Connecticut: Association for Death Education and Counseling.

Lieberman, M. 1989. Group properties and outcomes: A study of group norms in self-help groups for widows and widowers. *International Journal of Group Psychotherapy*, 39 (2):191–208.

Lieberman, M. 1994. "Must widows wear black: Growth beyond grief." Unpublished manuscript.

Lieberman, M. and L. Videka-Sherman. 1986. The impact of self-help groups on the mental health of widows and widowers. *American Journal of Orthopsychiatry*, 56 (3):435–449.

Lindemann, E. 1944. Symptomatology and management of acute grief. *American Journal of Orthopsychiatry*, 101:141–148.

Lister, L. 1991. Men and grief: A review of research. *Smith College Studies in Social Work*, 61 (3):220–235.

Lopata, H. 1979. *Women as Widows: Support Systems*. New York: Elsevier Press.

Lopata, H. 1996. *Current Widowhood: Myths and Realities*. Thousand Oaks, Cal.: Sage Publications.

Lund, D., M. Caserta, and M. Dimond. 1993. The course of spousal bereavement in later life. In M. Stroebe. and W. Stroebe, eds. *Handbook of Bereavement: Theory, Research, and Intervention*, pp. 240–254. New York : Cambridge University Press.

Marris, P. 1986. *Loss and Change*. London: Routledge and Kegan Paul.

Martin, A. 1991. The power of empathic relationships: Bereavement therapy with a lesbian widow. In C. Silverstein, ed. *Gays, Lesbians, and Their Therapists*, pp. 172–200. New York: W.W. Norton.

Martin, J. and L. Dean. 1993. Effects of AIDS-related bereavement and HIV-related illness on psychological distress among gay men: A 7-year longitudinal study, 1985–1991. *Journal of Consulting and Clinical Psychology*, 61 (1):94–103.

Martin, T. and K. Doka. 2000. *Men Don't Cry . . . Women Do: Transcending Stereotypes of Grief*. Philadelphia: Brunner/Mazel.

Matthews, S. 1979. *The Social World of Old Women: Management of Self Identity*. Beverly Hills, Cal.: Sage Publications.

Meagher, D. 1989. The counselor and the disenfranchised griever. In K. Doka, ed. *Disenfranchised Grief: Recognizing Hidden Sorrow*, pp. 313–333. New York: Lexington Books.

Mendola, M. 1980. *The Mendola Report: A New Look at Gay Couples*. New York: Crown.

Miller, J. 1986. *Toward a New Psychology of Women*. Boston: Beacon Press.

Mirkin, M. 1994. *Women in Context: Toward a Feminist Reconstruction of Psychotherapy*. New York: Guilford Press.

Modrein, M. and N. Wyers. 1990. Lesbian and gay couples: Where they turn when help is needed. *Journal of Gay and Lesbian Psychotherapy*, 1 (3):89–104.

Moss, M. and S. Moss. 1985. Some aspects of the elderly widow(er)'s persistent tie with the deceased spouse. *Omega*, 15 (3):195–205.

Moss, S., M. Moss, and R. Rubenstein. 1997. Middle-aged son's reactions to father's death. *Omega*, 34:259–277.

Murphy, P. and K. Perry. 1988. Hidden grievers. *Death Studies*, 12:451–462.

Neimeyer, R. 1998. *Lessons of Loss: A Guide to Coping*. New York: McGraw-Hill.

Neimeyer, R. 2001. *Meaning Reconstruction and the Experience of Loss*. Washington, D.C.: American Psychological Association.

Neugarten, B. and H. Hagestad. (1976) Age and the life course. In E. Shanas and R. Binstock, eds. *Handbook of Aging and the Social Sciences,* pp. 35–55. New York: Van Nostrand Reinhold.

Neugabauer, R, J. Rabkin, J. Williams, R. Remien, R. Goetz, and J. Gorman. 1992. *American Journal of Psychiatry,* 149 (10):1374–1379.

"New Yorkers tying the knot at lowest rate since 70s." *New York Times,* Jan. 9, 2000, Metro section, p. 21.

Nord, D. 1996. Issues and implications in the counseling of survivors of multiple AIDS-related losses. *Death Studies,* 20:389–413.

Oktay, J. and C. Walter. 1991. *Breast Cancer in the Life Course:Women's Experiences.* New York: Springer.

Osterweis, M., F. Solomon, and M. Green. 1984. *Bereavement: Reactions, Consequences, and Care.* Washington, D.C.: National Academy Press.

Parkes, C. 1972. *Bereavement: Studies of Grief in Adult Life.* New York: International Universities Press.

Parkes, C. 1993. Bereavement as a psychosocial transition: Processes of adaptation to change. In M. Stroebe and W. Stroebe, eds. *Handbook of Bereavement: Theory, Research, and Intervention,* pp. 91–101. New York: Cambridge University Press.

Peplau, L. and H. Amaro 1982. Understanding lesbian relationships. In W. Paul, J. Weinrich, J. Gonsiorek, and M. Hotvedt, eds. *Homosexuality: Social, Psychological, and Biological Issues.* Beverly Hills, Cal.: Sage.

Pesek, E. 2002. The role of support groups in disenfranchised grief. In K. Doka, ed. *Disenfranchised Grief: New Directions, Challenges, and Strategies for Practice,* pp. 127–133. Champaign, Ill.: Research Press.

Pine, V. 1989. Death, loss, and disenfranchised grief. In K. Doka, ed. *Disenfranchised Grief: Recognizing Hidden Sorrow.* New York: Lexington Books.

Rando, T. 1984. *Grief, Dying and Death: Clinical Interventions for Caregivers.* Champaign, Ill.: Research Press.

Rando, T. 1993. *Treatment of Complicated Mourning,* Champaign, Ill.: Research Press.

Raphael, B., W. Middleton, N. Martinek, and V. Misso. (1993) Counseling and therapy of the bereaved. In W. Stroebe, M. Stroebe, and R. Hansson, eds. *Handbook of Bereavement: Theory, Research and Intervention,* pp. 427–453. New York: Cambridge University Press.

Richards, T. 1999. "Spiritual aspects of loss among partners of men with AIDS: Postbereavement follow-up." *Death Studies,* 23:105–127.

Richmond, B. and M. Ross. 1995. Death of a partner: Responses to AIDS-related bereavement. In L. Sherr, ed. *Grief and AIDS,* pp.161–179. New York: John Wiley.

Roach, M. and G. Kitson. 1989. Impact of forewarning on adjustment to widowhood and divorce. In D. Lund, ed. *Older Bereaved Spouses,* pp. 185–200. New York: Hemisphere.

Romanoff, B. 2001. Research as therapy: The power of narrative to effect change. In R. Neimeyer, ed. *Meaning Reconstruction and the Experience of Loss,* pp. 245–257. Washington, D.C.: The American Psychological Association.

Rosenberg, H. (1991). *Vital Statistics,* Vol. 2, Part A. Tables 1–34. Washington, D.C.: National Center for Health Statistics.

Rubin, S. 1999. The two-track model of bereavement: Overview, retrospect, and prospect. *Death Studies,* 23:681–714.

Samaritan Hospice (2000). Conversations with group leaders of young widows' and widowers' support groups.

Sanders, C. 1989. *Grief: The Morning After.* New York: John Wiley.

Sarton, M. 1993. *The Education of Harriet Hatfield.* New York: W.W. Norton.

Schuchter, S. 1986. *Dimensions of Grief: Adjusting to the Death of a Spouse.* San Francisco: Jossey-Bass.

Schuchter, S. and S. Zisook. 1993. The course of normal grief. In M. Stroebe, W. Stroebe, and R. Hansson, eds. *Handbook of Bereavement: Theory, Research, and Intervention,* pp. 23–43. New York: Cambridge University Press.

Schwartzberg, S. 1996. *A Crisis of Meaning: How Gay Men Are Making Sense of AIDS.* Oxford: Oxford University Press.

Shaffer, S. 1993. Young widows: Rebuilding identity and personal growth following spousal loss. (Doctoral Dissertation, University of San Francisco, 1993.) Abstract in *Dissertation Abstracts International,* 54/01:94.

Shernoff, M. 1998. Gay widowers: Grieving in relation to trauma and social supports. *Journal of the Gay and Lesbian Medical Association,* 2 (1):27–33.

Shernoff, M. 1998. *Gay Widowers: Life After the Death of a Partner.* New York: Harrington Park Press.

Siegal, R. and D. Hoefer, 1981. Bereavement counseling for gay individuals. *American Journal of Orthopsychiatry,* 35:517–525.

Silverman, P. 1970. The widow as caregiver in a program of preventive intervention with other widows. *Mental Hygiene,* 54 (4):540–547.

Silverman, P. (1986). *Widow to Widow.* New York: Springer.

Silverman, P., S. Nickman, and J. Worden. 1992. The child's reconstruction of a dead parent. *American Journal of Orthopsychiatry,* 62:494–503.

Simos, B. 1979. *A Time to Grieve: Loss as a Human Experience.* New York: Family Service Association of America.

Sklar, F. and S. Hartley. 1990. Close friends as survivors. *Omega: Journal of Death and Dying,* 22 (2):103–112.

Slater, S. and J. Mencher. 1991. The lesbian life cycle: A contextual approach. *American Journal of Orthopsychiatry,* 61 (3):272–382.

Sowell, R., M. Bramlett, D. Gueldner, and G. Martin. 1991. The lived experience of survival and bereavement following the death of a lover from AIDS. *Image: The Journal of Nursing Scholarship,* 23 (2):89–93.

Stroebe, M., H. Schut, and W. Stroebe. 1998. Trauma and grief: A comparative analysis. In J. Harvey, ed. *Perspectives on Loss: A Sourcebook,* pp. 81–96. Washington, D.C.: Taylor and Francis.

Stroebe, M. and W. Stroebe. 1983. Who suffers more? Sex differences in health risks of the widowed. *Psychological Bulletin,* 93 (2):279–301.

Stroebe, M., W. Stroebe, and R. Hansson. 1988. Bereavement research: An historical introduction. *Journal of Social Issues,* 44:1–18.

Stroebe, W. and M. Stroebe. 1987. *Bereavement and Health: The Psychological and Physical Consequences of Partner Loss.* New York: Cambridge University Press.

Stylianos, S. and M. Vachon. 1999. The role of social support in bereavement. In M. Stroebe, W. Stroebe, and R. Hansson, eds. *Handbook of Bereavement: Theory, Research and Intervention,* pp. 397–410. New York: Cambridge University Press.

Walter, C. 1997. Support groups for widows and widowers. In G. Grief and P. Ephross, eds. *Group Work with Populations at Risk,* pp. 69–83. New York: Oxford University Press.

Walter, C. 2000. "The loss of a partner." Invitational presentation at Pennsylvania Hospice Network Annual Conference, Harrisburg, Penn.

Walter, T. 1996. A new model of grief: Bereavement and biography. *Mortality,* 1 (1):7–25.

Weenolsen, P. 1988. *Transcendence of Loss Over the Lifespan.* New York: Hemisphere Publishing.

White, M. 1997. *Narratives of Therapists' Lives.* Adelaide, Australia: Dulwich Centre Publications.

Worden, J. 1991. *Grief Counseling and Grief Therapy: A Handbook for the Mental Health Practitioner,* 2d ed. New York: Springer Publishing.

Worden, J. 2002. *Grief Counseling and Grief Therapy: A Handbook for the Mental Health Practitioner,* 3d ed. New York: Springer Publishing.

Worden, J. and P. Silverman. 1993. Grief and depression in newly widowed parents with school age children. *Omega,* 27 (3):251–261.

Wortman, C. and R. Silver. 1989. The myths of coping with loss. *Journal of Consulting and Clinical Psychology,* 57:349–357.

Yalom, I. and S. Vinogradov. 1988. Bereavement groups: Techniques and themes. *International Journal of Group Psychotherapy,* 38 (4):419–446.

Zucker, R. 2000. Becoming prepared for life: An interview with Phyllis Silverman. *The Grief and Healing Newsletter,* Spring, 1, 7.

Trolley, B., 216, 218

Walter, C (1997), 2, 14–15, 19, 20, 37, 169, 212
Walter, C. (with Oktay, 1991), 34, 49, 209
Weenolsen, P, 50
Weeping. *See* Crying
White, M., 236
Widowers: narratives and analyses—Frank, 63–70, 212, 216; narratives and analyses—George, 77–83; narratives and analyses—John, 51–57, 212, 216; review of literature, 19–21, 70–71
Widows: and gay men whose partners died from AIDS, similarities and differences in grieving, 34; and lesbian partners, similarities and differences in grieving, 34–35; review of literature, 15–19, 37–38, 70–71; young, mortality, heightened awareness of one's own, 37
Widows, narratives and analyses: Flora, 71–77, 216–17; Kristen, 38–51, 212–13, 215–16, 251; Marion, 57–63, 210
Williams, J., 28–29
Withdrawal from friends, 3, 195–96

Women's intuitive pattern of grieving, 22
Worden, J., 3, 55, 89, 220, 221, 222, 223

Yalom, I., 14, 15
Yearning and searching, 4
Young bereaved partners (under age 65): interventions for young widows, 230–31; mortality, heightened awareness of one's own, 37; support groups for young widows, 42–44
Young bereaved partners (under age 65), narratives and analyses: Alisa, 124–29; David, 148–53, 206, 207, 211, 250; Denise, 175–85, 208, 250; Don, 153–58, 205, 207, 210, 214; Francine, 110–16, 206, 217; Frank, 63–70, 212, 216; Gretchen, 169–75, 205, 213; Jim, 134–43, 215, 217; John, 51–57, 212, 216; Kristen, 38–51, 212–13, 215–16, 251; Laura, 116–24, 204, 206, 207; Lea, 185–94, 204, 208, 217–18; Marie, 90–95, 204; Marion, 57–63, 210; Pat, 194–97, 204, 205, 208, 211, 218; Pauline, 162–69, 205, 211, 213; Tom, 143–48, 204, 205–6, 207, 217